Assessment and Evaluation Masters

Glencoe

Algebra

Concepts and Applications

Glencoe
McGraw-Hill

New York, New York   Columbus, Ohio   Woodland Hills, California   Peoria, Illinois

Glencoe/McGraw-Hill

*A Division of The **McGraw·Hill** Companies*

Send all inquiries to:
The McGraw-Hill Companies
8787 Orion Place
Columbus, OH 43240-4027

ISBN: 0-07-821550-1

Algebra
Assessment and Evaluation Masters

1 2 3 4 5 6 7 8 9 10   055   07 06 05 04 03 02 01 00

CONTENTS

Book Materials

Preparing for Standardized Tests
Answer Sheet

1. (A) (B) (C) (D) (E)

2. (A) (B) (C) (D) (E)

3. (A) (B) (C) (D) (E)

4. (A) (B) (C) (D) (E)

5. (A) (B) (C) (D) (E)

6. (A) (B) (C) (D) (E)

7. (A) (B) (C) (D) (E)

8. (A) (B) (C) (D) (E)

9.

	$\oslash$	$\oslash$	
$\odot$	$\odot$	$\odot$	$\odot$
	0	0	0
1	1	1	1
2	2	2	2
3	3	3	3
4	4	4	4
5	5	5	5
6	6	6	6
7	7	7	7
8	8	8	8
9	9	9	9

10. Show your work.

Chapter 1 Test, Form 1A

1

Write the letter for the correct answer in the blank at the right of each problem.

Write an algebraic expression for each verbal expression.

1. five more than six times x

   A. $6x - 5$ **B.** $(5 + 6)x$ **C.** $6x + 5$ **D.** $5x - 6$

   1. _____

2. twelve less than the quotient of a and c

   A. $12 - \frac{a}{c}$ **B.** $\frac{a - 12}{c}$ **C.** $\frac{a}{12 - c}$ **D.** $\frac{a}{c} - 12$

   2. _____

Write an equation for each sentence.

3. Seventeen minus p equals 35.

   A. $p - 17 = 35$ **B.** $17 - p = 35$
   C. $17 = p - 35$ **D.** $17 = 35 - p$

   3. _____

4. Thirty plus the product of eight and m equals eleven.

   A. $30 + 8m = 11$ **B.** $38m = 11$
   C. $30m + 8 = 11$ **D.** $30(8 + m) = 11$

   4. _____

For Questions 5–6, find the value of each expression.

5. $16 + 32 \div 4 - 10$

   A. 2   **B.** 8   **C.** 14   **D.** 18

   5. _____

6. $60 \div 12 \times (11 - 6)$

   A. 1   **B.** 10   **C.** 25   **D.** 49

   6. _____

7. Name the property of equality shown by the statement below.

   If $y = x - 7$ and $x = 12$, then $y = 12 - 7$.

   A. Transitive   **B.** Symmetric   **C.** Reflexive   **D.** Substitution

   7. _____

8. Evaluate the algebraic expression $\frac{r + 12}{3(s - 2)}$ if $r = 66$ and $s = 4$.

   A. 11   **B.** 13   **C.** 15   **D.** 26

   8. _____

Name the property shown by each statement.

9. $14 + (16 + n) = (14 + 16) + n$

   A. Associative (×)   **B.** Associative (×)
   C. Commutative (+)   **D.** Commutative (×)

   9. _____

10. $x \cdot (y \cdot z) = (y \cdot z) \cdot x$

    A. Associative (+)   **B.** Associative (×)
    C. Commutative (+)   **D.** Commutative (×)

    10. _____

Simplify each expression.

11. $32 + (28 + w)$

    A. $28 + 32w$ **B.** $60w$ **C.** $60 + w$ **D.** $(32 + 28) + w$

    11. _____

12. $(7 \cdot k) \cdot 11$

    A. $77k$ **B.** $18k$ **C.** $7 \cdot (k \cdot 11)$ **D.** $77 + k$

    12. _____

13. $16c + 38 - 11c$

    A. $38 + 27c$ **B.** $38 + 5c$ **C.** $43c$ **D.** 43

    13. _____

Simplify each expression.

14. $3(9ab + 15ab)$

    A. $42ab$ **B.** $72ab$ **C.** $72 + 3ab$ **D.** $27ab + 15ab$ 14. _____

15. $6(g - 4) + 5g + h$

    A. $11g - 3h$ **B.** $11g - 4 + h$ **C.** $6g + 2 + h$ **D.** $11g - 24 + h$ 15. _____

16. $14n + 6r + 7r - 5n$

    A. $19n + 13r$ **B.** $9n + r$ **C.** $22nr$ **D.** $9n + 13r$ 16. _____

Solve each problem. Use any strategy.

17. Alex has a collection of 75 baseball and football cards. He has 23 more football cards than baseball cards. How many football cards does he have?

    A. 23 cards   **B.** 26 cards   **C.** 49 cards   **D.** 52 cards   17. _____

18. How many ways are there to make 35¢ using dimes, nickels, and pennies?

    A. 20 ways   **B.** 16 ways   **C.** 12 ways   **D.** 10 ways   18. _____

19. Suppose you deposit $275 into an account today that pays 4% annual interest. How much money will be in your account three years from now?

    A. $33   **B.** $286   **C.** $287   **D.** $308   19. _____

For Questions 20–22, refer to the frequency table.

Number of 3-Point Baskets in a Basketball Game Last Season		
Number	**Tally**	**Frequency**
0–1	‖	2
2–3	‖‖‖ I	6
4–5	‖‖‖	5
6–7	‖‖‖‖	4
8–9	I	1

20. In how many games did the team have at least four 3-point baskets?

    A. 5 games   **B.** 6 games

    C. 9 games   **D.** 10 games   20. _____

21. In how many games did the team have fewer than six 3-point baskets?

    A. 5 games   **B.** 11 games

    C. 13 games   **D.** 17 games   21. _____

22. Suppose you add a Cumulative Frequency column to the table. What would be the entry in this column for the 6–7 entry in the Number column?

    A. 8   **B.** 13   **C.** 17   **D.** 18   22. _____

The stem-and-leaf plot gives the number of home runs hit by Major League Baseball's leading home-run hitter for each season from 1980 through 1999.

```
Stem | Leaf
   3 | 1 9
   4 | 0 0 0 2 3 3 3 4 6 7 8 9
   5 | 0 1 2 8
   6 | 5
   7 | 0          3|1 = 31
```

23. What was the greatest number of home runs hit during one season?

    A. 20   **B.** 31   **C.** 65   **D.** 70   23. _____

24. How many leading home-run hitters had more than 50 home runs?

    A. 5   **B.** 6   **C.** 7   **D.** 16   24. _____

25. How many home runs did the leading home-run hitters hit most frequently?

    A. 40   **B.** 40 and 43   **C.** 43   **D.** 40, 43, and 70   25. _____

Bonus How many groups of 3 students can you choose from 6 students?

    A. 6   **B.** 15   **C.** 18   **D.** 20   **Bonus** _____

1

Chapter 1 Test, Form 1B

Write the letter for the correct answer in the blank at the right of each problem.

Write an equation for each sentence.

1. Six plus a number m equals 11.
   A. $6 = m + 11$ **B.** $6 - m = 11$
   C. $6 + m = 11$ **D.** $m = 6 + 11$ 1. _____

2. Twenty minus the product of ten and w equals eight.
   A. $(20 - 10)w = 8$ **B.** $10w = 8$
   C. $20 - 10 = 8w$ **D.** $20 - 10w = 8$ 2. _____

Write an algebraic expression for each verbal expression.

3. four less than nine times y
   A. $9y - 4$ **B.** $(9 - 4)y$ **C.** $4y - 9$ **D.** $4(9) - y$ 3. _____

4. the sum of two and the quotient of r and s
   A. $2 + \dfrac{r}{s}$ **B.** $\dfrac{r + 2}{s}$ **C.** $\dfrac{r}{2 + s}$ **D.** $\dfrac{r}{12} + s$ 4. _____

For Questions 5–6, find the value of each expression.

5. $40 - 25 \div 5 + 8$
   A. 11   **B.** 21   **C.** 27   **D.** 43   5. _____

6. $(20 + 7) \div 9 + 18$
   A. 1   **B.** 21   **C.** 27   **D.** 54   6. _____

7. Evaluate the algebraic expression $\dfrac{a + 16}{2c - 4}$ if $a = 8$ and $c = 5$.
   A. 2   **B.** 4   **C.** 6   **D.** 8   7. _____

8. Name the property of equality shown by the statement below.
   If $8 = x$, then $x = 8$.
   A. Transitive   **B.** Symmetric   **C.** Reflexive   **D.** Substitution   8. _____

Name the property shown by each statement.

9. $4 \cdot (m \cdot 6) = 4 \cdot (6 \cdot m)$
   A. Associative (+)   **B.** Associative (×)
   C. Commutative (+)   **D.** Commutative (×)   9. _____

10. $(t + 7) + 5 = t + (7 + 5)$
    A. Associative (+)   **B.** Associative (×)
    C. Commutative (+)   **D.** Commutative (×)   10. _____

Simplify each expression.

11. $4 \cdot (3 \cdot z)$
    A. $7z$ **B.** $12z$ **C.** $(4 \cdot 3) \cdot z$ **D.** $12 + z$ 11. _____

12. $16 + n + 44$
    A. $16n + 44$ **B.** $60n$ **C.** $60 + n$ **D.** $16 + 44n$ 12. _____

13. $14w - 23 - 6w + 3$
    A. $8w + 20$ **B.** $20w - 20$ **C.** $40w$ **D.** $8w - 20$ 13. _____

Simplify each expression.

14. $9(st + 5st)$
   A. $14st$ **B.** $46st$ **C.** $54st$ **D.** $9st + 45st$ **14.** _____

15. $c + d + 4(c - 5)$
   A. $5c + d - 20$ **B.** $5c + 19d$ **C.** $d - 15c$ **D.** $5c + d - 5$ **15.** _____

16. $6a - 3b + 10b - 2a$
   A. $16a - 5b$ **B.** $3a + 8b$ **C.** $11ab$ **D.** $4a + 7b$ **16.** _____

Solve each problem. Use any strategy.

17. Myra has a collection of 42 pop and country CDs. She has 20 more country CDs than pop CDs. How many country CDs does she have?
   A. 11 CDs   **B.** 20 CDs   **C.** 22 CDs   **D.** 31 CDs   **17.** _____

18. How many ways are there to make 30¢ using dimes, nickels, and pennies?
   A. 20 ways   **B.** 16 ways   **C.** 12 ways   **D.** 10 ways   **18.** _____

19. Suppose you deposit $300 into an account today that pays 3% annual interest. How much money will be in your account three years from now?
   A. $27   **B.** $309   **C.** $327   **D.** $345   **19.** _____

For Questions 20–22, refer to the frequency table.

Number of 3-Point Baskets in a Basketball Game Last Season		
Number	Tally	Frequency
0–1	|||	3
2–3	||||	4
4–5	⊔⊔⊔ ||	7
6–7	||	2
8–9			1

20. In how many games did the team have at least four 3-point baskets?
   A. 3 games   **B.** 4 games
   C. 7 games   **D.** 10 games   **20.** _____

21. In how many games did the team have fewer than six 3-point baskets?
   A. 3 games   **B.** 7 games
   C. 14 games   **D.** 16 games   **21.** _____

22. Suppose you add a Cumulative Frequency column to the table. What would be the entry in this column for the 6–7 entry in the Number column?
   A. 7   **B.** 14   **C.** 16   **D.** 17   **22.** _____

The stem-and-leaf plot gives the number of points scored by the winning team in each Super Bowl played from 1967 through 2000.

```
Stem | Leaf
   1 | 4 6 6 6
   2 | 0 0 1 3 3 4 4 6 7 7 7 7
   3 | 0 1 1 2 3 4 5 5 5 7 8 8 9
   4 | 2 6 9
   5 | 2 5        1|4 = 14
```

23. What was the greatest number of points scored in a Super Bowl game?
   A. 55   **B.** 52   **C.** 27   **D.** 14   **23.** _____

24. How many winning teams scored fewer than 30 points in a Super Bowl?
   A. 5   **B.** 6   **C.** 16   **D.** 17   **24.** _____

25. How many points did the winning team score most frequently?
   A. 16   **B.** 27   **C.** 35   **D.** 16, 27, and 35   **25.** _____

Bonus How many groups of 4 students can you choose from 6 students?
   A. 12   **B.** 15   **C.** 20   **D.** 24   **Bonus** _____

1 Chapter 1 Test, Form 2A

Write an algebraic expression for each verbal expression.

1. fifteen increased by the quotient of n and 6

   1. _____

2. eleven less than the product of x and y

   2. _____

Write a verbal expression for each algebraic expression.

3. $3r - 5$

   3. _____

4. $\dfrac{n}{12}$

   4. _____

Write an equation for each sentence.

5. Fifty divided by w is the same as five times z.

   5. _____

6. Twenty equals eight more than the product of 6 and a.

   6. _____

Evaluate each algebraic expression if $a = 6$ and $c = 8$.

7. $\dfrac{5ac}{2(c - a)}$

   7. _____

8. $\dfrac{17 + 3a}{2c - 9}$

   8. _____

9. $[7a - 3(c - 2)] \div 4$

   9. _____

10. $(2c + a)(3c - 4a)$

    10. _____

Name the property shown by each statement.

11. If $18 = n + 5$, then $n + 5 = 18$.

    11. _____

12. $14 - (20 \div 4) = 14 - 5$

    12. _____

13. $(f + g) + h = (g + f) + h$

    13. _____

14. $5 \cdot (s \cdot t) = (5 \cdot s) \cdot t$

    14. _____

15. $6(4w - 3z) = (6 \cdot 4w) - (6 \cdot 3z)$

    15. _____

Simplify each expression.

16. $17 + (w + 23)$

    16. _____

17. $(18c) \cdot 5$

    17. _____

18. $(11 + 3n) + 25$

    18. _____

19. $6 \cdot m \cdot 12$

    19. _____

20. $8(3w + x - w)$

    20. _____

21. $(12m + 4n) + (3m + 7n)$

    21. _____

22. $6(11xy - 8)$

    22. _____

23. $4(3d) + 7(2d - 5)$

    23. _____

Solve each expression. Use any strategy.

24. Mario is 16 years older than his youngest sister, Mercedes. Together, their ages total 36 years. How old is each person?

24. _____

25. Austin has 42 paperback books that are either mysteries or science fiction. If he has 16 more mysteries than science fiction books, how many mysteries does he have?

25. _____

26. How many ways are there to make 45¢ using quarters, dimes, and nickels?

26. _____

27. Hue put $450 into an account that pays interest at an annual rate of 3%. How much will her account have in two years?

27. _____

Determine whether each is a good sample. Write yes or no.

28. Every other person on a school's parent advisory committee is surveyed to determine how many people support passage of a school bond to build a new elementary building.

28. _____

29. Every fifth student in 9th grade is surveyed to find the average weekly number of hours they spend on homework.

29. _____

For Questions 30–31, refer to the frequency table.

30. How many U.S. states were added after 1860?

30. _____

31. Suppose a cumulative frequency histogram of the data is to be constructed. What should be the height of the bar labeled 1861–1900?

Dates of Statehood for the 50 States in the United States		
Year	Tally	Frequency
1781–1820	卌 卌 卌 卌 III	23
1821–1860	卌 卌	10
1861–1900	卌 卌 II	12
1901–1940	III	3
1941–1980	II	2

31. _____

The stem-and-leaf plot gives the number of points scored by the winning team in each NCAA Men's Division I Basketball Championship game from 1970 through 1999.

```
Stem | Leaf
   5 | 4 9
   6 | 3 3 6 7 8
   7 | 1 2 2 4 5 6 6 6 7 7 8
   8 | 0 0 1 3 4 4 6 7 9
   9 | 2 4
  10 | 3          10|3 = 103
```

32. What number of points did the winning team score most frequently?

32. _____

33. How many times did the winning team score less than 80 points?

33. _____

Bonus How can you tell the difference between a histogram and a cumulative frequency histogram just by looking at the bars?

Bonus _____

Chapter 1 Test, Form 2B

1

Write an algebraic expression for each verbal expression.

1. sixteen less than b

1. _____

2. nine more than seven times k

2. _____

Write a verbal expression for each algebraic expression.

3. $c + 10$

3. _____

4. $5w$

4. _____

Write an equation for each sentence.

5. Four times h equals 20.

5. _____

6. Three is equal to 12 divided by z.

6. _____

Evaluate each algebraic expression if r = 6 and s = 8.

7. $\dfrac{3 \cdot 6 + 4 \cdot r}{r + s}$

7. _____

8. $\dfrac{2rs}{s - 4}$

8. _____

9. $r(3s - 10)$

9. _____

10. $(r + 5)(s - 3)$

10. _____

Name the property shown by each statement.

11. If $n - 3 = 8$ and $n = 11$, then $11 - 3 = 8$.

11. _____

12. If $10 = x$, then $x = 10$.

12. _____

13. $(j + 5) + 8 = j + (5 + 8)$

13. _____

14. $a \cdot b = b \cdot a$

14. _____

15. $4(p + 3) = (4 \cdot p) + (4 \cdot 3)$

15. _____

Simplify each expression.

16. $14 + r + 7$

16. _____

17. $6 \cdot (9w)$

17. _____

18. $(2 + t + 8)(5 - 4)$

18. _____

19. $7 \cdot h \cdot 12$

19. _____

20. $6z + 2z + z$

20. _____

21. $4n + 8t + 3t + 5n$

21. _____

22. $5(12 + 3c)$

22. _____

23. $4(6x + 1) - 8x$

23. _____

Chapter 1 Test, Form 2B *(continued)*

Solve each expression. Use any strategy.

24. Alyssa is 11 years older than her younger brother, Darrin. Together, their ages total 25 years. How old is each person?

24. _____

25. How many ways are there to make 45¢ using dimes and nickels?

25. _____

26. Yuji put $200 into an account that pays interest at an annual rate of 5%. How much will his account have in three years?

26. _____

27. Janine has a collection of 28 figurines that are young girls and boys. If she has 4 more girl figurines than boy figurines, how many of her figurines are boys?

27. _____

Determine whether each is a good sample. Write yes or no.

28. The tenth person on each page of a city telephone directory is called and asked for an opinion on the city's bus system.

28. _____

29. The class presidents at a large high school are surveyed to determine the average number of hours that students spend each week working at a job after school.

29. _____

For Questions 30–31, refer to the frequency table.

30. How many U.S. states were added after 1900?

31. Suppose a cumulative frequency histogram of the data is to be constructed. What should be the height of the bar labeled 1821–1860?

Dates of Statehood for the 50 States in the United States		
Year	Tally	Frequency
1781–1820	卌 卌 卌 卌 III	23
1821–1860	卌 卌	10
1861–1900	卌 卌 II	12
1901–1940	III	3
1941–1980	II	2

30. _____

31. _____

The stem-and-leaf plot gives the number of points scored by the winning team in each NCAA Women's Division I Basketball Championship game from 1982 through 1999.

```
Stem | Leaf
   5 | 6
   6 | 0 2 7 8 9
   7 | 0 0 0 2 6 6 8
   8 | 3 4 8
   9 | 3 7        5|6 = 56
```

32. What number of points did the winning team score most frequently?

32. _____

33. How many times did the winning team score more than 70 points?

33. _____

Bonus How can a stem-and-leaf plot be used to display data values that have three digits?

Bonus _____

Chapter 1 Open-Ended Assessment

Instructions: Demonstrate your knowledge by giving a clear, concise solution for each problem. Be sure to include all relevant drawings and to justify your answers. You may show your solution in more than one way or investigate beyond the requirements of the problem.

1. In the table below, write at least three words or phrases used to indicate each mathematical operation.

Addition	Subtraction	Multiplication	Division

2. Simplify each expression. Indicate the properties used in each step.

   a. $5n + 11t - 3n - 6t$ **b.** $8(4b + 9d - 3d)$

3. The table at the right shows the temperature at noon in a small town each day for the past three weeks.

Noon Temperature (°F)
70 69 75 80 71 65 66
69 81 84 78 72 72 75
77 69 70 78 82 83 81

   a. Make a frequency table to organize the data. Choose appropriate temperature intervals.

Noon Temperature (°F)		
Temp.	Tally	Frequency

   b. Construct a cumulative frequency histogram to display the data. Use the temperature intervals you chose in part a.

4. The table at the right shows students' scores on a 25-point algebra quiz.

Quiz Scores
16 20 24 23 19 22 25 25
25 18 19 23 22 19 12 11
19 17 8 20 19 15 16 14

   a. Make a stem-and-leaf plot of the quiz scores.

Stem	Leaf

   b. What score occurred most frequently?

   c. How many students scored at least 20 points on the quiz?

Chapter 1 Mid-Chapter Test
(Lessons 1–1 through 1–4)

Write an algebraic expression for each verbal expression.

1. the quotient of a number m and 8

1. _____

2. a number v increased by 11

2. _____

3. six less than the product of 5 and d

3. _____

Write an equation for each sentence.

4. Ten is equal to 20 divided by x.

4. _____

5. Twelve minus the product of four and b equals three.

5. _____

Evaluate each algebraic expression if w = 4 and x = 5.

6. $[(16 - 2x) + w] \div x$

6. _____

7. $(5w - 2x)(w + x)$

7. _____

8. $\dfrac{3wx - 8 \cdot 7}{4(x - w)}$

8. _____

Name the property shown by each statement.

9. If $a = 16$, then $a \div 8 = 16 \div 8$.

9. _____

10. If $14 - 3x = 4x + 1$, then $4x + 1 = 14 - 3x$.

10. _____

11. $8 \cdot 7 \cdot 5 = 8 \cdot 5 \cdot 7$

11. _____

12. $(6 + 11) + 9 = 6 + (11 + 9)$

12. _____

13. $101 + 79 = 79 + 101$

13. _____

Simplify each expression.

14. $16 + (y + 14)$

14. _____

15. $13 \cdot (p \cdot 7)$

15. _____

16. $8c + 12c - 7c$

16. _____

17. $5(9s + 6t - 4s)$

17. _____

18. $3wx + 11x + 7wx$

18. _____

19. $6(2b + 3) + b - 8$

19. _____

20. $2(k + 3m) + 3(2k + m)$

20. _____

Algebra: Concepts and Applications

NAME _____ DATE _____ PERIOD _____

Chapter 1 Quiz A
(Lessons 1–1 through 1–3)

1. Write an algebraic expression for the verbal expression below.

   eight less than the quotient of a and b

   1. _____

2. Write a verbal expression for the algebraic expression $rs + 5$.

   2. _____

3. Write a sentence for the equation $2n - 3 = 10$.

   3. _____

Find the value of each expression.

4. $20 \div 5 - 12 \div 6$

   4. _____

5. $11 + 4 \cdot 7 - 20$

   5. _____

6. $18 + 9(7 - 2)$

   6. _____

Simplify each expression.

7. $6 \cdot x \cdot 8$

   7. _____

8. $(24 + w) + 16$

   8. _____

Name the property shown by each statement.

9. $(7 \cdot 8) \cdot 5 = 7 \cdot (8 \cdot 5)$

   9. _____

10. $(a + b) + c = (b + a) + c$

   10 _____

1

NAME _____ DATE _____ PERIOD _____

Chapter 1 Quiz B
(Lessons 1–4 through 1–7)

For Questions 1–2, simplify the expression.

1. $5h + 3(4h + 9)$

   1. _____

2. $6(c + 2d) + 5(2c + d)$

   2. _____

3. How many ways are there to make 50¢ using quarters, dimes, and nickels?

   3. _____

4. Jesse owns 75 music cassettes and CDs. If he has 15 more CDs than cassettes, how many CDs does he have?

   4. _____

Determine whether each is a good sample. Write yes or no.

5. Ten band students are asked to name their favorite musician.

   5. _____

6. Everyone riding the cross-town bus at 3 P.M. is surveyed to determine the inner-city residents' opinion of the new token system being used on the buses.

   6. _____

The table shows the class results on a 25-point quiz. Use the table for Questions 7–8.

Quiz Scores
21 15 25 24 19 15 18
19 16 20 21 25 18 21
23 21 12 17 20 17 10

7. If a stem-and-leaf plot is made for the data, how many leaves will there be for the stem 2?

   7. _____

8. What score occurred most frequently?

   8. _____

NAME _____ DATE _____ PERIOD _____

Chapter 1 Cumulative Review

For Questions 1–2, write an algebraic expression for each verbal expression. *(Lesson 1–1)*

1. the sum of 7 and 8 times a number t

2. eleven less than the quotient of c and 4

3. Write an equation for the sentence below. *(Lesson 1–1)*

     Twenty is equal to n *divided by 8.*

Evaluate each algebraic expression if $u = 3$, $v = 7$, and $w = 5$. *(Lesson 1–2)*

4. $\dfrac{6 \cdot w + 5 \cdot 2}{v - w}$

5. $8[17 - (u + v)] - 6v$

6. $(2u + w)(20 - uw)$

Name the property shown by each statement. *(Lessons 1–3, 1–4)*

7. $(11 \cdot 5) \cdot 6 = 11 \cdot (5 \cdot 6)$

8. $(9 \cdot d) + (9 \cdot h) = 9(d + h)$

Simplify each expression. *(Lessons 1–3, 1–4)*

9. $12 + z + 38$

10. $8(3w + 2x) - 9w + 4x$

Solve each problem. Use any strategy. *(Lesson 1–5)*

11. Twins Diana and Riana are each 6 years older than their younger brother Kyle. Together, their three ages total 21 years. How old is Kyle?

12. Adam collects stamps and coins. He has a total of 54 stamps and coins. If he has 20 more coins than stamps, how many stamps does he have?

The frequency table shows the results of a survey of students. *(Lesson 1–6)*

13. How many students were surveyed?

14. How many students saw fewer than two movies?

Movies Seen Last Month		
Number	**Tally**	**Frequency**
0	ЖЖ	5
1	ЖЖ II	7
2	ЖЖ IIII	9
3	IIII	4

The line graph shows the number of cellular phone subscribers in the U.S. from 1990 through 1999. *(Lesson 1–7)*

15. Describe the general trend in the number of subscribers.

16. Estimate the number of subscribers for the year 1999.

U.S. Cellular Phone Use

Number of Subscribers (millions)

Year

1. _____

2. _____

3. _____

4. _____

5. _____

6. _____

7. _____

8. _____

9. _____

10. _____

11. _____

12. _____

13. _____

14. _____

15. _____

16. _____

Write the letter for the correct answer in the blank at the right of each problem.

1. Which statement is false?
   A. An algebraic expression contains at least one variable and at least one mathematical operation.
   B. A numerical expression contains only numbers and mathematical operations.
   C. A variable stands for a known number; its value is always the same.
   D. An equation is a sentence that contains an equals sign.

   1. _____

2. Which is the equation for the sentence below?

   Seven less than six times n is 41.
   A. $7 - 6n = 41$ B. $6n - 7 = 41$ C. $41 - 7 = 6n$ D. $7 = 6n - 41$

   2. _____

3. All of the following are examples of algebraic expressions except
   A. $4 - 6m$.   B. $\frac{x}{10}$.   C. $\frac{5}{r} - 8$.   D. $\frac{7-3}{5-1}$.

   3. _____

4. Find the value of $18 + (24 \div 8) - 5 \cdot 3$.
   A. 0   B. 6   C. 12   D. 48

   4. _____

5. Name the property of equality shown by the statement below.

   If $g + 14 = 31$ and $g = 17$, then $17 + 14 = 31$.
   A. Transitive Property   B. Symmetric Property
   C. Reflexive Property   D. Substitution Property

   5. _____

6. Evaluate $\frac{3(r + 2s)}{rs - 13}$ if $r = 8$ and $s = 5$.
   A. 2   B. 3   C. 5   D. 8

   6. _____

For Questions 7–8, name the property shown by the statement.

7. $(14 + n) + 16 = (n + 14) + 16$
   A. Associative (+)   B. Associative (×)
   C. Commutative (+)   D. Commutative (×)

   7. _____

8. $x \cdot z = z \cdot x$
   A. Associative (+)   B. Associative (×)
   C. Commutative (+)   D. Commutative (×)

   8. _____

9. Which of the following is a counterexample showing that the following statement is false?

   Subtraction of whole numbers is associative.
   A. $(10 - 8) - 5 \neq (8 - 10) - 5$ B. $10 - (8 - 5) \neq (10 - 8) - 5$
   C. $10 - (8 + 5) \neq (10 - 8) + 5$ D. $10 - (8 - 5) = 10 - 3$

   9. _____

10. Simplify $2(7j + 8k) + 3(2j - 5k)$.
    A. $20j + 31k$ B. $20j + 3k$ C. $20j + k$ D. $21jk$

    10. _____

11. Simplify $4(3ab - 4) + 2(ab + 9)$.
    A. $14ab + 2$ B. $14ab + 5$ C. $10ab - 14$ D. $24ab + 30$

    11. _____

12. Which statement is true?
    A. A term is a number or the product or quotient of numbers.
    B. Two algebraic expressions are equivalent whenever their variables are replaced by the same value.
    C. You can write an algebraic expression in simplest form by writing an equivalent expression having no like terms and no parentheses.
    D. The variable that appears in the first term of an algebraic expression is the coefficient of the expression.

    12. _____

Solve each problem. Use any strategy.

13. Angela has $94 in bills, none greater than $10. She has four $10 bills. If she has 6 fewer $5 bills than $1 bills, how many $5 bills and how many $1 bills does she have?
    A. 14 $5 bills, 8 $1 bills   B. 10 $5 bills, 4 $1 bills
    C. 9 $5 bills, 15 $1 bills   D. 8 $5 bills, 14 $1 bills

    13. _____

14. Distance traveled *d* equals the product of the rate *r* and the time *t*. How far will a bicycle racer travel if he averages 24 miles per hour for 4 hours?
    A. 6 mi   B. 28 mi   C. 86 mi   D. 96 mi

    14. _____

15. Using quarters, dimes, and nickels, you can make 30¢ in
    A. 4 ways.   B. 5 ways.   C. 6 ways.   D. 7 ways.

    15. _____

For Questions 16–18, refer to the frequency table.

Runs Scored in a Softball Game Last Season		
Runs	**Tally**	**Frequency**
0–2	⊦⊦⊦⊦ I	6
3–5	⊦⊦⊦⊦ IIII	9
6–8	⊦⊦⊦⊦ II	7
9–11	III	3
12–14	II	2

16. In how many games did the team score more than 5 runs?
    A. 7 games   B. 12 games
    C. 15 games   D. 21 games

    16. _____

17. Which number of runs did the team score most frequently in a game?
    A. 3–5 runs   B. 6–8 runs
    C. 9–11 runs   D. 12–14 runs

    17. _____

18. If the team lost every game in which they scored fewer than 4 runs, how many games did they lose?
    A. 6 games   B. 9 games
    C. 15 games   D. Cannot be determined.

    18. _____

The stem-and-leaf plot gives the number of points scored by the winning team in the Super Bowl each year from 1967 through 2000.

```
Stem | Leaf
   1 | 4 6 6 6
   2 | 0 0 1 3 3 4 4 6 7 7 7 7
   3 | 0 1 1 2 3 4 5 5 5 7 8 8 9
   4 | 2 6 9
   5 | 2 5          1|4 = 14
```

19. In how many games was the winning score a multiple of 5?
    A. 3 games   B. 4 games   C. 7 games   D. 8 games

    19. _____

20. How many winning teams scored at least 35 points in the game?
    A. 18 teams   B. 12 teams   C. 9 teams   D. 3 teams

    20. _____

Chapter 1 Answer Key

Form 1A

Page 1

1. C
2. D
3. B
4. A
5. C
6. C
7. D
8. B
9. A
10. D
11. C
12. A
13. B

Page 2

14. B
15. D
16. D
17. C
18. A
19. D
20. D
21. C
22. C
23. D
24. A
25. B
Bonus D

Form 1B

Page 3

1. C
2. D
3. A
4. A
5. D
6. B
7. B
8. B
9. D
10. A
11. B
12. C
13. D

Page 4

14. C
15. A
16. D
17. D
18. B
19. C
20. D
21. C
22. C
23. A
24. C
25. B
Bonus B

Chapter 1 Answer Key

Form 2A

1. $15 + \dfrac{n}{6}$

2. $xy - 11$

3. Sample answer: 5 less than the product of 3 and r

4. Sample answer: the quotient of n and 12

5. $\dfrac{50}{w} = 5z$

6. $20 = 6a + 8$

7. 60

8. 5

9. 6

10. 0

11. Symmetric Property of Equality

12. Substitution Property of Equality

13. Commutative Property (+)

14. Associative Property (×)

15. Distributive Property

16. $w + 40$

17. $90c$

18. $3n + 36$

19. $72m$

20. $16w + 8x$

21. $15m + 11n$

22. $66xy - 48$

23. $26d - 35$

24. Mario, 26; Mercedes, 10

25. 29 mysteries

26. 8 ways

27. $477

28. no

29. yes

30. 17 states

31. 45

32. 76 points

33. 18 times

Bonus In a cumulative frequency histogram, the bars increase in height from left to right.

Chapter 1 Answer Key
Form 2B

Page 7

1. $b - 16$
2. $7k + 9$
3. Sample answer: 10 more than c
4. Sample answer: the product of 5 and w
5. $4h = 20$
6. $3 = \dfrac{12}{z}$
7. 3
8. 24
9. 84
10. 55
11. Substitution Property of Equality
12. Symmetric Property of Equality
13. Associative Property (+)
14. Commutative Property (×)
15. Distributive Property
16. $r + 21$
17. $54w$
18. $10 + t$
19. $84h$
20. $9z$
21. $9n + 11t$
22. $60 + 15c$
23. $16x + 4$

Page 8

24. Alyssa, 18; Darrin, 7
25. 5 ways
26. $230
27. 12 boys
28. yes
29. no
30. 5 states
31. 33
32. 70 points
33. 9 times

Bonus. The digits in the first two place values form the stem and the third digit forms the leaf.

Chapter 1 Answer Key
Open-Ended Assessment
Sample Answers
Page 9

1.

Addition	Subtraction	Multiplication	Division
plus	minus	times	divided by
sum	difference	product	quotient
increased by	decreased by	multiplied by	ratio
more than	less than		

2. a. $5n + 11t - 3n - 6t$
$= 5n - 3n + 11t - 6t$ *Comm. (+)*
$= (5n - 3n) + (11t - 6t)$ *Assoc. (+)*
$= (5 - 3)n + (11 - 6)t$ *Distrib.*
$= 2n + 5t$ *Substit.*

b. $8(4b + 9d - 3d)$
$= 8[4b + (9d - 3d)]$ *Assoc. (+)*
$= 8[4b + (9 - 3)d]$ *Distrib.*
$= 8(4b + 6d)$ *Substit.*
$= (8 \cdot 4b) + (8 \cdot 6d)$ *Distrib.*
$= 32b + 48d$ *Substit.*

3. a.

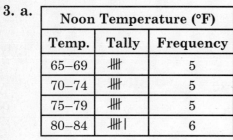

Noon Temperature (°F)		
Temp.	Tally	Frequency
65–69	⊞	5
70–74	⊞	5
75–79	⊞	5
80–84	⊞|	6

b.

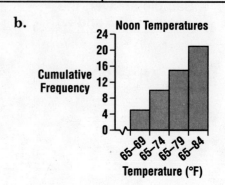

4. a.

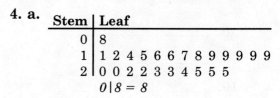

Stem	Leaf
0	8
1	1 2 4 5 6 6 7 8 9 9 9 9 9
2	0 0 2 2 3 3 4 5 5 5

$0|8 = 8$

b. 19

c. 10 students

Chapter 1 Answer Key

Mid-Chapter Test
Page 10

1. $\dfrac{m}{8}$

2. $v + 11$

3. $5d - 6$

4. $10 = \dfrac{20}{x}$

5. $12 - 4b = 3$

6. 2

7. 90

8. 1

9. Division Property of Equality

10. Reflexive Property of Equality

11. Commutative ($\times$)

12. Associative ($+$)

13. Commutative ($+$)

14. $y + 30$

15. $91p$

16. $13c$

17. $25s + 30t$

18. $10wx + 11x$

19. $13b + 10$

20. $8k + 9m$

Quiz A
Page 11

1. $\dfrac{a}{b} - 8$

2. 5 more than the product of r and s

3. Two times n minus 3 equals 10.

4. 2

5. 19

6. 63

7. $48x$

8. $w + 40$

9. Associative ($\times$)

10. Commutative ($+$)

Quiz B
Page 11

1. $17h + 27$

2. $16c + 17d$

3. 10 ways

4. 45 CDs

5. no

6. no

7. 10 leaves

8. 21

Chapter 1 Answer Key

Cumulative Review — Page 12

1. $7 + 8t$
2. $\dfrac{c}{4} - 11$
3. $20 = \dfrac{n}{8}$
4. 20
5. 14
6. 55
7. Associative Prop. ($\times$)
8. Distributive Prop.
9. $50 + z$
10. $15w + 20x$
11. 3 years old
12. 17 stamps
13. 25 students
14. 12 students
15. It is increasing.
16. Sample answer: about 85 million

Standardized Test Practice — Page 13

1. C
2. B
3. D
4. B
5. D
6. A
7. C
8. D
9. B
10. C
11. A

Page 14

12. C
13. D
14. D
15. B
16. B
17. A
18. D
19. C
20. B

2

Chapter 2 Test, Form 1A

Write the letter for the correct answer in the blank at the right of each problem.

1. Which of the following sentences is true?
   A. $|-3| > -|-3|$
   B. $2 < |-2|$
   C. $|-5| < |-3|$
   D. $-5 > -3$

   1. _____

2. Name the coordinate of C on the number line at the right.

   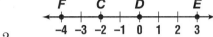

   A. -4
   B. -2
   C. 2
   D. 3

   2. _____

3. Order -8, 6, -7, 7, and 0 from greatest to least.
   A. $-8, -7, 0, 6, 7$
   B. $-8, 7, -7, 6, 0$
   C. $7, 6, 0, -7, -8$
   D. $7, 6, 0, -8, -7$

   3. _____

4. Evaluate $-|14| + |-7|$.
   A. -21
   B. -7
   C. 7
   D. 21

   4. _____

For Questions 5–6, refer to the coordinate plane at the right.

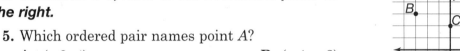

5. Which ordered pair names point A?
   A. $(-3, 4)$
   B. $(-4, -3)$
   C. $(3, -4)$
   D. $(4, -3)$

   5. _____

6. In which quadrant is point C located?
   A. I
   B. II
   C. No quadrant; it lies on the y-axis.
   D. No quadrant; it lies on the x-axis.

   6. _____

7. Which of the following points is located in Quadrant III?
   A. $(-2, -4)$
   B. $(-6, 0)$
   C. $(-5, 3)$
   D. $(1, -2)$

   7. _____

8. The graph of $P(x, y)$ satisfies the condition that $y < 0$. In which quadrant(s) could point P be located?
   A. III only
   B. IV only
   C. II or III
   D. III or IV

   8. _____

9. Which ordered pair names a point that lies on the y-axis and below the x-axis?
   A. $(-1, -4)$
   B. $(-6, 0)$
   C. $(0, -3)$
   D. $(0, 2)$

   9. _____

10. Find the sum: $-18 + (-24)$.
    A. -42
    B. -32
    C. -6
    D. 6

    10. _____

11. What is the value of k if $40 + (-58) + 32 = k$?
    A. 130
    B. 50
    C. 16
    D. 14

    11. _____

12. Simplify $15z + (-23z) + 25z$.
    A. $27z$
    B. $17z$
    C. $63z$
    D. $-7z$

    12. _____

13. A basketball player averages 24 points per game. In her next four games, she scores 5 points above her average, 4 points below her average, 6 points below her average, and 11 points above her average. How many points total is she above or below average for the four games?
    A. 6 below   B. 4 below   C. 4 above   D. 6 above   13. _____

14. Find the difference: $-12 - (-5)$.
    A. -17 B. -7 C. 7   D. 17   14. _____

15. Evaluate $20 - a + b$ if $a = 18$ and $b = -5$.
    A. 43   B. 33   C. -3 D. -7 15. _____

16. Simplify $-14d - 8d - (-21d)$.
    A. $-d$ B. $-43d$ C. $-15d$ D. d 16. _____

17. The week that your rent is due your paycheck is \$462. If your rent is \$275, how much money do you have left for the week after paying your rent?
    A. \$87   B. \$177   C. \$187   D. \$737   17. _____

18. Find the product: $-2(3)(-1)(5)(-2)$.
    A. -60 B. -30 C. 30   D. 60   18. _____

19. Evaluate $-2xy + 3z$ if $x = 8$, $y = -1$, and $z = -5$.
    A. 31   B. 1   C. -1 D. -31 19. _____

20. What is the product of -5, -6, and -2?
    A. -70 B. -60 C. 60   D. 70   20. _____

21. Simplify $-2(-3r)(5s)$.
    A. $6r + 5s$ B. $11r + s$ C. $25rs$ D. $30rs$ 21. _____

22. Find the quotient: $-125 \div (-5)$.
    A. -120 B. -24 C. 24   D. 25   22. _____

23. Find the value of s if $-84 \div 12 = s$.
    A. 72   B. 7   C. -7 D. -8 23. _____

24. Evaluate $\frac{mp - n}{-3}$ if $m = -5$, $n = 6$, and $p = -3$.
    A. -7 B. -3 C. 3   D. 7   24. _____

25. Over a six-year period, the enrollment of a school decreased from 812 to 482. What was the average change in enrollment for each of those six years?
    A. -330 B. -55 C. -45 D. -38 25. _____

Bonus Simplify $\frac{-96}{-6} - (-2)(-9)$.
    A. -2 B. 0   C. 2   D. 34   **Bonus** _____

2

Chapter 2 Test, Form 1B

Write the letter for the correct answer in the blank at the right of each problem.

1. Name the coordinate of Z on the number line at the right.

   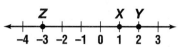

   A. 3   **B.** 2

   C. 1   **D.** −3   1. _____

2. Order −4, 2, −1, −3, and −2 from least to greatest.

   A. −1, −2, −3, −4, 2   **B.** −2, −1, 2, −3, −4

   C. −4, −3, −2, −1, 2   **D.** 2, −1, −2, −3, −4   2. _____

3. Which of the following sentences is true?

   A. $-|2| < |-2|$ **B.** $-4 > -3$

   C. $6 > |-7|$ **D.** $|-1| < 1$ 3. _____

4. Evaluate $|5| - |-2|$.

   A. 7   **B.** 3   **C.** −3   **D.** −7   4. _____

5. Which of the following points is located in Quadrant II?

   A. $(-4, 0)$ **B.** $(-2, 7)$ **C.** $(5, -1)$ **D.** $(-3, -4)$ 5. _____

For Questions 6–7, refer to the coordinate plane at the right.

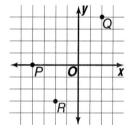

6. Which ordered pair names point P?

   A. $(0, 4)$ **B.** $(4, 0)$

   C. $(-4, 0)$ **D.** $(0, -4)$ 6. _____

7. In which quadrant is point Q located?

   A. I   **B.** II

   C. III   **D.** IV   7. _____

8. The graph of $P(x, y)$ satisfies the conditions that $x < 0$ and $y > 0$. In which quadrant is point P located?

   A. I   **B.** II   **C.** III   **D.** IV   8. _____

9. Which ordered pair names a point that lies on the x-axis and to the left of the y-axis?

   A. $(0, -3)$ **B.** $(4, 0)$ **C.** $(0, 0)$ **D.** $(-1, 0)$ 9. _____

10. What is the value of m if $m = 13 + (-27)$?

    A. −40   **B.** −24   **C.** −14   **D.** 40   10. _____

11. Simplify $-4k + (-2k) + 8k$.

    A. $-2k$ **B.** $2k$ **C.** $14k$ **D.** $6k$ 11. _____

12. Find the sum: $-50 + 28$.

    A. −78   **B.** −32   **C.** −22   **D.** 78   12. _____

13. In four days, a golfer has rounds of four over par (+4), 1 under par (−1), 2 over par (+2) and 3 under par (−3). What is the golfer's overall score for the four days?

    A. −1   **B.** +1   **C.** +2   **D.** +4   13. _____

14. Evaluate $y - x$ if $x = 12$ and $y = -8$.

    A. −20   **B.** −4   **C.** 4   **D.** 20   14. _____

15. On January 13, the low temperature was 12°F. The next day, the low temperature dropped by 25°. What was the low temperature on January 14?

    A. −37°F   **B.** −25°F   **C.** −13°F   **D.** 37°F   15. _____

16. Find the difference: $-9 - 5$.

    A. 45   **B.** 14   **C.** −4   **D.** −14   16. _____

17. Simplify $-6p - (-9p)$.

    A. $-3p$ **B.** $3p$ **C.** $-15p$ **D.** $15p$ 17. _____

18. Evaluate $-2\ell m - n$ if $\ell = -1$, $m = 2$, and $n = -3$.

    A. −7   **B.** −4   **C.** 1   **D.** 7   18. _____

19. Simplify $-5(-4t)$.

    A. $20t$ **B.** $-9t$ **C.** $-t$ **D.** $-20t$ 19. _____

20. Find the product: $-8(-6)$.

    A. −56   **B.** −48   **C.** 14   **D.** 48   20. _____

21. What is the value of n if $n = (-6)(3)(-3)$?

    A. −54   **B.** −36   **C.** 36   **D.** 54   21. _____

22. Evaluate $\frac{fg}{-2}$ if $f = -4$ and $g = 2$.

    A. 4   **B.** 3   **C.** 1   **D.** −4   22. _____

23. Find the quotient: $54 \div (-3)$.

    A. −18   **B.** −16   **C.** 16   **D.** 18   23. _____

24. Find the value of b if $b = -72 \div (-18)$.

    A. −6   **B.** −4   **C.** 4   **D.** 6   24. _____

25. Over eight years, the population of a town decreased from 1000 to 800. What was the average change in population for each of the eight years?

    A. −200   **B.** −25   **C.** 25   **D.** 200   25. _____

Bonus Simplify $\frac{9}{-3} - (-4)(2)$.

     A. −11   **B.** −5   **C.** 5   **D.** 11   Bonus _____

2

Chapter 2 Test, Form 2A

1. Graph the set of numbers {3, −1, 0} on a number line.

1.
```
←─┼─┼─┼─┼─┼─→
 -1  0  1  2  3
```

For Questions 2–4, replace each ● with < or > to make a true sentence.

2. $|-10|$ ● 11

2. _____

3. -6 ● -8

3. _____

4. -3 ● $-|-2|$

4. _____

5. Evaluate $-|-6| - |0|$.

5. _____

For Questions 6–9, use the coordinate plane at the right.

6. What ordered pair names point P?

6. _____

7. What ordered pair names point R?

7. _____

8. In what quadrant is point S located?

8. _____

9. In what quadrant is point T located?

9. _____

10. In what quadrant is the point $D(-4, 8)$ located?

10. _____

For Questions 11–13, find each sum.

11. $18 + (-27) + 46$

11. _____

12. $-36 + (-8) + 20$

12. _____

13. $50 + (-36) + (-12)$

13. _____

14. During one week the Dow Jones Industrial average, the most commonly used measure of the stock market, rises 43 points, falls 11 points, rises 38 points, rises 69 points, and falls 148 points. By how many points is it up or down overall for the week?

14. _____

15. Evaluate $-26 + |z| + y$ if $y = -8$ and $z = -15$.

15. _____

Find each difference.

16. $22 - (-9)$

16. _____

17. $-8 - (-12)$

17. _____

18. $-30 - (-8) - (-25)$

18. _____

19. $45 - (-18) - 75$

19. _____

20. Simplify $-28k - (-18k) - 14k$.

20. _____

21. What is the difference in elevation between the highest point in California, Mount Whitney, which towers 4421 meters above sea level, and the lowest point in California, Death Valley, which lies 86 meters below sea level?

21. _____

For Questions 22–24, find each product.

22. $-2(-3)(-3)$

22. _____

23. $4(-2)(-1)(5)(-2)$

23. _____

24. $-12(-2)(-1)$

24. _____

25. A small company buys 8 chairs, each at a price of $40 less than the regular price, and 6 lamps, each at a price of $15 less than the regular price. What number describes the price the company pays in all compared to the regular price?

25. _____

26. Evaluate $3xz - 8y$ if $x = 4$, $y = -1$, and $z = -2$.

26. _____

27. Find the next term in the pattern $2, -8, 32, -128, \ldots$.

27. _____

For Questions 28–30, find each quotient.

28. $\dfrac{57}{-3}$

28. _____

29. $-120 \div (-15)$

29. _____

30. $\dfrac{-100}{-4}$

30. _____

31. The acceleration a of an object (in feet per second squared) is given by $a = \dfrac{s_2 - s_1}{t}$, where t is the time in seconds, s_1 is the speed at the beginning of the time, and s_2 is the speed at the end of the time. What is the acceleration of a car that brakes from a speed of 114 feet per second to a speed of 18 feet per second in 6 seconds?

31. _____

32. Evaluate $\dfrac{z - x}{y}$ if $x = -6$, $y = -4$, and $z = 10$.

32. _____

33. Over a five-year period, the value of a house increased from $135,000 to $150,000. What was the average change in value for each of these five years?

33. _____

Bonus From Sunday to Monday, the minimum daily humidity drops 3%. Over the next three days, it rises 8%, rises 16%, and then drops 21%. What is the average daily change when you compare the minimum humidity on Thursday to the minimum humidity on Sunday?

Bonus _____

2

Chapter 2 Test, Form 2B

For Questions 1–3, replace each ● with < or > to make a true sentence.

1. -5 ● -7

2. 3 ● $|-4|$

3. $-|-2|$ ● 1

4. Evaluate $|-4| + |-8|$.

5. Graph the set of numbers $\{-2, 1, 0\}$ on a number line.

1. _____

2. _____

3. _____

4. _____

5.

$$\xleftarrow{\hspace{0.3cm}}\overset{\displaystyle+\ \ +\ \ +\ \ +\ \ +}{\underset{\text{-3 \ -2 \ -1 \ \ 0 \ \ 1}}{\hspace{0.3cm}}}\xrightarrow{\hspace{0.3cm}}$$

For Questions 6–9, use the coordinate plane at the right.

6. In what quadrant is point B located?

7. In what quadrant is point C located?

8. What ordered pair names point A?

9. What ordered pair names point E?

10. In what quadrant is the point $R(6, -2)$ located?

11. Evaluate $-4 + b + |c|$ if $b = 7$ and $c = -2$.

6. _____

7. _____

8. _____

9. _____

10. _____

11. _____

For Questions 12–14, find each sum.

12. $6 + (-3) + 9$

13. $-21 + (-15) + 31$

14. $-12 + 18 + (-20)$

12. _____

13. _____

14. _____

15. During one week a small town reservoir falls 3 feet, drops 2 feet, rises 3 feet, rises 1 foot, and falls 1 foot. By how many feet does the reservoir rise or fall overall for the week?

15. _____

For Questions 16–19, find each difference.

16. $9 - (-5)$

17. $-15 - (-32)$

18. $-6 - (-5)$

19. $-11 - (-28) - 3$

16. _____

17. _____

18. _____

19. _____

20. Simplify $8b - 5b - (-3b)$.

20. _____

21. The temperature dropped 42°F overnight from yesterday's high temperature of 25°F. What is the temperature this morning?

21. _____

22. Find the next term in the pattern $3, -15, 75, \ldots$.

22. _____

23. Evaluate $2x - 3y$ when $x = -5$ and $y = -4$.

23. _____

For Questions 24–26, find each product.

24. $4(6)(-2)$

24. _____

25. $-2(3)(-1)(5)$

25. _____

26. $3(-3)(-2)(-1)$

26. _____

27. You and several friends go together to buy detergent from a warehouse store. By buying 12 economy boxes, you get a price that is $2 less per box than the regular price. What number describes the price you pay for the total purchase compared to the regular price?

27. _____

28. Evaluate $\dfrac{a - c}{b}$ if $a = 16$, $b = -4$, and $c = -8$.

28. _____

For Questions 29–31, find each quotient.

29. $-42 \div (-3)$

29. _____

30. $\dfrac{-150}{25}$

30. _____

31. $\dfrac{64}{-4}$

31. _____

32. The acceleration a of an object (in feet per second squared) is given by $a = \dfrac{s_2 - s_1}{t}$, where t is the time in seconds, s_1 is the speed at the beginning of the time, and s_2 is the speed at the end of the time. What is the acceleration of a sled testing child car seats that goes from a speed of 88 feet per second to a speed of 0 feet per second in 2 seconds?

32. _____

33. Over the past three years, the zoo's attendance figures have decreased from 185,000 to 176,000. What is the average change in attendance for each of the last three years?

33. _____

Bonus From Sunday to Monday, the maximum daily temperature in a small pond rises 1°F. Over the next three days, it rises 4°F, falls 1°F, and then falls 8°F. What is the average daily change when you compare the maximum temperature on Thursday to the maximum temperature on Sunday?

Bonus _____

Chapter 2 Open-Ended Assessment

Instructions: Demonstrate your knowledge by giving a clear, concise solution to each problem. Be sure to include all relevant drawings and to justify your answers. You may show your solution in more than one way or investigate beyond the requirements of the problem.

1. Refer to the coordinate plane at the right.

   a. Write the ordered pair that names each point.

   b. Multiply the x- and y-coordinates of each point by -2.

   c. Graph the new points. Label the point corresponding to A as X, the point corresponding to B as Y, and the point corresponding to C as Z.

   d. Describe how the new triangle is related to the original triangle.

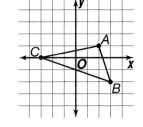

2. Now we will investigate more generally what happens to points when their x- and/or y-coordinates are multiplied by a negative number.

   a. Pick a negative integer n. Fill out the table below, in which you will choose one point (a, b) in each quadrant, and then multiply one or both coordinates by n.

Quadrant of (a, b)	I	II	III	IV
Coordinates of (a, b)				
Coord. and quad. of (na, b)				
Coord. and quad. of (a, nb)				
Coord. and quad. of (na, nb)				

   b. How does multiplying one or both coordinates of a point by a negative number change the quadrant in which a point lies?

3. In an investment club, members pool their money and their knowledge to invest in the stocks of various companies. Members share any profits or losses equally.

   a. One club charges each member a $250 initial investment and monthly investments of $30. In its first year, the 15-member club loses $1320. In its second year, the club makes a $990 profit. Write and evaluate an expression to find each member's net gain or loss after two years.

   b. Another club charges each member a $150 initial investment and monthly investments of $20. In its first year, the 25-member club loses $1750. In its second year, the club makes a $1200 profit. Write and evaluate an expression to find each member's net gain or loss after two years.

   c. Compare the results of the two investment clubs.

Chapter 2 Mid-Chapter Test
(Lessons 2–1 through 2–3)

For Questions 1–2, name the coordinate of each point on the number line at the right.

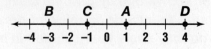

1. C 1. _____

2. D 2. _____

Replace each ● with < or > to make a true sentence.

3. -8 ● -2 3. _____

4. $|-3|$ ● $-|-2|$ 4. _____

5. 4 ● -5 5. _____

6. -6 ● $|-7|$ 6. _____

Order each set of numbers from greatest to least.

7. $-12, 10, -8, 0, 3$ 7. _____

8. $-4, 6, -5, -3, 2, 5$ 8. _____

Graph each point on the same coordinate plane.

9. $P(3, 0)$

10. $Q(-2, -1)$

11. $R(4, -3)$

9–11.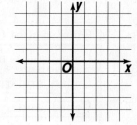

For Questions 12–15, use the coordinate plane at the right.

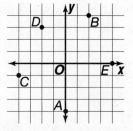

12. What ordered pair names point A?   12. _____

13. What ordered pair names point D?   13. _____

14. In what quadrant is point C located?   14. _____

15. In what quadrant is point B located?   15. _____

For Questions 16–18, find each sum.

16. $-9 + 18$ 16. _____

17. $84 + (-35) + (-27)$ 17. _____

18. $-8 + 4 + (-9) + 15$ 18. _____

19. Simplify $12x + (-9x) + 6x$.   19. _____

20. Evaluate $-11 + y + z$ if $y = -4$ and $z = 8$.   20. _____

NAME _____ DATE _____ PERIOD _____

Chapter 2 Quiz A
(Lessons 2–1 and 2–2)

1. Graph the set of numbers $\{3, -2, 0\}$ on a number line.

1.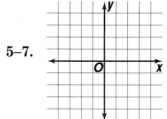

For Questions 2–3, replace each ● with < or > to make a true sentence.

2. $|-12| \; \bullet \; -10$

2. _____

3. $-8 \; \bullet \; -|-7|$

3. _____

4. Evaluate $-|-6| - |-2|$.

4. _____

For Questions 5–7, graph each point on the same coordinate plane.

5. $A(2, -3)$

6. $B(3, 4)$

7. $C(-3, -4)$

5–7.

8. In what quadrant is the point $T(4, -1)$ located?

8. _____

2

NAME _____ DATE _____ PERIOD _____

Chapter 2 Quiz B
(Lessons 2–3 through 2–6)

1. Find the sum: $-11 + 8 + (-7)$.

1. _____

2. Evaluate $a + b + (-12)$ if $a = -16$ and $b = 28$.

2. _____

3. Find the difference: $120 - (-54)$.

3. _____

4. Write and evaluate an expression to find the difference (in the number of floors) between the 21st story of a building and the parking level three stories below the ground floor.

4. _____

5. Find the product: $-2(7)(-3)(-1)$.

5. _____

6. Evaluate $(-2s)(5t)$ if $s = -1$ and $t = 8$.

6. _____

7. What is the value of b if $b = -90 \div (-15)$?

7. _____

8. Over the past four years, the value of a car has decreased from $22,000 to $12,000. What is the average change in value for each of the last four years?

8. _____

Chapter 2 Cumulative Review

1. Write an equation for the sentence below. *(Lesson 1–1)*
   Six less than four times a is the same as eleven more than the
   product of b and c.

   1. _____

2. Find the value of $6 + 2(7 - 4) \div 6$. *(Lesson 1–2)*

   2. _____

3. Name the property shown by the statement below. *(Lesson 1–3)*
   $$8 + 6 \cdot (5 \cdot 11) = 8 + (6 \cdot 5) \cdot 11$$

   3. _____

4. Simplify $6(2x - 3) - 4x$. *(Lesson 1–4)*

   4. _____

5. Mrs. Esposito buys apples at $2 per pound and walnuts at
   $5 per pound. If she spends three times as much on walnuts
   as apples and her total bill is $20, how many pounds of apples
   does she buy? *(Lesson 1–5)*

   5. _____

6. The frequency table gives the
   number of goals a soccer team
   scored in 11 games. In how many
   games did the team score at
   least two goals? *(Lesson 1–6)*

Goals	Frequency
0	2
1	3
2	4
3	1
4	1

   6. _____

7. What kind of a graph or plot is best to use to display how a
   quantity changes over time? *(Lesson 1–7)*

   7. _____

8. Order 11, -25, 36, -64, -2, and 3 from least to greatest.
   (Lesson 2–1)

   8. _____

**For Questions 9–10, refer to the coordinate
plane at the right.** *(Lesson 2–2)*

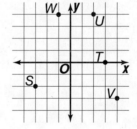

9. Write the ordered pair that names
   point W.

   9. _____

10. Name the quadrant in which point V
    is located.

    10. _____

11. Find the sum: $-22 + (-31)$. *(Lesson 2–3)*

    11. _____

12. Evaluate $-a + b - c$ if $a = -12$, $b = 22$, and $c = -8$.
    (Lesson 2–4)

    12. _____

13. At 20°F with a 5-mile-per-hour wind, the windchill factor is
    16°F. At this temperature with a 45-mile-per-hour wind, the
    windchill factor drops 38°F. What is the windchill factor at
    20°F with a 45-mile-per-hour wind? *(Lesson 2–4)*

    13. _____

14. Find the product of -2, 3, -1, and 8. *(Lesson 2–5)*

    14. _____

15. Evaluate $\frac{3xy}{-4}$ if $x = -6$ and $y = 2$. *(Lesson 2–6)*

    15. _____

16. Find the quotient: $(-126) \div (-9)$. *(Lesson 2–6)*

    16. _____

2

Chapter 2 Standardized Test Practice
(Chapters 1–2)

Write the letter for the correct answer in the blank at the right of the problem.

1. Write an equation for the sentence below.

   Three less than the quotient of b and 5 equals 4 more than twice b.

   A. $\frac{b}{5} - 3 = 6b$ **B.** $\frac{b-3}{5} = 4 + 2b$

   C. $\frac{b}{5} - 3 = 2b + 4$ **D.** $3 - \frac{b}{5} = 4 + 2b$ 1. _____

2. Annie buys a pair of pants for \$25 and several T-shirts for \$8 each. Write an expression for her total cost if she buys n T-shirts.

   A. $n(8 + 25)$ **B.** $25 + 8n$ **C.** $25 + \frac{8}{n}$ **D.** $25n + 8$ 2. _____

3. Find the value of $14 \div 2 + 5 \cdot 2 - 3$.
   A. 1   **B.** 2   **C.** 14   **D.** 21   3. _____

4. Name the property of equality shown by the statement below.

         If $2b - 10 = 5x$ and $5x = 15$, then $2b - 10 = 15$.
   A. Reflexive Property of Equality
   B. Transitive Property of Equality
   C. Symmetric Property of Equality
   D. Multiplication Property of Equality   4. _____

5. Name the property shown by the statement below.

         $6 \cdot (5 + 3) = 6 \cdot (3 + 5)$
   A. Commutative Property of Addition
   B. Commutative Property of Multiplication
   C. Associative Property of Addition
   D. Associative Property of Multiplication   5. _____

6. Simplify $3(4 - 2a) + 8(a + 6)$.
   A. $20 + 14a$ **B.** $2a + 60$ **C.** $60 - 2a$ **D.** $50 + 14a$ 6. _____

7. How many ways are there to make \$1.20 using quarters and/or dimes?
   A. 2   **B.** 3   **C.** 4   **D.** 5   7. _____

8. Use the frequency table to determine how many out of 20 students wear shoes larger than size 7.

   A. 7   **B.** 12
   C. 15   **D.** 16   8. _____

Shoe Size	Frequency
6	4
7	1
8	7
9	5
10	3

9. The stem-and-leaf plot shows the number of times students ran the length of a football field in 15 minutes. How many students ran this length fewer than 25 times?
   A. 4   **B.** 5   **C.** 7   **D.** 8   9. _____

Stem	Leaf
1	6 9
2	0 3 5 6
3	1 2 2 4 8

   3|1 = 31

10. You want to show how the number of computers per 100 students has changed in your state over the past 20 years. The most appropriate way to display your data would be a
    A. histogram.
    B. stem-and-leaf plot.
    C. cumulative frequency table.
    D. line graph.

10. _____

11. Which of the following statements is true?
    A. $|-5| < |-3|$
    B. $-|-5| > -|3|$
    C. $-3 > -5$
    D. $|-5| < 3$

11. _____

12. Evaluate $|-8| - |9|$.
    A. -17 B. -1 C. 1   D. 17

12. _____

For Questions 13–14, refer to the coordinate plane at the right.

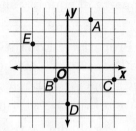

13. What ordered pair names point D?
    A. $(-3, 0)$ B. $(0, 3)$
    C. $(3, 0)$ D. $(0, -3)$

13. _____

14. In which quadrant is point E located?
    A. I   B. II
    C. III   D. IV

14. _____

15. Find the sum: $-15 + (-11) + 20$.
    A. 16   B. 6   C. -6 D. -16

15. _____

16. Simplify $-8b + (-3b) - (-5b) - 4b$.
    A. $2b$ B. $-2b$ C. $-10b$ D. $-20b$

16. _____

17. Evaluate $-12 - x + y$ when $x = -6$ and $y = -4$.
    A. -22 B. -10 C. -2 D. 2

17. _____

18. Find the value of p if $-2(3)(-1)(-5) = p$.
    A. -30 B. -11 C. 30   D. 60

18. _____

19. What is the value of k if $-216 \div 9 = k$?
    A. -24 B. -22 C. 22   D. 24

19. _____

20. Over seven years, the number of books in a school library increased from 1160 to 2000. What was the average change in the number of books in the library for each of the seven years?
    A. 115   B. 120   C. 134   D. 840

20. _____

Chapter 2 Answer Key

Form 1A

Page 21

1. __A__
2. __B__
3. __C__
4. __B__
5. __D__
6. __C__
7. __A__
8. __D__
9. __C__
10. __A__
11. __D__
12. __B__

Page 22

13. __D__
14. __B__
15. __C__
16. __A__
17. __C__
18. __A__
19. __B__
20. __B__
21. __D__
22. __D__
23. __C__
24. __B__
25. __B__

Bonus __A__

Form 1B

Page 23

1. __D__
2. __C__
3. __A__
4. __B__
5. __B__
6. __C__
7. __A__
8. __B__
9. __D__
10. __C__
11. __B__
12. __C__

Page 24

13. __C__
14. __A__
15. __C__
16. __D__
17. __B__
18. __D__
19. __A__
20. __D__
21. __D__
22. __A__
23. __A__
24. __C__
25. __B__

Bonus __C__

Chapter 2 Answer Key
Form 2A

Page 25

1.

-1 0 1 2 3

2. <

3. >

4. <

5. −6

6. (−4, 2)

7. (2, 4)

8. IV

9. III

10. II

11. 37

12. −24

13. 2

14. down 9

15. −19

16. 31

17. 4

18. 3

19. −12

Page 26

20. −24k

21. 4507 m

22. −18

23. −80

24. −24

25. −$410

26. −16

27. 512

28. −19

29. 8

30. 25

31. −16 ft per second squared

32. −4

33. $3000

Bonus   0%

Chapter 2 Answer Key

Form 2B

Page 27

1. \>

2. \<

3. \<

4. 12

5.

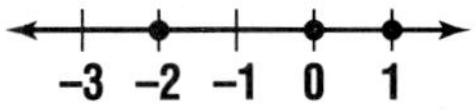

6. Point *B* lies on the *x*-axis. It is not located in a quadrant.

7. IV

8. (4, 3)

9. (−4, −2)

10. IV

11. 5

12. 12

13. −5

14. −14

15. falls 2 ft

16. 14

17. 17

18. −1

19. 14

Page 28

20. 6*b*

21. −17°F

22. −375

23. 2

24. −48

25. 30

26. −18

27. −$24

28. −6

29. 14

30. −6

31. −16

32. −44 ft per second squared

33. −3000

Bonus −1°F

Chapter 2 Answer Key

1. a. $A(2, 1)$, $B(3, -2)$, $C(-3, 0)$

   b. $(-4, -2)$, $(-6, 4)$, $(6, 0)$

   c.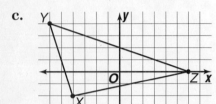

   d. The new triangle has the same shape, but its sides seem to be twice as long. It also seems to be rotated halfway around the origin.

2. a. A sample table is shown below for $n = -3$.

Quadrant of (a, b)	I	II	III	IV
Coordinates of (a, b)	$(2, 3)$	$(-1, 3)$	$(-3, -3)$	$(1, -2)$
Coord. and quad. of (na, b)	$(-6, 3)$; II	$(3, 3)$; I	$(9, -3)$; IV	$(-3, -2)$; III
Coord. and quad. of (a, nb)	$(2, -9)$; IV	$(-1, -9)$; III	$(-3, 9)$; II	$(1, 6)$; I
Coord. and quad. of (na, nb)	$(-6, -9)$; III	$(3, -9)$; IV	$(9, 9)$; I	$(-3, 6)$; II

   b. Multiplying the x-coordinate by a negative number moves the point horizontally to the quadrant next to it. Multiplying the y-coordinate by a negative number moves the point vertically to the quadrant above or below it. Multiplying both coordinates by a negative number moves the point to the quadrant diagonally across from it.

3. a. $\dfrac{\$990 - \$1320}{15} = -\$22$

   b. $\dfrac{\$1200 - \$1750}{25} = -\$22$

   c. Both clubs lost the same amount per person, $22, but members of the first club invested $970 each, while those in the second club invested $630 each.

Chapter 2 Answer Key

Mid-Chapter Test
Page 30

1. _____ **−1** _____
2. _____ **4** _____

3. _____ **<** _____
4. _____ **>** _____
5. _____ **>** _____
6. _____ **<** _____

7. _____ **10, 3, 0, −8, −12** _____
8. _____ **6, 5, 2, −3, −4, −5** _____

9–11.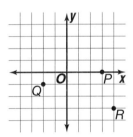

12. _____ **(0, −4)** _____
13. _____ **(−2, 3)** _____
14. _____ **III** _____
15. _____ **I** _____

16. _____ **9** _____
17. _____ **22** _____
18. _____ **2** _____

19. _____ **9x** _____
20. _____ **−7** _____

Quiz A
Page 31

1.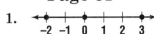

2. _____ **>** _____
3. _____ **<** _____
4. _____ **−8** _____

5–7.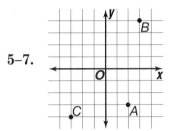

8. _____ **IV** _____

Quiz B
Page 31

1. _____ **−10** _____
2. _____ **0** _____
3. _____ **174** _____

4. _____ **21 − (−3) = 24** _____
5. _____ **−42** _____
6. _____ **80** _____
7. _____ **6** _____

8. _____ **−$2500** _____

Chapter 2 Answer Key

Cumulative Review
Page 32

1. $4a - 6 = bc + 11$
2. 7
3. Associative Property ($\times$)
4. $8x - 18$
5. $2\frac{1}{2}$ lb
6. 6
7. line graph
8. $-64, -25, -2, 3, 11, 36$
9. $(-1, 4)$
10. IV
11. -53
12. 42
13. $-22°F$
14. 48
15. 9
16. 14

Standardized Test Practice
Page 33   Page 34

1. C
2. B
3. C
4. B
5. A
6. B
7. B
8. C
9. A

10. D
11. C
12. B
13. D
14. B
15. C
16. C
17. B
18. A
19. A
20. B

3

Chapter 3 Test, Form 1A

Write the letter for the correct answer in the blank at the right of each problem.

1. Which sentence is true?

   A. $\frac{4}{5} > \frac{9}{12}$ B. $\frac{2}{7} < \frac{2}{9}$ C. $\frac{3}{2} = \frac{2}{3}$ D. $\frac{4}{18} > \frac{2}{6}$

   1. _____

2. Write the numbers $\frac{2}{11}$, $-\frac{1}{3}$, -0.35, and $\frac{2}{13}$ from least to greatest.

   A. $-\frac{1}{3}$, -0.35, $\frac{2}{11}$, $\frac{2}{13}$ B. $-\frac{1}{3}$, -0.35, $\frac{2}{13}$, $\frac{2}{11}$

   C. -0.35, $-\frac{1}{3}$, $\frac{2}{13}$, $\frac{2}{11}$ D. -0.35, $-\frac{1}{3}$, $\frac{2}{11}$, $\frac{2}{13}$

   2. _____

3. A nursery school teacher is planning to buy fish-shaped crackers for snack time. Which is the best buy?

   A. a $3\frac{1}{2}$ oz package for $0.69   B. a 12 oz package for $1.89

   C. a 32 oz package for $4.89   D. a 48 oz package for $7.99

   3. _____

4. Find $\frac{2}{3} + \frac{4}{7} - \frac{8}{9}$.

   A. $-\frac{2}{63}$ B. $\frac{1}{3}$ C. $\frac{22}{63}$ D. $1\frac{61}{63}$

   4. _____

5. Evaluate $-a + b$ if $a = 0.81$ and $b = -0.49$.

   A. -1.3 B. -1.2 C. -0.32 D. 0.32

   5. _____

6. An 8- by 10-inch photograph is framed as shown at the right with a $1\frac{3}{8}$-inch mat and a $\frac{3}{4}$-inch frame. What are the outer dimensions of the frame?

   A. $10\frac{1}{8} \times 12\frac{1}{8}$ in.   B. $11\frac{1}{2} \times 13\frac{1}{2}$ in.

   C. $12\frac{1}{4} \times 14\frac{1}{4}$ in.   D. $12\frac{1}{2} \times 14\frac{1}{2}$ in.

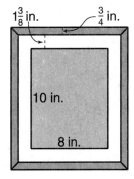

$1\frac{3}{8}$ in. $\frac{3}{4}$ in.

10 in.

8 in.

   6. _____

7. What is the median of 29, 46, 35, 45, 32, and 45?

   A. 16   B. $38\frac{2}{3}$ C. 40   D. 45

   7. _____

8. What is the range of the data in the stem-and-leaf plot?

   A. 18   B. 75

   C. 83.4   D. 85

Stem	Leaf
7	5 5 5 8
8	4 6 7 9
9	2 3 7|5 = 75

   8. _____

9. Salma earned the following scores on her algebra quizzes this term: 78, 86, 94, 87, 98, and 90. What is her mean quiz score to the nearest tenth?

   A. 88.5   B. 88.8   C. 89.0   D. 90.5

   9. _____

10. Find the solution of $72 - \frac{y + 26}{7} = 65$ if the replacement set is {20, 21, 22, 23}.

    A. 20   B. 21   C. 22   D. 23

    10. _____

11. Solve $m = \dfrac{56 \div 8 - 4}{11 + 16 - 18}$.

    A. $\dfrac{1}{15}$ B. $\dfrac{3}{11}$ C. $\dfrac{1}{3}$ D. $3\dfrac{1}{9}$

    11. _____

12. To convert a temperature from degrees Fahrenheit to degrees Celsius, the formula $C = \dfrac{5(F - 32)}{9}$ can be used. Which of the following Fahrenheit temperatures corresponds to a temperature of 30°C?

    A. 83°F   B. 84°F   C. 85°F   D. 86°F

    12. _____

13. Write the equation that corresponds to the algebra tile model shown.

    A. $-4 + x = 6$ B. $4 + x = -6$
    C. $4x + 1 = -6$ D. $4 + x = 6$

    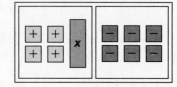

    13. _____

14. Solve $y + (-6) = 9$. Use algebra tiles if necessary.

    A. 15   B. 3   C. -3 D. -15

    14. _____

For Questions 15–16, solve each equation.

15. $\dfrac{7}{8} = f - \left(-\dfrac{5}{24}\right)$

    A. $\dfrac{1}{12}$ B. $\dfrac{2}{3}$ C. $1\dfrac{1}{12}$ D. $1\dfrac{7}{24}$

    15. _____

16. $g + 4.86 = 2.59$

    A. -2.37 B. -2.27 C. 2.37   D. 7.45

    16. _____

17. Which equation corresponds to the statement *the sum of x and 10.4 is -3.8*?

    A. $x = 10.4 - 3.8$ B. $x - 10.4 = -3.8$
    C. $x + 10.4 = -3.8$ D. $x - 3.8 = 10.4$

    17. _____

For Questions 18–19, solve each equation.

18. $|s - 12| - 5 = 9$

    A. $\{-2, 26\}$ B. $\{2, 26\}$ C. $\{8, 16\}$ D. $\varnothing$

    18. _____

19. $-2 = 4 + |x - 4|$

    A. $\{-2, 10\}$ B. $\{-2, 2\}$ C. $\{2, 6\}$ D. $\varnothing$

    19. _____

20. To audition for a chorus line, a dancer must be within $1\dfrac{1}{2}$ inches of 5 feet 9 inches. Which equation can be used to find h, the tallest and shortest height a dancer can be to audition?

    A. $|h - 5.9| = 1.5$ B. $|h - 69| = 1.5$
    C. $|1.5 + h| = 69$ D. $h - 1.5 = 69$

    20. _____

Bonus A school has $6500 budgeted for textbooks. The principal wants to buy 120 new geography textbooks for $39.95 each. How much money will be left in the textbook budget after the purchase?

     A. $1706   B. $1765   C. $1820   D. $4794

     Bonus _____

3

Chapter 3 Test, Form 1B

Write the letter for the correct answer in the blank at the right of each problem.

1. Write the numbers $\frac{3}{4}$, $-\frac{5}{6}$, 0.6, and -0.8 from least to greatest.

   A. -0.8, $-\frac{5}{6}$, 0.6, $\frac{3}{4}$ **B.** $-\frac{5}{6}$, -0.8, $\frac{3}{4}$, 0.6

   C. $-\frac{5}{6}$, -0.8, 0.6, $\frac{3}{4}$ **D.** 0.6, $\frac{3}{4}$, -0.8, $-\frac{5}{6}$ 1. _____

2. Which is the best buy for popcorn at a movie?
   A. 6 cups for \$2   **B.** 9 cups for \$3
   C. 15 cups for \$4   **D.** 21 cups for \$5   2. _____

3. Which sentence is true?
   A. $\frac{2}{3} > \frac{3}{4}$ **B.** $\frac{4}{5} > \frac{7}{11}$ **C.** $\frac{3}{7} < \frac{2}{5}$ **D.** $\frac{4}{10} = \frac{5}{2}$ 3. _____

4. Evaluate $b - c$ if $b = \frac{4}{9}$ and $c = \frac{1}{6}$.

   A. $\frac{11}{18}$ **B.** $\frac{1}{3}$ **C.** $\frac{5}{18}$ **D.** $\frac{1}{5}$ 4. _____

5. Find $-2.49 + 1.85$.
   A. -4.34 **B.** -0.64 **C.** -0.54 **D.** 0.64   5. _____

6. For three babysitting jobs one weekend Quyen earns \$12.75, \$18.50, and \$6.50. He buys a CD for \$12.95 and pays his sister the \$5.90 he owes her. How much of his babysitting earnings does he have left?
   A. \$18.30   **B.** \$18.90   **C.** \$19.10   **D.** \$25.10   6. _____

7. What is the mode of the data in the stem-and-leaf plot?

Stem	Leaf
1	7 8
2	1 6 6 8
3	4 5 6 9

   $1 \mid 7 = 17$

   A. 26   **B.** 27
   C. 28   **D.** 85   7. _____

8. What is the median of 26, 16, 23, 17, 39, 26, 20, and 22?
   A. 26   **B.** 23.6   **C.** 23   **D.** 22.5   8. _____

9. Use the table to find the mean high temperature over the five days shown.

Day	M	Tu	W	Th	F
High temp. (°F)	46	37	42	40	30

   A. 39°F   **B.** 40°F   **C.** 41°F   **D.** 42°F   9. _____

10. Solve $\frac{10 - 4 + 11}{2 \cdot 4 + 3} = f$.

    A. $2\frac{3}{11}$ **B.** $1\frac{6}{11}$ **C.** $1\frac{3}{14}$ **D.** $-\frac{5}{11}$ 10. _____

11. Find the solution of $\frac{c+4}{3} + 7 = 12$ if the replacement set is $c = \{10, 11, 12, 13\}$.

   A. 10   **B.** 11   **C.** 12   **D.** 13   11. _____

12. It costs Samantha $25 to rent a table at the local craft fair. If she sells n refrigerator magnets for $3.50 each, her net income I is given by the formula $I = 3.5n - 25$. If she makes a net income of $76.50, how many magnets has she sold?

   A. 27   **B.** 28   **C.** 29   **D.** 30   12. _____

13. Which equation corresponds to the algebra tile model shown?

   A. $6 = x - 2$ **B.** $-6 = x + 2$

   C. $6x = x + 2$ **D.** $x + 6 = -2$

   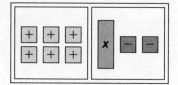

   13. _____

14. Solve $x - 2 = -5$. Use algebra tiles if necessary.

   A. -7 **B.** -3 **C.** 3   **D.** 7   14. _____

For Questions 15–16, solve each equation.

15. $m + \frac{2}{3} = -\frac{4}{9}$

   A. $\frac{10}{9}$ **B.** $\frac{2}{9}$ **C.** $-\frac{2}{9}$ **D.** $-\frac{10}{9}$ 15. _____

16. $-8 = k - 19$

   A. -27 **B.** 9   **C.** 11   **D.** 27   16. _____

17. Which equation corresponds to the statement *fifteen less than x is −28*?

   A. $x - 15 = -28$ **B.** $x + 15 = -28$

   C. $x - 15 = 28$ **D.** $15 - x = -28$ 17. _____

For Questions 18–19, solve each equation.

18. $|z + 5| = 12$

   A. $\{-13, 3\}$ **B.** $\{-17, 7\}$ **C.** $\{-7, 17\}$ **D.** $\{7, 17\}$ 18. _____

19. $|-8 + x| - 2 = 4$

   A. $\{2, 14\}$ **B.** $\varnothing$ **C.** $\{-10, 2\}$ **D.** $\{6, 10\}$ 19. _____

20. Projected enrollment for your school is 850. If the actual enrollment is within 40 students of the projected figure, which equation can be used to find e, the greatest and least possible enrollments?

   A. $|e - 40| = 850$ **B.** $e = 850 - 40$

   C. $|850 - 40| = e$ **D.** $|e - 850| = 40$ 20. _____

Bonus Derek has a 10-foot board. If he cuts four shelves that are each 18 inches (without waste) from the board, how many inches long is the piece of wood that he has left?

   A. 44 in.   **B.** 48 in.   **C.** 52 in.   **D.** 60 in.   **Bonus** _____

3

Chapter 3 Test, Form 2A

For Questions 1–4, replace each ● with <, >, or = to make a true sentence.

1. $-\dfrac{3}{7}$ ● $\dfrac{1}{11}$

1. _____

2. 16.109 ● 16.111

2. _____

3. $\dfrac{6}{9}$ ● $\dfrac{7}{11}$

3. _____

4. $-\dfrac{2}{3}$ ● $-\dfrac{12}{18}$

4. _____

5. Write the numbers $\dfrac{5}{6}$, 0.8, $-\dfrac{1}{3}$, -0.3, and $\dfrac{5}{7}$ from least to greatest.

5. _____

Find each sum or difference.

6. $-68.92 - (-42.27) + 12.54$

6. _____

7. $\dfrac{7}{5} - \dfrac{3}{10} - \dfrac{6}{15}$

7. _____

For Questions 8–9, evaluate each expression if a = 0.65, b = 1.28, and c = $-\dfrac{5}{2}$.

8. $8.91 + b - c$

8. _____

9. $-a - (-b) + 4.2$

9. _____

10. During one week Ms. Davis made deposits in her checking account of \$562.90 and \$450.32, and wrote a check for \$837.10. By how much did her checking account increase or decrease during the week?

10. _____

11. What is the median of the data in the stem-and-leaf plot?

Stem	Leaf
4	2 6 8
5	0 1 7 9
6	1 4 5
7	3 4

$4\,|\,2 = 4.2$

11. _____

12. What is the range of 108, 92, 85, 96, 129, and 142?

12. _____

13. What is the mean of the data in Question 12?

13. _____

14. Find the solution of $80 + 35x = 1095$ if the replacement set is $\{28, 29, 30, 31\}$.

14. _____

15. Solve $8 \cdot 3 - 42 \div 7 = k$.

15. _____

45 *Algebra: Concepts and Applications*

3

16. Dominic's Pizzeria charges $12.50 plus $0.85 per topping for any large deep-dish pizza. A SuperDeluxe costs $19.30. Does it have 6, 7, 8, or 9 toppings?

16. _____

17. Solve $-6 + y = 2$. Use algebra tiles if necessary.

17. _____

18. Write the equation that corresponds to the algebra tile model shown.

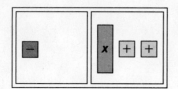

18. _____

For Questions 19–21, solve each equation.

19. $14.82 + a = -10.47$

19. _____

20. $\frac{11}{12} + b = \frac{5}{6}$

20. _____

21. $c - 0.62 = -0.23$

21. _____

22. Write and solve the equation that corresponds to the statement *14 less than x equals −2*.

22. _____

For Questions 23–24, solve each equation.

23. $|-14 + p| = 10$

23. _____

24. $6 + |q - 2| = -1$

24. _____

25. A number x must be no more than $\frac{1}{12}$ from $2\frac{1}{3}$. Find the least and greatest possible values for x.

25. _____

Bonus Eric makes a double recipe of cookie dough and enough pizza dough for two large pizzas. A single cookie recipe calls for $1\frac{2}{3}$ cups of flour. Altogether, Eric uses $9\frac{1}{12}$ cups of flour. Write and solve an equation to find the amount of flour that Eric uses for the pizza dough.

Bonus _____

3

Chapter 3 Test, Form 2B

For Questions 1–4, replace each ● with <, >, or = to make a true sentence.

1. $-\frac{3}{5}$ ● -0.75

1. _____

2. $\frac{5}{12}$ ● $\frac{4}{9}$

2. _____

3. $\frac{4}{14}$ ● $\frac{16}{56}$

3. _____

4. -2 ● $-\frac{5}{2}$

4. _____

5. Write the numbers $\frac{4}{3}$, 1.2, -0.2, $-\frac{1}{6}$, and $\frac{3}{4}$ from least to greatest.

5. _____

Find each sum or difference.

6. $-\frac{2}{3} - \left(-\frac{4}{9}\right) + \frac{1}{6}$

6. _____

7. $-14.39 + 6.56$

7. _____

For Questions 8–9, evaluate each expression if p = 0.75, q = −1.6, and r = 0.8.

8. $r + 2.1 - q$

8. _____

9. $p + q - (-0.7)$

9. _____

10. On December 31, the high temperature was $-10.2°F$. Over the next three days the temperature rose $39.4°F$. What was the high temperature on January 3?

10. _____

11. Find the mode of 1.6, 2.4, 2.1, 1.7, 2.4, 1.9, 2.3, and 2.1.

11. _____

12. What is the median of the data in the stem-and-leaf plot?

Stem	Leaf
2	9
3	1 3 3 5
4	2 4 6 9

$2\,|\,9 = 29$

12. _____

13. What is the mean of the data in Question 12?

13. _____

14. Solve $6.9 - (-4.7) - 5.8 = p$.

14. _____

15. Find the solution of $\frac{y - 8}{12} = 3$ if the replacement set is {44, 45, 46, 47}.

15. _____

16. It costs \$3.50 to rent bowling shoes and \$2.50 to bowl one game. The cost of bowling n games is given by the formula $C = \$3.50 + \$2.50n$. If it costs Satchi \$11 for one evening of bowling, did she bowl 2, 3, 4, or 5 games?

16. _____

17. Write the equation that corresponds to the algebra tile model shown.

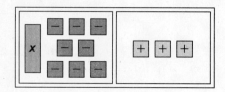

17. _____

18. Solve $y + (-4) = -3$. Use algebra tiles if necessary.

18. _____

For Questions 19–21, solve each equation.

19. $f - \left(-\frac{7}{10}\right) = -\frac{4}{5}$

19. _____

20. $d + 6.4 = -8.5$

20. _____

21. $g - 11 = -15$

21. _____

22. Write and solve the equation that corresponds to the statement *the sum of −12 and x is 15*.

22. _____

For Questions 23–24, solve each equation.

23. $|k - 5| = 4$

23. _____

24. $-2 + |m + 6| = 4$

24. _____

25. A number y is no more than 0.2 from 14.39. Find the least and greatest possible values of y.

25. _____

Bonus Two empty boxes weigh 1.8 pounds and 1.4 pounds. After the boxes are filled, they weigh 48.3 pounds together. Write and solve an equation to find x, the weight of the contents of the two boxes.

Bonus _____

3 Chapter 3 Open-Ended Assessment

Instructions: Demonstrate your knowledge by giving a clear, concise solution to each problem. Be sure to include all relevant drawings and to justify your answers. You may show your solution in more than one way or investigate beyond the requirements of the problem.

1. Your English class has been assigned to do book reports. The table below shows the book selections of six of your classmates, the number of pages in each book, and how far in the book each student has read. The table also gives the estimated number of pages each student will read in a day.

Name	Title of Book	Pages in Book	Current Page	Estimated Pages/Day
Aaron	*Tales from a Troubled Land*	128	88	20
Meesha	*The Swiss Family Robinson*	246	96	30
Karl	*David Copperfield*	583	373	70
Domingo	*Have Spacesuit Will Travel*	255	140	23
Emily	*Walden*	221	101	40
Fred	*Alaska*	868	518	50

a. How would you judge which student has read farthest in her or his book? Who do you think will finish first? Explain.

b. The table shows that the students are reading at different rates. Write an equation for each student to find p, the page number he or she will be on n days from now.

c. All of the students must finish their reading within 7 days, so that they have enough time to write book reviews. Use {1, 2, 3, 4, 5, 6, 7} as the replacement set for n to determine how many days it will take each student to finish her or his book.

2. Jammal's honors club is selling T-shirts for Spirit Week at his high school. There are 1025 students in the school. Jammal orders 600 T-shirts for $8.50 each, and spends $32.50 on advertising.

a. Suppose the club sells 415 shirts at $12.95 each. Will the club make a profit? If so, how much?

b. After selling 415 shirts, the club drops the price by $1.45 and sells 165 more. What is the profit or loss now?

c. The manufacturer gives Jammal $4 each for returning the unsold T-shirts. What is the final profit or loss?

3 Chapter 3 Mid-Chapter Test
(Lessons 3–1 through 3–4)

For Questions 1–3, replace each ● with <, >, or = to make a true sentence.

1. -1.06 ● -1.60

2. $\frac{5}{8}$ ● $\frac{2}{3}$

3. $\frac{7}{11}$ ● $\frac{7}{12}$

1. _____

2. _____

3. _____

4. Write $\frac{4}{3}$, -1.3, $-\frac{3}{2}$, -0.9, and $\frac{4}{5}$ in order from least to greatest.

4. _____

Find each sum or difference.

5. $\frac{5}{9} - \frac{5}{3} + \frac{5}{6}$

6. $-2.6 + 6.2 - (-4.8)$

5. _____

6. _____

For Questions 7–8, evaluate each expression if p = 17.82, q = −4.29, and r = 11.56.

7. $-p + q$

8. $q - r$

7. _____

8. _____

9. What is the total number of yards of fabric necessary to make a skirt, jacket, and vest if the skirt requires $1\frac{3}{4}$ yards, the jacket $2\frac{7}{16}$ yards, and the vest $\frac{5}{8}$ yards?

9. _____

For Questions 10–12, refer to the set of data below.

   3, 7, 5, 3, 9, 8, 3, 4

10. Find the mean.

11. Find the range.

12. Find the median and the mode(s).

10. _____

11. _____

12. _____

13. On the first four tests of the semester Alexa received grades of 78, 88, 92, and 98. What is the minimum score she needs to make on the fifth test to have a mean score of at least 90?

13. _____

14. Find the solution of $\frac{x + 2}{-2 - 5} = -3$ if the replacement set is {18, 19, 20, 21}.

14. _____

15. Solve $p = \frac{18 - 11 - 3}{24 \div 3 - 2}$.

15. _____

16. The surface area S of a rectangular box with length ℓ, width w, and height h is given by $S = 2\ell w + 2\ell h + 2wh$. Suppose a box has a length of 12 inches, a width of 5 inches, and a surface area of 222 square inches. Is the box 3, 4, or 5 inches tall?

16. _____

NAME _____ DATE _____ PERIOD _____

Chapter 3 Quiz A
(Lessons 3–1 through 3–3)

1. Replace the ● with $<$, $>$, or $=$ to make a true sentence.

$$-\frac{2}{7} \bullet -\frac{3}{11}$$

1. _____

2. Write $\frac{4}{5}$, 0.85, $-\frac{2}{3}$, -0.68, and $\frac{5}{6}$ in order from least to greatest.

2. _____

3. Find $12.1 - (-14.6) - 8.4$.

3. _____

Use the stem-and-leaf plot to find the indicated values.

Stem	Leaf
7	6 9
8	0 4 4 8
9	1 3 7 9

$7|6 = 76$

4. mean

4. _____

5. median and mode(s)

5. _____

NAME _____ DATE _____ PERIOD _____

Chapter 3 Quiz B
(Lessons 3–4 through 3–7)

1. Find the solution for $-\frac{36}{4} - a = 5$ if the replacement set is $\{-16, -15, -14, -13\}$.

1. _____

2. Solve $-6 = h + (-2)$. Use algebra tiles if necessary.

2. _____

3. This year 92 students signed up to play in an intramural basketball league consisting of 8 teams. This was 14 students more than the number who signed up last year. Write an equation to find s, the number of students who signed up last year.

3. _____

4. Solve $-\frac{7}{36} + b = \frac{1}{2}$.

4. _____

5. Three years ago a baseball card collector bought a rare card for $175. Its value now is estimated to be within $25 of $290. Write and solve an equation to find the lowest and highest estimates for the card's value.

5. _____

1. Write an equation for the sentence *six less than the product of 7 and k equals 20. (Lesson 1–1)*

   1. _____

2. Evaluate $14(a - 2 \div 2) - 8(6 - a)$ if $a = 4$. *(Lesson 1–2)*

   2. _____

3. Name the property shown by the statement below. *(Lesson 1–3)*
$$8 + 4 \cdot 3 = 8 + 3 \cdot 4$$

   3. _____

For Questions 4–5, order the numbers from least to greatest.

4. $-6, -15, 14, -8, 7, -1$ *(Lesson 2–1)*

   4. _____

5. $\frac{4}{5}, 0.45, -\frac{5}{6}, -0.7, -\frac{3}{4}$ *(Lesson 3–1)*

   5. _____

6. Write the ordered pair that names point S. In which quadrant is S located? *(Lesson 2–2)*

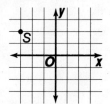

   6. _____

7. On its first three plays in a football game, the offense gains 6 yards, loses 5 yards, and then gains 7 yards. Write an equation that could be used to find y, the number of yards needed on the fourth play for the overall 10-yard gain required for a first down. *(Lesson 2–3)*

   7. _____

For Questions 8–10, find each sum or difference.

8. $-14 + 6 + (-11) + (-5)$ *(Lesson 2–3)*

   8. _____

9. $-9 - (-16)$ *(Lesson 2–4)*

   9. _____

10. $-\frac{3}{4} + \frac{5}{6} - \frac{2}{3}$ *(Lesson 3–2)*

   10. _____

11. Evaluate $q - p$ if $p = -\frac{1}{2}$ and $q = -\frac{1}{6}$. *(Lesson 3–2)*

   11. _____

12. Find the mean of 94, 100, 89, 97, and 78. *(Lesson 3–3)*

   12. _____

13. Your little sister Selena has six quarters in her pocket. To buy n bags of her favorite candy, which costs \$0.89 a bag, she needs to borrow $m = 0.89n - 1.5$ dollars. If she asks you for \$2.06, does she plan to buy 3, 4, 5, or 6 bags of candy? *(Lesson 3–4)*

   13. _____

Solve each equation.

14. $a - \frac{1}{2} = \frac{7}{8}$ *(Lesson 3–6)*

   14. _____

15. $11.8 + 6.4 = c - 8.7$ *(Lesson 3–6)*

   15. _____

16. $|-b - 16.2| = 13.8$ *(Lesson 3–7)*

   16. _____

3 Chapter 3 Standardized Test Practice
(Chapters 1–3)

Write the letter for the correct answer in the blank at the right of the problem.

1. Which of the following expressions is *not* equivalent to the other three?

   A. 8 less than the quotient of 4 and n

   B. $8 - \frac{4}{n}$

   C. the quotient of 4 and n decreased by 8

   D. $\frac{4}{n} - 8$

   1. _____

2. Use the order of operations to find the value of $6 \times 8 - 12 \div 6 + 6$.

   A. 3   **B.** 12   **C.** 40   **D.** 52

   2. _____

3. Name the property of equality shown by the statement below.

   If $x + 8 = 10$, then $10 = x + 8$.

   A. Symmetric   **B.** Substitution   **C.** Transitive   **D.** Reflexive

   3. _____

4. Name the property shown by the statement below.

   $3 \cdot (4 \cdot r) = (3 \cdot 4) \cdot r$

   A. Commutative Property ($\times$)   **B.** Symmetric Property ($\times$)

   C. Associative Property ($\times$)   **D.** Reflexive Property ($\times$)

   4. _____

5. Simplify $2(3x + 4y) - 2(x - 2y)$.

   A. $4x + 12y$ **B.** $8x + 8y$ **C.** $4x + 8y$ **D.** $4x + 2y$

   5. _____

6. One box weighs three times as much as another box. Together they weigh 72 pounds. How much does the heavier box weigh?

   A. 18 lb   **B.** 24 lb   **C.** 48 lb   **D.** 54 lb

   6. _____

7. Your class plans to survey the school about students' favorite types of music. You ask 200 students randomly selected to choose their favorite among rock, jazz, rap, country, classical, or other. Which would be the *most* appropriate method to display your data?

   A. stem-and-leaf plot   **B.** histogram

   C. line graph   **D.** frequency table

   7. _____

8. Which of the following has the greatest value?

   A. $|4| + |-3|$ **B.** $0 - |5|$ **C.** $|-7| - |2|$ **D.** $|6| - |-1|$

   8. _____

9. What are the coordinates of point A?

   A. (2, 1)   **B.** (−1, 2)

   C. (2, −1)   **D.** (1, −2)

   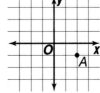

   9. _____

10. In which quadrant is point A located?

    A. I   **B.** II   **C.** III   **D.** IV

    10. _____

11. Simplify $-18a + 7a + (-11a)$.

    A. 0   **B.** $-14a$ **C.** $-22a$ **D.** $-36a$ **11.** _____

12. Find $3(-2)(4)(-1)$.

    A. -24 **B.** -20 **C.** 20   **D.** 24   **12.** _____

13. Evaluate $\frac{-a - (-b)}{c}$ if $a = -4$, $b = 5$, and $c = -3$.

    A. -3 **B.** $-\frac{1}{3}$ **C.** $\frac{1}{3}$ **D.** 3   **13.** _____

14. Which of the following statements is true?

    A. $\frac{4}{9} > \frac{4}{7}$ **B.** $-\frac{2}{3} < -\frac{5}{8}$ **C.** $\frac{5}{6} < -\frac{7}{6}$ **D.** $\frac{3}{4} > \frac{4}{3}$ **14.** _____

15. Find the value of $y - z$ if $y = -1.94$ and $z = -3.33$.

    A. -5.27 **B.** -1.39 **C.** 1.39   **D.** 5.27   **15.** _____

16. What is the median of the data in the stem-and-leaf plot?

Stem	Leaf
5	5
6	0
7	4 8
8	6 9 9
9	7 $5\,|\,5 = 55$

    A. 78.5   **B.** 82

    C. 86   **D.** 89   **16.** _____

17. Find the solution of $30 + 18x = 246$ if the replacement set is $\{12, 13, 14, 15\}$.

    A. 12   **B.** 13   **C.** 14   **D.** 15   **17.** _____

18. Solve $y - \frac{7}{10} = -\frac{1}{15}$.

    A. $\frac{23}{30}$ **B.** $\frac{2}{3}$ **C.** $\frac{19}{30}$ **D.** $-\frac{23}{30}$ **18.** _____

19. The low temperature for the day is $-14.2°F$. The high temperature for the day is $28.4°F$. By how many degrees did the temperature change during the day?

    A. $-42.6°F$ **B.** $-14.2°F$ **C.** $14.2°F$ **D.** $42.6°F$ **19.** _____

20. Solve $|14 + x| - 12 = -4$.

    A. $\varnothing$ **B.** $\{-22, -6\}$ **C.** $\{-8, 8\}$ **D.** $\{-18, -10\}$ **20.** _____

Chapter 3 Answer Key

1. __A__

2. __C__

3. __C__

4. __C__

5. __A__

6. __C__

7. __C__

8. __A__

9. __B__

10. __D__

11. __C__

12. __D__

13. __B__

14. __A__

15. __B__

16. __B__

17. __C__

18. __A__

19. __D__

20. __B__

Bonus __A__

1. __C__

2. __D__

3. __B__

4. __C__

5. __B__

6. __B__

7. __A__

8. __D__

9. __A__

10. __B__

11. __B__

12. __C__

13. __A__

14. __B__

15. __D__

16. __C__

17. __A__

18. __B__

19. __A__

20. __D__

Bonus __B__

Chapter 3 Answer Key
Form 2A

1. $<$

2. $<$

3. $>$

4. $=$

5. $-\frac{1}{3}, -0.3, \frac{5}{7}, 0.8, \frac{5}{6}$

6. -14.11

7. $\frac{7}{10}$

8. 12.69

9. 4.83

10. $176.12 increase

11. 5.8

12. 57

13. $108\frac{2}{3}$

14. 29

15. 18

16. 8

17. 8

18. $-1 = x + 2$

19. -25.29

20. $-\frac{1}{12}$

21. 0.39

22. $x - 14 = -2; \ 12$

23. $\{4, 24\}$

24. $\varnothing$

25. $2\frac{1}{4}, \ 2\frac{5}{12}$

Bonus $2\left(1\frac{2}{3}\right) + x = 9\frac{1}{12}; \ 5\frac{3}{4}$ c

Chapter 3 Answer Key
Form 2B

Page 47

1. $>$

2. $<$

3. $=$

4. $>$

5. $-0.2, -\dfrac{1}{6}, \dfrac{3}{4},$ $1.2, \dfrac{4}{3}$

6. $-\dfrac{1}{18}$

7. -7.83

8. 4.5

9. -0.15

10. $29.2°F$

11. 2.1 and 2.4

12. 35

13. 38

14. 5.8

15. 44

Page 48

16. 3

17. $x - 8 = 3$

18. 1

19. $-\dfrac{3}{2}$

20. -14.9

21. -4

22. $x + (-12) = 15;$ 27

23. $\{1, 9\}$

24. $\{-12, 0\}$

25. $14.19, 14.59$

Bonus $1.8 + 1.4 + x = 48.3; 45.1$ lb

Chapter 3 Answer Key

Open-Ended Assessment
Sample Answers
Page 49

1. a. I would divide the pages read by each student by the total number of pages in her or his book. I would compare the fractions to see who has read the greatest portion of her or his book. Aaron has read the greatest portion of his book: $\frac{88}{128} = \frac{11}{16}$ or 0.6875. Aaron should also finish first, because he has only $128 - 88 = 40$ pages left to read, and at 20 pages per day, it will take him only 2 days to finish.

b. Aaron: $p = 88 + 20n$
Meesha: $p = 96 + 30n$
Karl: $p = 373 + 70n$
Domingo: $p = 140 + 23n$
Emily: $p = 101 + 40n$
Fred: $p = 518 + 50n$

c. Aaron will finish in 2 days; Karl and Emily will finish in 3 days; Meesha and Domingo will finish in 5 days; Fred will finish in 7 days.

2. a. $241.75 profit

b. $2139.25 profit

c. $2219.25 profit

Chapter 3 Answer Key

1. _____>_____

2. _____<_____

3. _____>_____

4. $-\frac{3}{2}$, -1.3, -0.9, $\frac{4}{5}$, $\frac{4}{3}$

5. $-\frac{5}{18}$

6. 8.4

7. -22.11

8. -15.85

9. $4\frac{13}{16}$

10. 5.25

11. 6

12. 4.5; 3

13. 94

14. 19

15. $\frac{2}{3}$

16. 3 in.

1. _____<_____

2. -0.68, $-\frac{2}{3}$, $\frac{4}{5}$, $\frac{5}{6}$, 0.85

3. 18.3

4. 87.1

5. 86; 84

1. -14

2. -4

3. $s + 14 = 92$

4. $\frac{25}{36}$

5. $|x - 290| = 25$; $265, $315

Chapter 3 Answer Key

Cumulative Review
Page 52

1. $7k - 6 = 20$

2. 26

3. **Commutative Prop. (×)**

4. $-15, -8, -6, -1, 7, 14$

5. $-\frac{5}{6}, -\frac{3}{4}, -0.7, 0.45, \frac{4}{5}$

6. $(-3, 2)$; II

7. $6 + (-5) + 7 + y = 10$

8. -24

9. 7

10. $-\frac{7}{12}$

11. $\frac{1}{3}$

12. 91.6

13. 4

14. $1\frac{3}{8}$

15. 26.9

16. $\{-30, -2.4\}$

Standardized Test Practice
Page 53

1. B

2. D

3. A

4. C

5. A

6. D

7. D

8. A

9. C

10. D

Page 54

11. C

12. D

13. A

14. B

15. C

16. B

17. A

18. C

19. D

20. B

Chapter 4 Test, Form 1A

Write the letter for the correct answer in the blank at the right of each problem.

1. Find $\left(-\frac{2}{3}\right)\left(-\frac{9}{4}\right)$.

   A. $-\frac{3}{2}$ B. $-\frac{8}{27}$ C. $\frac{8}{27}$ D. $\frac{3}{2}$ 1. _____

2. Simplify $(1.5)(-4.3k)$.

   A. $-3.2k$ B. $-6.65k$ C. $-6.45k$ D. $-2.8k$ 2. _____

3. On weekdays Mr. Brown budgets $5.75 a day for lunch. How much does he budget for weekday lunches for four weeks?

   A. $23   B. $28.75   C. $115   D. $161   3. _____

4. Evaluate $\frac{4}{5}x + \frac{2}{3}y$ if $x = -5$ and $y = 6$.

   A. -1 B. 0 C. 2 D. 8 4. _____

5. Find the number of possible outcomes of spinning each of the spinners shown once. An outcome consists of an ordered pair of the form (*color, color*).

   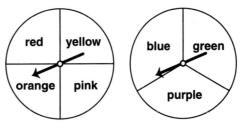

   A. 7   B. 9

   C. 12   D. 16   5. _____

6. At the local diner the daily special consists of eggs (fried, scrambled, or poached), toast or hash browns, bacon or sausage, and orange juice or coffee. How many different breakfast specials are possible?

   A. 24   B. 18   C. 15   D. 9   6. _____

7. Find $-28 \div (-5.6)$.

   A. 5.5   B. 5   C. -5 D. -5.5 7. _____

8. Evaluate $-\frac{h}{f}$ if $f = \frac{2}{3}$ and $h = \frac{1}{9}$.

   A. $\frac{2}{27}$ B. $-\frac{2}{27}$ C. $-\frac{1}{9}$ D. $-\frac{1}{6}$ 8. _____

9. How many $3\frac{1}{2}$-inch pieces can be cut from a ribbon that is 63 inches long?

   A. 18   B. 20   C. 21   D. 22   9. _____

10. Solve $-\frac{15}{22}p = \frac{5}{11}$.

    A. $\frac{3}{2}$ B. $\frac{2}{3}$ C. $-\frac{2}{3}$ D. $-\frac{3}{2}$ 10. _____

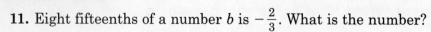
11. Eight fifteenths of a number b is $-\frac{2}{3}$. What is the number?

   A. $\frac{5}{4}$ B. $\frac{4}{5}$ C. $-\frac{4}{5}$ D. $-\frac{5}{4}$

   11. _____

12. It costs $7.00 for a bag of apples. If the apples are $1.25 per pound, how many pounds are in the bag?

   A. 5.2 B. 5.6 C. 6 D. 8.75

   12. _____

13. Solve $82.5 - 2y = -40.3$.

   A. 61.4 B. 42.2 C. 21.1 D. -21.1

   13. _____

14. A gardener buys three trees and two bags of fertilizer at $4.29 per bag. If the total bill is $64.08, which equation could you use to find n, the cost of one tree?

   A. $\frac{3}{n} + 2(4.29) = 64.08$ B. $3n + 2(4.29) = 64.08$

   C. $3n = 64.08 + 2(4.29)$ D. $4.29(2 + 3n) = 64.08$

   14. _____

15. What is the solution of $-3 = \frac{r-4}{6}$?

   A. -22 B. -14 C. $3\frac{1}{2}$ D. 6

   15. _____

16. Solve $5x - 120 = 35x + 60$.

   A. -1.5 B. -2 C. -4.5 D. -6

   16. _____

17. Thirteen more than eight times a number k is equal to 62 less than five times k. Find the number.

   A. 4 B. -16 C. -25 D. -225

   17. _____

18. Solve $14(2 - x) + 22 = 20 - 12x$.

   A. -25 B. $1\frac{2}{13}$ C. 15 D. 25

   18. _____

19. Find the solution of $4(2.5 - 2y) = -3(y + 2)$.

   A. -8 B. $-1\frac{5}{16}$ C. $1\frac{3}{5}$ D. $3\frac{1}{5}$

   19. _____

20. There are 18 students in the writing club. The sponsor agrees to buy each student a notebook at $4.50 each and some pens at $0.89 each. If the total for these supplies is $177.12, which equation represents the number of pencils n each student gets?

   A. $18(4.50) + 0.89n = 177.12$ B. $4.50 + 18(0.89n) = 177.12$
   C. $18(4.50 + 0.89n) = 177.12$ D. $18n(4.50 + 0.89n) = 177.12$

   20. _____

Bonus Twice a number added to the sum of 5 times the number and -10 is equal to 6 times the number subtracted from the sum of the number and 2. What is the number?

   A. 6 B. 4 C. 1 D. -4

   Bonus _____

4

Chapter 4 Test, Form 1B

Write the letter for the correct answer in the blank at the right of each problem.

1. Simplify $(9x)(4.5y)$.
   A. $13.5xy$ B. $2xy$ C. $40.5xy$ D. $40.5x + y$ 1. _____

2. Find $\left(\frac{2}{5}\right)\left(\frac{15}{8}\right)$.
   A. $\frac{16}{75}$ B. $\frac{3}{4}$ C. $\frac{6}{7}$ D. $\frac{17}{13}$ 2. _____

3. Evaluate $8.4a - 0.5ab$ if $a = 5$ and $b = 4$.
   A. 22   B. 30   C. 32   D. 40   3. _____

4. It takes $\frac{3}{8}$ cup of syrup to make one gallon of punch. How many cups of syrup does it take to make six gallons of punch?
   A. $1\frac{1}{8}$ B. $2\frac{1}{8}$ C. $2\frac{1}{4}$ D. $2\frac{1}{2}$ 4. _____

5. At the appetizer table are carrots, celery, broccoli, and red pepper along with two dips, dill and blue cheese. How many different choices of dip and vegetable are available?
   A. 6   B. 8   C. 10   D. 12   5. _____

6. Find the number of possible arrangements of two songs if you pick the first song from a CD that has 12 tracks and the second from a CD that has 9 tracks.
   A. 21   B. 81   C. 108   D. 120   6. _____

7. Evaluate $-\frac{j}{k}$ if $j = \frac{2}{5}$ and $k = -\frac{3}{10}$.
   A. $\frac{4}{3}$ B. $\frac{3}{25}$ C. $-\frac{3}{25}$ D. $-\frac{4}{3}$ 7. _____

8. Find $-6.8 \div 17$.
   A. -4 B. -0.4 C. -0.34 D. 4   8. _____

9. It takes $\frac{5}{8}$ yard of canvas to make a tote bag. If Sara has 10 yards of canvas, how many tote bags can she make?
   A. 12   B. 14   C. 16   D. 18   9. _____

10. Solve $-1.6r = 4$.
    A. -6.4 B. -2.5 C. -2.4 D. 6.4 10. _____

11. How many $8.75 calendars can you buy with $100?
    A. 9   B. 10   C. 11   D. 85   11. _____

12. Thirty-two times x is 20. Find x.

   A. $\frac{4}{9}$ 　　　　 B. $\frac{5}{8}$ 　　　　 C. $\frac{8}{5}$ 　　　　 D. 640

   12. _____

13. You want to buy a CD player that costs $100. You get paid $6 per hour. Which equation could you use to find out how many hours you must work in order to buy the CD player and still have $80 left over?
   A. $6n - 100 = 80$ 　　　　　　 B. $6n = 100 - 80$
   C. $6(80n) = 100$ 　　　　　　 D. $100 - 6n = 80$

   13. _____

14. Find the value of z in the equation $\frac{z + 2}{1.2} = -5$.

   A. -2.5 　　　 B. -4 　　　 C. -5.83 　　　 D. -8

   14. _____

15. Solve $\frac{7}{2} - 3x = -1$.

   A. $-\frac{3}{2}$ 　　　 B. $-\frac{5}{6}$ 　　　 C. $\frac{5}{6}$ 　　　 D. $\frac{3}{2}$

   15. _____

16. Ten less than five times a number y equals fifty more than twice y. Find the number.

   A. $13\frac{1}{3}$ 　　　 B. 20 　　　 C. 25 　　　 D. $36\frac{2}{3}$

   16. _____

17. Solve $20 - 4x = 8x - 4$.
   A. 6 　　　 B. 2 　　　 C. -2 　　　 D. -6

   17. _____

18. What is the value of m in $6(2m + 4) = 8m + 4$?
   A. -5 　　　 B. -1 　　　 C. 0 　　　 D. 7

   18. _____

19. Solve $8(x - 2) = x + 19$.

   A. $\frac{3}{7}$ 　　　 B. 3 　　　 C. $3\frac{8}{9}$ 　　　 D. 5

   19. _____

20. Three sisters have enrolled in four dance classes each. The registration fee for the dance school is $20 per student. If their parents pay a total of $1200, write an equation to find s, the cost of one class.
   A. $3(20) + 4s = 1200$ 　　　　 B. $3(20 + 4s) = 1200$
   C. $20 + 3(4s) = 1200$ 　　　　 D. $3s(20 + 4) = 1200$

   20. _____

Bonus The difference of 8 times a number and 3 times the number is equal to twice the number added to the sum of 4 times the number and 11. What is the number?

   A. -11 　　　 B. -1 　　　 C. 1 　　　 D. 11 　　　 **Bonus** _____

4

Chapter 4 Test, Form 2A

Find each product.

1. $\left(\frac{3}{14}\right)\left(\frac{7}{9}\right)$

1. _____

2. $(8.8)(-6.5)$

2. _____

For Questions 3–4, simplify each expression.

3. $\left(\frac{2}{3}x\right)\left(-\frac{5}{4}y\right)$

3. _____

4. $-2.2(-4.5a)$

4. _____

5. How many outcomes are possible if a six-sided number cube is tossed three times?

5. _____

6. There are many English two-letter words consisting of a vowel followed by a consonant, such as AN, ON, OF, and IS. How many two-letter combinations consisting of a vowel followed by a consonant are possible if there are 5 vowels and 21 consonants?

6. _____

Find each quotient.

7. $7.8 \div 0.6$

7. _____

8. $\frac{2}{9} \div \frac{3}{2}$

8. _____

For Questions 9–10, evaluate each expression if $c = \frac{5}{6}$, $d = \frac{1}{4}$, and $e = \frac{9}{2}$.

9. $\frac{-e}{c}$

9. _____

10. $\frac{8c}{d}$

10. _____

11. A 5-pound bag of whole wheat flour contains $18\frac{3}{4}$ cups. A batch of cookies calls for $1\frac{2}{3}$ cups of flour. Write an equation representing the number of batches b the bag of flour will make. Then solve the equation.

11. _____

Solve each equation.

12. $-\frac{8}{63}b = -\frac{4}{9}$

12. _____

13. $\frac{3}{5} = \frac{9}{10}b$

13. _____

14. $-0.3c = 27$

14. _____

For Questions 15–17, solve each equation.

15. $-55 - 4n = 13$

15. _____

16. $\frac{x - 17}{8} = 7$

16. _____

17. $\frac{x}{9} + 14 = 9$

17. _____

18. Ms. Singh buys 3 pounds of Jungle Jellies at $4.65 per pound and 2 pounds of Rainbow Ripple. If her total bill is $20.95, how much did the Rainbow Ripple cost per pound?

18. _____

For Questions 19–20, solve each equation.

19. $6x - 18 = 4x + 8$

19. _____

20. $\frac{2}{3}n + 4 = 10 - \frac{4}{3}n$

20. _____

21. Eleven less than four times a number f equals seven more than three times f. Write an equation to represent the problem. Then solve the equation to find the number.

21. _____

22. Alex and Beth are running partners. Alex lives 0.4 mile from the park. Beth lives 0.8 mile from the park. To run equal distances, Alex runs from his house to the park, eight times around the park, and then home, while Beth runs from home, six times around the park, and then home. Write and then solve an equation to find the distance once around the park.

22. _____

For Questions 23–24, solve each equation.

23. $8(2x - 3) + 5 = 61$

23. _____

24. $\frac{3(x + 12)}{5} = x + 2$

24. _____

25. A trapezoid has bases of length x meters and $(x + 6)$ meters. Its height is 4 meters. Find the lengths of the bases if the area is 64 square meters.

25. _____

Bonus A restaurant has two types of lunch specials. A sandwich platter gives you a choice of three types of sandwiches and either fries or soup. A hot platter offers three kinds of entrees, rice or potatoes, and one of two vegetables. How many lunch special choices are possible?

Bonus _____

4

Chapter 4 Test, Form 2B

Simplify each expression.

1. $\frac{3}{4}(-24t)$

1. _____

2. $(0.8p)(3.5q)$

2. _____

For Questions 3–4, find each product.

3. $\left(-\frac{3}{4}\right)\left(\frac{8}{9}\right)$

3. _____

4. 8×4.6

4. _____

5. How many different footwear combinations are possible given three pairs of shoes and eight pairs of socks? Assume that shoes and socks are worn as matched pairs only.

5. _____

6. How many combinations are possible if a fair coin is tossed four times?

6. _____

Evaluate each expression if $x = \frac{4}{3}$, $y = \frac{4}{5}$, and $z = -\frac{1}{15}$.

7. $\frac{x}{z}$

7. _____

8. $-\frac{y}{x}$

8. _____

Find each quotient.

9. $20 \div 0.2$

9. _____

10. $-\frac{4}{5} \div \frac{2}{5}$

10. _____

For Questions 11–13, solve each equation.

11. $-36 = -\frac{6}{7}p$

11. _____

12. $24y = 60$

12. _____

13. $\frac{2}{5}q = -12$

13. _____

14. A Scout troop has collected $62.40 for dues. Each Scout has paid $7.80 in dues. Write an equation representing the number of Scouts n in the troop. Then solve the equation.

14. _____

For Questions 15–17, solve each equation.

15. $3x - 4 = 3.8$ 15. _____

16. $\frac{40 - x}{7} = 7$ 16. _____

17. $\frac{x}{3} - 9 = -2$ 17. _____

18. Julio buys a pair of pants that cost $27.50 and five T-shirts. If the total bill is $95, how much does each T-shirt cost?   18. _____

For Questions 19–20, solve each equation.

19. $5x + 11 = 8x - 13$ 19. _____

20. $\frac{4}{7}x + 5 = \frac{3}{7}x - 1$ 20. _____

21. An older brother has saved $15 and receives $10 per week for allowance. The younger brother has saved $50, but receives only $7.50 per week for allowance. Assume that neither brother spends any money. Write and then solve an equation to find how many weeks it will be until the two brothers have saved the same amount.   21. _____

22. Five more than three times a number y is equal to twelve less than four times y. Write an equation that you could use to find y. Then solve the equation to find the number.   22. _____

For Questions 23–24, solve each equation.

23. $6(y - 2) + 5 = -13$ 23. _____

24. $\frac{5(x - 3)}{4} = x + 1$ 24. _____

25. A store charges $5 to monogram a person's initials on a backpack. Mrs. Salas spends $262.50 to buy monogrammed backpacks for her seven children. Find c, the cost of one backpack before monogramming.   25. _____

Bonus A couple is expecting their first child. If it is a boy, they plan to name him Jason, Jacob, or Jared. For a middle name, they will choose Ray or Charles. If it is a girl, they will name her Rebecca or Rochelle. For a middle name, they will choose Leigh, Anne, or Lynne. How many possible names there are for the child?   Bonus _____

4

Chapter 4 Open-Ended Assessment

Instructions: Demonstrate your knowledge by giving a clear, concise solution to each problem. Be sure to include all relevant drawings and to justify your answers. You may show your solution in more than one way or investigate beyond the requirements of the problem.

The baseball batting average is one of the most commonly used sports statistics. It is expressed as a three-digit decimal between 0.000 (for a batter who has had no hits when at bat) to 1.000 (for a batter who has gotten a hit every time at bat). Batting averages are calculated by dividing the number of hits by the number of times at bat.

$$\text{batting average} = \frac{\text{number of hits}}{\text{times at bat}}$$

In the major leagues a batting average between 0.300 and 0.350 is considered excellent, with anything over 0.350 extremely rare. Suppose a player named Enrique Peña, expected to be an exceptional hitter, has gotten off to a mediocre start, with 36 hits in his first 150 at-bats, for a batting average of 0.240.

1. Enrique tells his coach he knows he can do better. He claims that he can bat 0.400 in his next 50 at-bats.
   a. Write and solve an equation for how many hits Enrique must make in his next 50 at-bats to average 0.400 for these at-bats.
   b. Assume that Enrique backs up his claim in part a. Find the average of 0.240 and 0.400. Is this Enrique's batting average for his first 200 at-bats? Explain. If not, find his actual average.

2. Assume that Enrique continues his red-hot 0.400 streak for n at-bats after his original 150 at-bats. Then the number of hits he will make in these n at-bats is hits = average · at-bats, or $0.4n$.
   a. Write an expression for the total number of hits so far in the season.
   b. Suppose Enrique makes 26 hits while batting 0.400. Write an equation using the expression in part 2a for the total number of hits so far in the season. Then solve it to find n.
   c. What is Enrique's season batting average to this point?

3. It is possible to find how long Enrique must keep up the 0.400 streak to reach an overall average of 0.300.
   a. Write an expression using n as defined in Question 2 for the total number of at-bats so far in Enrique's season.
   b. Using the formula hits = average · at-bats again and the expression in part 3a, write an expression for the total number of hits when Enrique's overall average is 0.300.
   c. The expressions in parts 2a and 3b both describe the total number of hits. Use this fact to write an equation expressing this relationship. This equation describes how many at-bats with a 0.400 average it will take Enrique to reach a season average of 0.300. Solve the equation for n.
   d. How many at-bats will Enrique have to this point? Verify that his batting average is now 0.300.

4

Chapter 4 Mid-Chapter Test
(Lessons 4–1 through 4–4)

For Questions 1–3, find each product.

1. $(6.5)(4.8)$

1. _____

2. $\left(-\frac{2}{3}\right)\left(\frac{9}{8}\right)$

2. _____

3. $\left(-\frac{8}{5}\right)\left(-\frac{15}{16}\right)$

3. _____

4. Solve $x = \left(\frac{9}{10}\right)\left(\frac{5}{9}\right) + \left(\frac{1}{2}\right)(-1)$ to find the value of x.

4. _____

5. A scientist marks plant specimens with an ID made up of a letter followed by a digit from 1 to 5. How many specimen labels are possible?

5. _____

6. How many different kinds of sundae are possible if you can choose one of three kinds of ice cream (vanilla, chocolate, and strawberry), one of three kinds of topping (fudge, butterscotch, or strawberry), and then specify with or without nuts and with or without whipped cream?

6. _____

7. Refer to Question 6. Your friend loves strawberry and would like both strawberry ice cream and strawberry topping. From how many sundae combinations does your friend have to choose?

7. _____

For Questions 8–9, find each quotient.

8. $49.5 \div 4.5$

8. _____

9. $-1\frac{3}{5} \div \frac{2}{5}$

9. _____

10. Evaluate $\frac{4y}{x}$ if $x = \frac{3}{4}$ and $y = \frac{1}{2}$.

10. _____

11. A class has raised $156 to buy gloves for homeless children. If a pair of gloves costs $6.50, how many pairs can the class buy?

11. _____

For Questions 12–13, solve each equation.

12. $-\frac{2}{3}x = 18$

12. _____

13. $18n = 63$

13. _____

14. Find the value of p in the equation $\frac{p}{8} = 7\frac{1}{4}$.

14. _____

15. Five sixths of a number m equals -80. What is the number?

15. _____

16. The cost of admission to an aquarium for 45 students is $382.50. Write and solve an equation to find f, the student admission fee.

16. _____

4

Chapter 4 Quiz A
(Lessons 4–1 through 4–3)

1. Find $\left(\dfrac{3}{20}\right)\left(-\dfrac{5}{6}\right)$.

1. _____

2. How much is a worker who earns $12.40 an hour paid for 7.8 hours of work?

2. _____

3. How many snacks consisting of a drink and a food from the lists shown below are possible?

Drink	**Food**
orange juice	pretzels
apple juice	popcorn
fruit punch	carrots
	cheese and crackers

3. _____

4. A coin is tossed and a number from 1 to 4 is chosen at random. Write all of the outcomes in the sample space as ordered pairs.

4. _____

5. Evaluate $-\dfrac{a}{b}$ if $a = \dfrac{3}{4}$ and $b = -\dfrac{3}{8}$.

5. _____

6. In a one-mile race, runners circle a track $4\dfrac{2}{5}$ times. If it takes four runners per team to run a two-mile relay, how many laps does each runner have to run?

6. _____

- -

4

Chapter 4 Quiz B
(Lessons 4–4 through 4–7)

1. Four sevenths of a number b is 28. Write and solve an equation to find the number.

1. _____

For Questions 2–5, solve each equation.

2. $21 = 4.2s$

2. _____

3. $\dfrac{s + 2}{6} = -3$

3. _____

4. $\dfrac{3}{4}x + 2 = \dfrac{1}{2}x - 3$

4. _____

5. $\dfrac{6(20 - 5s)}{5} - 10 = -4$

5. _____

6. Video club members get a $1.50 discount on each rental when they rent more than five tapes. When a member rents seven tapes, the total bill is $15.75. Write and solve an equation to find x, the regular rental price for one tape.

6. _____

4

Chapter 4 Cumulative Review

1. Write an equation for the sentence below. *(Lesson 1–1)*
   The difference of twice b and 7 is equal to the quotient of
   16 and 3 times d.

   1. _____

2. Simplify $5(4n - 2p) - 3(2p - 3n)$. *(Lesson 1–4)*

   2. _____

3. The weights in pounds of 12 dogs in a kennel are given below.
   Make a stem-and-leaf plot of the weights. *(Lesson 1–7)*
   $$24, 40, 32, 58, 54, 21, 78, 55, 46, 79, 60, 51$$

   3. _____

4. Anchara has a balance of $450 in her checking account. Find
   her new balance after she makes deposits of $50 and $75 and
   withdrawals of $15, $28, and $42. *(Lesson 2–3)*

   4. _____

**For Questions 5–6, evaluate each expression if $x = -6$, $y = 2$,
and $z = -4$.** *(Lessons 2–5, 2–6)*

5. $-3x - 5y$

   5. _____

6. $\frac{y - x}{z}$

   6. _____

7. Find the value of $\frac{5}{18} - \frac{4}{9} + \frac{2}{3}$. *(Lesson 3–2)*

   7. _____

8. What is the mean of 28, 18, 21, 30, 23, and 24? *(Lesson 3–3)*

   8. _____

9. Solve $-\frac{5}{6} + n = -\frac{7}{12}$. *(Lesson 3–6)*

   9. _____

10. To win a prize, you must guess the number of jelly beans in a
    jar to within 30. There are 627 jelly beans in the jar. Write
    and solve an equation to find the least and greatest possible
    winning estimates. *(Lesson 3–7)*

    10. _____

11. Simplify $\frac{1}{2}\left(-\frac{2}{3}b\right) + \left(\frac{3}{4}b\right)\left(\frac{4}{9}\right)$. *(Lesson 4–1)*

    11. _____

12. Rosa can choose from two skirts, two belts, and five blouses.
    How many outfits are possible? *(Lesson 4–2)*

    12. _____

13. Henri earns $158.70 for 23 hours of work. How much is he
    paid per hour? *(Lesson 4–3)*

    13. _____

14. Sam brought $17 to the arcade. He buys two sodas for $0.75
    each and popcorn for $3.50. Arcade games cost $0.75. Write
    and solve an equation to find n, the number of games he can
    afford to play. *(Lesson 4–4)*

    14. _____

Solve each equation. *(Lessons 4–6, 4–7)*

15. $\frac{5}{3}n + 4 = -\frac{7}{3}n - 28$

    15. _____

16. $180 = 15(2 - t)$

    16. _____

4 Chapter 4 Standardized Test Practice
(Chapters 1–4)

Write the letter for the correct answer in the blank at the right of the problem.

1. Which of the following sentences is *not* equivalent to the other three?
   A. Four less than twice x equals 18.
   B. $4 - 2x = 18$
   C. Two times x minus four equals 18.
   D. $18 = 2x - 4$

   1. _____

2. Use the order of operations to find the value of $18 \div 6 + 3 \cdot 5 - 4$.
   A. 2   B. 6   C. 10   D. 14

   2. _____

3. Refer to the frequency table. How many times does a number less than or equal to 16 occur?
   A. 2   B. 3
   C. 9   D. 13

Number	Frequency
11	2
14	7
16	4
19	3
20	1

   3. _____

4. Which of the following would be the most appropriate way to display data about the price of movie theater tickets over the past eighty years?
   A. histogram   B. frequency table
   C. stem-and-leaf plot   D. line graph

   4. _____

5. Write -5, $|-3|$, $-|-4|$, $-|2|$, and 1 in order from least to greatest.
   A. $1, -|2|, |-3|, -|-4|, -5$ B. $-5, -|-4|, |-3|, -|2|, 1$
   C. $-5, -|-4|, -|2|, 1, |-3|$ D. $-5, |-3|, -|2|, 1, -|-4|$

   5. _____

6. Which of the following ordered pairs represents a point in Quadrant II?
   A. $(-5, 2)$ B. $(-3, 0)$ C. $(4, -1)$ D. $(-2, -5)$

   6. _____

7. During one week, Alicia makes credit card purchases of $28, $35, and $52. She also makes a payment of $200. If she owed $600 at the beginning of the week, what is her new balance at the end of the week?
   A. $285   B. $515   C. $685   D. $715

   7. _____

8. Evaluate $z + x - y$ if $x = -18$, $y = 14$, and $z = 35$.
   A. -39 B. -29 C. 3   D. 31

   8. _____

9. Which of the following sentences is true?
   A. $\frac{4}{7} > \frac{3}{5}$ B. $\frac{2}{5} < \frac{3}{7}$ C. $\frac{2}{3} < \frac{7}{12}$ D. $\frac{1}{2} < \frac{6}{13}$

   9. _____

4

Chapter 4 Standardized Test Practice
(Chapters 1–4) *(continued)*

10. Find $\frac{2}{5} + \frac{1}{10} + \frac{4}{15}$.

   A. $\frac{7}{30}$ **B.** $\frac{11}{30}$ **C.** $\frac{19}{30}$ **D.** $\frac{23}{30}$

10. _____

11. What is the mean of the set of data below?

       4.8, 6.4, 5.5, 4.3, 5.0

   A. 5.0   **B.** 5.2   **C.** 5.4   **D.** 5.6

11. _____

12. Find the solution of $\frac{x}{4} + \frac{12}{x} = 4$ if the replacement set is {4, 6, 8, 10}.

   A. 4   **B.** 6   **C.** 8   **D.** 10

12. _____

13. Solve $|-7 + x| + 4 = 12$. Check your solution.

   A. $-1, 1$ **B.** $-1, 15$ **C.** $-9, 15$ **D.** $-9, 23$

13. _____

14. Simplify $\left(-\frac{4}{7}x\right)\left(-\frac{21}{44}y\right)$.

   A. $\frac{3}{11}xy$ **B.** $-\frac{25}{51}xy$ **C.** $-\frac{3}{11}xy$ **D.** $\frac{11}{3}xy$

14. _____

15. Spinner A has the digits 1, 2, and 3 on it, Spinner B has the digits 4, 5, and 6 on it, and Spinner C has the digits 7, 8, and 9 on it. How many three-digit combinations (in the order Spinner A, Spinner B, Spinner C) can be formed by spinning each spinner once?

   A. 6   **B.** 9   **C.** 18   **D.** 27

15. _____

16. Find $18 \div 0.4$.

   A. 7.2   **B.** 27   **C.** 45   **D.** 72

16. _____

17. What is the solution of $\frac{2}{7}t = 14$?

   A. 4   **B.** 42   **C.** 49   **D.** 98

17. _____

18. Julia has $42 to go to the circus. The admission price is $18. How many souvenir mugs can she buy for her friends if each mug costs $1.50?

   A. 16   **B.** 20   **C.** 36   **D.** 40

18. _____

19. Twenty-seven less than eight times b equals eighteen more than five times b. Find b.

   A. -3 **B.** $\frac{9}{13}$ **C.** $\frac{13}{9}$ **D.** 15

19. _____

20. What is the solution of $\frac{4(2 - x)}{5} - 10 = -2$?

   A. 17   **B.** -8 **C.** -12 **D.** -32

20. _____

Chapter 4 Answer Key

Page 61

1. ___D___

2. ___C___

3. ___C___

4. ___B___

5. ___C___

6. ___A___

7. ___B___

8. ___D___

9. ___A___

10. ___C___

Page 62

11. ___D___

12. ___B___

13. ___A___

14. ___B___

15. ___B___

16. ___D___

17. ___C___

18. ___D___

19. ___D___

20. ___C___

Bonus ___C___

Page 63

1. ___C___

2. ___B___

3. ___C___

4. ___C___

5. ___B___

6. ___C___

7. ___A___

8. ___B___

9. ___C___

10. ___B___

11. ___C___

Page 64

12. ___B___

13. ___A___

14. ___D___

15. ___D___

16. ___B___

17. ___B___

18. ___A___

19. ___D___

20. ___B___

Bonus ___A___

Chapter 4 Answer Key
Form 2A

1. $\dfrac{1}{6}$

2. -57.2

3. $-\dfrac{5}{6}xy$

4. $9.9a$

5. 216

6. 105

7. 13

8. $\dfrac{4}{27}$

9. $-5\dfrac{2}{5}$

10. $26\dfrac{2}{3}$

11. $1\dfrac{2}{3}b = 18\dfrac{3}{4};\ 11$

12. $\dfrac{7}{2}$

13. $\dfrac{2}{3}$

14. -90

15. -17

16. 73

17. -45

18. $\$3.50$

19. 13

20. 3

21. $4f - 11 = 3f + 7;$ 18

22. $2(0.4) + 8p =$ $2(0.8) + 6p;$ 0.4 mi

23. 5

24. 13

25. 13 m and 19 m

Bonus 18

Chapter 4 Answer Key
Form 2B

Page 67

1. $-18t$

2. $2.8pq$

3. $-\dfrac{2}{3}$

4. 36.8

5. 24

6. 16

7. -20

8. $-\dfrac{3}{5}$

9. 100

10. -2

11. 42

12. 2.5

13. -30

14. $7.80n = 62.40;$ 8

Page 68

15. 2.6

16. -9

17. 21

18. $\$13.50$

19. 8

20. -42

21. $15 + 10w = 50 + 7.5w;$ 14 weeks

22. $3y + 5 = 4y - 12;\ 17$

23. -1

24. 19

25. $\$32.50$

Bonus 12

Chapter 4 Answer Key

Open-Ended Assessment
Sample Answers
Page 69

1. **a.** $\frac{h}{50} = 0.400$; 20 hits

   b. 0.320; no; The 0.240 average was for 150 at-bats, while the 0.400 was for only 50 at-bats, so his average for the first 200 at-bats will be closer to 0.240 than to 0.400. His actual average is $\frac{36 + 20}{150 + 50} = \frac{56}{200}$, or 0.280.

2. **a.** $36 + 0.4n$

   b. $36 + 0.4n = 62$; 65

   c. 0.288

3. **a.** $150 + n$

   b. $(0.300)(150 + n)$

   c. $36 + 0.4n = (0.300)(150 + n)$; 90

   d. 240; $\frac{36 + 0.4(90)}{240} = \frac{72}{240}$ or 0.300

Chapter 4 Answer Key

Mid-Chapter Test
Page 70

1. 31.2
2. $-\dfrac{3}{4}$
3. $\dfrac{3}{2}$
4. 0
5. 130
6. 36
7. 4
8. 11
9. -4
10. $2\dfrac{2}{3}$
11. 24
12. -27
13. 3.5
14. 58
15. -96
16. $45f = 382.50$; 8.50

Quiz A
Page 71

1. $-\dfrac{1}{8}$
2. 96.72
3. 12
4. (H, 1), (H, 2), (H, 3), (H, 4), (T, 1), (T, 2), (T, 3), (T, 4)
5. 2
6. $2\dfrac{1}{5}$

Quiz B
Page 71

1. $\dfrac{4}{7}b = 28$; 49
2. 5
3. -20
4. -20
5. 3
6. $7(x - 1.5) = 15.75$; 3.75

Chapter 4 Answer Key

Cumulative Review
Page 72

1. $2b - 7 = \dfrac{16}{3d}$

2. $29n - 16p$

3.
Stem	Leaf
2	1 4
3	2
4	0 6
5	1 4 5 8
6	0
7	8 9

$2|1 = 21$

4. $490

5. 8

6. -2

7. $\dfrac{1}{2}$

8. 24

9. $\dfrac{1}{4}$

10. $|e - 627| = 30;$ $597, 657$

11. 0

12. 20

13. 6.90

14. $17 - 2(0.75) -$ $3.50 = 0.75n;$ $16;$ 16 games

15. -8

16. -10

Standardized Test Practice
Page 73

1. B

2. D

3. D

4. D

5. C

6. A

7. B

8. C

9. B

Page 74

10. D

11. B

12. A

13. B

14. A

15. D

16. C

17. C

18. A

19. D

20. B

5

Chapter 5 Test, Form 1A

Write the letter for the correct answer in the blank at the right of each problem.

1. Find the value of y that makes $\frac{8}{3} = \frac{24}{y}$ a proportion.

   A. 6   **B.** 8   **C.** 9   **D.** 64   1. _____

2. Solve $\frac{b}{2} = \frac{b + 12}{8}$.

   A. 2   **B.** 2.4   **C.** 4   **D.** 16   2. _____

3. Convert 8.2 grams to milligrams.

   A. 0.0082 mg   **B.** 82 mg   **C.** 820 mg   **D.** 8200 mg   3. _____

4. A soft drink bottling plant can produce 120,000 cans of soft drink a day. At this rate, how long will it take to produce 15,000 cans?

   A. 2 h   **B.** 2.5 h   **C.** 3 h   **D.** 30 h   4. _____

5. On a kitchen blueprint, a cooktop is 2 inches wide. If an actual cooktop is 3 feet wide, find the scale of the model.

   A. 1:3   **B.** 1:18   **C.** 1:36   **D.** 1:72   5. _____

6. The Petronas Twin Towers in Kuala Lumpur, Malaysia, are officially the tallest buildings in the world at 452 meters above street level. If a scale of 1 centimeter = 4 meters is used to make a replica, how tall is the replica?

   A. 1.13 cm   **B.** 112 cm   **C.** 1.13 m   **D.** 2.008 m

                                                     6. _____

7. Express the ratio 8 to 5 as a percent.

   A. 1.6%   **B.** 16%   **C.** 62.5%   **D.** 160%   7. _____

8. Forty-eight percent of the students in a school attended their basketball team's playoff game. If there are 1500 students in the school, how many attended the game?

   A. 72   **B.** 720   **C.** 3125   **D.** 7200   8. _____

9. What number is 175% of 56?

   A. 9.8   **B.** 32   **C.** 98   **D.** 320   9. _____

10. How long will it take Mr. Brooks to earn $675 in interest if he invests $4500 at an annual rate of 5%?

   A. 2 yr   **B.** 2.5 yr   **C.** 3 yr   **D.** 5 yr   10. _____

11. Kaitlyn works at a fruit and nut shop. She mixes pecans that sell for $3.50 per pound with cashews that sell for $5.00 per pound. How many pounds of cashews should she mix with 4 pounds of pecans if she wants to sell the mixture for $4.00 per pound?

   A. 1 lb   **B.** 2 lb   **C.** 3 lb   **D.** 4 lb   11. _____

12. A sweater selling for $48 is now selling for $36. Find the percent of discount in the price.

  A. 25%   **B.** $33\frac{1}{3}$%   **C.** 75%   **D.** $133\frac{1}{3}$%

  12. _____

13. All gold jewelry at Gold Mart is on sale at a 40% discount. If a necklace originally cost $199, what is the sale price?

  A. $79.60   **B.** $109.60   **C.** $119.40   **D.** $187.06

  13. _____

14. The original price of a video is $16. If the sales tax rate is 6%, find the total price.

  A. $15.04   **B.** $16.10   **C.** $16.96   **D.** $18.06

  14. _____

15. Suppose you toss a pair of dice. Find the probability of tossing a sum less than 6.

  A. $\frac{1}{6}$ **B.** $\frac{1}{4}$ **C.** $\frac{1}{3}$ **D.** $\frac{5}{18}$

  15. _____

16. Find the probability of spinning a number greater than 3 using the spinner shown.

  A. $\frac{3}{8}$ **B.** $\frac{3}{5}$

  C. $\frac{5}{8}$ **D.** $\frac{3}{4}$

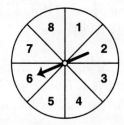

  16. _____

17. A quality-control inspector finds 3 faulty products out of 50 tested. What is the experimental probability of a single product passing inspection? Express the answer as a percent.

  A. 3%   **B.** 6%   **C.** 94%   **D.** 97%

  17. _____

18. A bag contains 5 red marbles, 2 blue marbles, and 3 green marbles. Find the odds of choosing a green marble at random.

  A. 3:7   **B.** 7:3   **C.** 3:10   **D.** 7:10

  18. _____

19. Two dice are rolled. Find the probability that an even number is rolled on one of the dice and the number 3 is rolled on the other.

  A. $\frac{1}{12}$ **B.** $\frac{1}{6}$ **C.** $\frac{1}{4}$ **D.** $\frac{2}{3}$

  19. _____

20. A card is drawn from a deck of ten cards numbered 1 through 10. Find the probability of drawing either a multiple of 3 or a 10.

  A. $\frac{3}{100}$ **B.** $\frac{1}{20}$ **C.** $\frac{2}{5}$ **D.** $\frac{1}{2}$

  20. _____

Bonus Suppose there is a 60% chance that it will rain for each of the next two days. Find the probability that it will *not* rain on either day.

  A. 3.6%   **B.** 16%   **C.** 40%   **D.** 60%

  Bonus _____

Write the letter for the correct answer in the blank at the right of each problem.

1. Find the value of y that makes $\frac{y}{18} = \frac{9}{2}$ a proportion.

   A. 4   **B.** 9   **C.** 81   **D.** 90   1. _____

2. Solve $\frac{y}{3} = \frac{y+6}{6}$.

   A. 2   **B.** 4   **C.** 6   **D.** 12   2. _____

3. Convert 250 meters to kilometers.

   A. 0.0025 km   **B.** 0.25 km   **C.** 2.5 km   **D.** 25 km   3. _____

4. A truck can travel 1200 miles on 80 gallons of gasoline. How far can it travel on 240 gallons of gasoline?

   A. 400 mi   **B.** 3600 mi   **C.** 4000 mi   **D.** 36,000 mi   4. _____

5. In a photograph in a magazine, a child is 4 inches tall. If the actual child is 4 feet tall, find the scale of the model.

   A. 1:4   **B.** 1:12   **C.** 1:48   **D.** 1:192   5. _____

6. The wings of an airplane are 50 feet wide. If a scale of 1 inch = 2.5 feet is used to construct a scale model, find the width of the wings of the model in inches.

   A. 7.2 in.   **B.** 20 in.   **C.** 25 in.   **D.** 125 in.   6. _____

7. Express $\frac{20}{16}$ as a percent.

   A. 1.25%   **B.** 12.5%   **C.** 80%   **D.** 125%   7. _____

8. Eight out of 50 students bought tickets to the play. Express this as a percent.

   A. 6.25%   **B.** 8%   **C.** 16%   **D.** 625%   8. _____

9. Twelve is 60% of what number?

   A. 7.2   **B.** 20   **C.** 72   **D.** 720   9. _____

10. How much interest will Ms. Hernandez earn if she invests $3200 at a rate of 4% for 5 years?

    A. $128   **B.** $288   **C.** $640   **D.** $3840   10. _____

11. Joelene works at a harvest shop. She packages red apples that sell for $1.25 per pound with yellow apples that sell for $1.75 per pound. How many pounds of yellow apples should she package with 3 pounds of red apples if she wants to sell the mixture for $1.60 per pound?

    A. 3 lb   **B.** 4 lb   **C.** 6 lb   **D.** 7 lb   11. _____

12. A television selling for $800 is on sale for $600. Find the percent of discount in the price.

   A. 25%   B. $33\frac{1}{3}\%$ C. 75%   D. $133\frac{1}{3}\%$

   12. _____

13. All books at Best Books are on sale at a 15% discount. Find the sale price of an art book that originally cost $40.

   A. $6   B. $25   C. $34   D. $46

   13. _____

14. The original price of a watch is $49. If the sales tax rate is 5%, find the total price.

   A. $46.55   B. $49.25   C. $50.45   D. $51.45

   14. _____

15. Suppose you toss a single die. Find the probability of tossing an even number.

   A. $\frac{1}{6}$ B. $\frac{1}{3}$ C. $\frac{1}{2}$ D. 1

   15. _____

16. Find the probability of spinning a number less than 5 using the spinner shown.

   A. $\frac{3}{8}$ B. $\frac{1}{2}$

   C. $\frac{5}{8}$ D. $\frac{4}{5}$

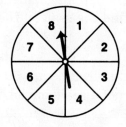

   16. _____

17. A kicker for a football team has completed 9 field goals out of 15 attempts. What is the experimental probability of the kicker scoring a field goal? Express the answer as a percent.

   A. 4%   B. 16%   C. 40%   D. 60%

   17. _____

18. A bag contains 7 red marbles, 3 blue marbles, and 6 green marbles. Find the odds of choosing a blue marble at random.

   A. 3:13   B. 13:3   C. 3:16   D. 7:16

   18. _____

19. Two dice are rolled. Find that probability that an odd number is rolled on one of the dice and the number 2 is rolled on the other.

   A. $\frac{1}{12}$ B. $\frac{1}{4}$ C. $\frac{1}{2}$ D. $\frac{2}{3}$

   19. _____

20. A card is drawn from a deck of ten cards numbered 1 through 10. Find the probability of drawing either a 5 or a multiple of 4.

   A. $\frac{1}{50}$ B. $\frac{1}{25}$ C. $\frac{3}{10}$ D. $\frac{2}{5}$

   20. _____

Bonus Suppose there is a 40% chance that it will rain for each of the next two days. Find the probability that it will *not* rain on either day.

   A. 36%   B. 40%   C. 60%   D. 64%   **Bonus** _____

5 Chapter 5 Test, Form 2A

In Questions 1–3, solve each proportion.

1. $\dfrac{5}{8} = \dfrac{x}{40}$

1. _____

2. $\dfrac{b}{4} = \dfrac{b-2}{3}$

2. _____

3. $\dfrac{12}{3d+1} = \dfrac{6}{5}$

3. _____

4. A recipe makes 5 quarts of punch. Convert this measurement to gallons.

4. _____

5. Tanya knows that her car can travel 420 miles on a full tank of gasoline. The gasoline tank holds 20 gallons. At this rate, how much gasoline is needed to travel 504 miles?

5. _____

6. A doll house is 2 feet wide. If it is a scale model of an actual house that is 32 feet wide, find the scale of the model.

6. _____

7. An "O gauge" train model is created using a scale of 1 : 48. The "Mikado," a World-War-II-era engine, measured 78 feet, 10 inches in length. How long is an "O gauge" model of the engine to the nearest inch?

7. _____

8. The scale on a map of Ohio is 1 inch = 20 miles. Find the actual distance from Columbus to Cleveland if the distance between them on the map is 7.2 inches.

8. _____

9. Express the ratio 9 out of 40 as a percent.

9. _____

10. 140 is 20% of what number?

10. _____

11. In the year 2010, 10.1% of the U.S. population is projected to be between the ages of 18 and 24. If the population will be about 298 million, about how many people will be in that age range? Round your answer to the nearest hundred thousand.

11. _____

12. In the 1996 presidential election, Bill Clinton received about 49% of the vote compared to 41% for Robert Dole. Other candidates received 10% of the vote. Make a circle graph of the data.

12. _____

13. How long will it take Mr. Ghoshal to earn $288 in interest if he invests $2400 at a rate of 4%?

13. _____

14. Laura opens a money market account that earns 5% annual interest. She wants to earn at least $200 in interest after 4 years. How much money should she deposit in the account?

14. _____

15. Alexis is selling tickets to the school play. Adult tickets cost $6.00, and student tickets cost $4.00. She sells twice as many student tickets as adult tickets. The total amount collected is $462. How many of each type of ticket did she sell?

15. _____

16. The cost of a car increases from $20,000 to $21,000 from one model year to the next. Find the percent of increase.

16. _____

17. Sweaters are on sale for 30% off the list price. If the list price of a sweater is $48, what is the sale price?

17. _____

18. The original price of a DVD player is $249. If the sales tax rate is 4%, find the total price.

18. _____

19. Suppose you roll a pair of dice. Find the probability that the second die shows a prime number.

19. _____

20. Find the probability of spinning a number that is not a 3 or less using the spinner shown.

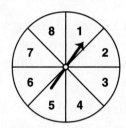

20. _____

21. The quarterback of a football game completes 28 out of 42 passes. What is the experimental probability of completing a pass?

21. _____

22. Suppose you have 5 quarters, 3 dimes, and 6 nickels in your pocket. You pick a coin at random. What are the odds that you choose a nickel?

22. _____

23. Suppose you toss four coins in a row. What is the probability that you toss four tails?

23. _____

24. A bag contains 4 red marbles and 2 green marbles. You withdraw one marble and record the color. You then replace the marble, shake the bag, and withdraw a second marble. Find the probability of choosing 2 green marbles.

24. _____

25. A card is drawn from a standard deck of 52 cards. What is the probability that the card is a king or a black card?

25. _____

Bonus A bag contains 5 red marbles, 8 blue marbles, and 3 green marbles. You withdraw one marble, replace it, and then withdraw another marble. What is the probability that you do *not* pick two red marbles?

Bonus _____

5

Chapter 5 Test, Form 2B

In Questions 1–3, solve each proportion.

1. $\dfrac{4}{3.2} = \dfrac{2}{x}$

1. _____

2. $\dfrac{z}{3} = \dfrac{z + 9}{12}$

2. _____

3. $\dfrac{16}{4d + 2} = \dfrac{8}{3}$

3. _____

4. A solution contains 2.2 liters of water. Convert this measurement to milliliters.

4. _____

5. Brandon can drive his car 30 miles on one gallon of gasoline. How many gallons does he need for a 165-mile trip?

5. _____

6. A toy airplane is 10 inches long. If the actual airplane is 75 feet long, find the scale of the model.

6. _____

7. An "N gauge" train model is created using a scale of 1 : 160. If an actual train engine, the "K−4," an early twentieth-century engine, is 45 feet long, what is the length of an "N gauge" model of the engine in inches?

7. _____

8. The actual distance from Fargo, North Dakota to Minneapolis, Minnesota is 240 miles. If the scale on a map is 1 inch = 20 miles, how long is a line on the map connecting the two cities?

8. _____

9. Express $\dfrac{7}{8}$ as a percent.

9. _____

10. What percent of 60 is 105?

10. _____

11. In the year 2010, 6.7% of the U.S. population is projected to be under the age of 5. If the population will be about 298 million, about how many people will be in that age range? Round your answer to the nearest hundred thousand.

11. _____

12. The grades for an algebra class are weighted so that tests are 45% of the grade, quizzes are 25%, homework is 20%, and projects are 10% of the grade. Make a circle graph of the data.

12. _____

13. How much interest will Ms. Williams earn if she invests $550 at 5% for 6 years?

13. _____

14. Manny opens a savings account that earns 6% annual interest. His goal is to earn $600 interest in 5 years. How much money does he need to deposit?

14. _____

15. An Internet company sells CDs for $10 and cassettes for $8. In one hour, they sold eight times as many CDs as cassettes. If their sales totaled $704, how many of each type did they sell?

15. _____

16. The cost of a computer decreases from $1500 to $1200 after 3 months. Find the percent of decrease.

16. _____

17. Jeans are on sale for 40% off the list price. If the original price of a pair of jeans is $48, find the sale price.

17. _____

18. Mr. Ortega buys a car for $16,500. A state sales tax of 4% is then added to the price of the car. What is the total price?

18. _____

19. Find the probability that the name of a month of the year, chosen at random, begins with a consonant.

19. _____

20. Find the probability of spinning a number that is a multiple of 3 using the spinner shown.

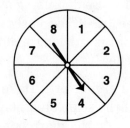

20. _____

21. A professional basketball player has scored on 105 out of 150 free throw attempts. What is the experimental probability of scoring on a free throw?

21. _____

22. A bag contains 7 red marbles, 3 blue marbles, and 6 green marbles. You choose a marble at random. What are the odds of choosing a green marble?

22. _____

23. Suppose you toss a coin and roll a die. What is the probability that you toss heads and roll a 4?

23. _____

24. A bag of candy has 6 orange pieces, 8 green pieces, and 11 red pieces. What is the probability that the first piece of candy you draw at random out of the bag is red or green?

24. _____

25. A card is drawn from a standard deck of 52 cards. What is the probability that the card is an ace or a red card?

25. _____

Bonus A bag contains 6 red marbles, 9 blue marbles, and 5 green marbles. You withdraw one marble, replace it, and then withdraw another marble. What is the probability that you do *not* pick two green marbles?

Bonus _____

5

Chapter 5 Open-Ended Assessment

Instructions: Demonstrate your knowledge by giving a clear, concise solution for each problem. Be sure to include all relevant drawings and to justify your answers. You may show your solutions in more than one way or investigate beyond the requirements of the problem.

1. A holiday punch recipe calls for $1\frac{3}{4}$ parts orange juice, 3 parts lemon-lime soft drink, and $2\frac{3}{4}$ parts cranberry juice.

   a. Describe how to determine how many pints of orange juice and cranberry juice to use if you plan to use 6 pints of lemon-lime soft drink.

   b. Describe how to rewrite the recipe using only whole number units.

   c. Using your results from part 1b, describe how to find how many pints of soft drink are needed to make one gallon of punch.

   d. Find what percent each ingredient is of the entire recipe. Then use the results to make a circle graph of the ingredients of the punch.

2. Suppose you are designing a rectangular recreation room to add to your house.

   a. Pick reasonable dimensions for the room. Then describe how you would determine a scale for a drawing of your plans.

   b. Sketch a simple floor plan, labeling the units. Give the actual dimensions and the scaled dimensions you are using.

   c. Describe how you could fit the floor plan drawn to scale on a sheet of $8\frac{1}{2}$- by 11-inch paper. What scale should you use to make the drawing as large as possible?

   d. You decide that your original recreation room is too small. You decide to increase each dimension by 20%. What are the new dimensions of the room and the new dimensions of a scale drawing using the scale you chose in part 2b?

   e. Calculate the floor area of the room as originally planned and in the larger version. What is the percent of increase of the area of the larger version from the area of the original version?

5

Chapter 5 Mid-Chapter Test
(Lessons 5–1 through 5–4)

In Questions 1–2, solve each proportion.

1. $\frac{4}{9} = \frac{x-2}{18}$

1. _____

2. $\frac{g}{3} = \frac{g+15}{12}$

2. _____

3. Convert 7 gallons to quarts.

3. _____

4. Kin Yui saves $20 a week from a part-time job. She needs to save $520 to buy a stereo system. At this rate, how long will it take her to save the money?

4. _____

5 An active man weighing 80 kilograms may consume 3600 calories a day. Using the same rate, how many calories would be consumed by an active man weighing 65 kilograms?

5. _____

6. A scale model of a playground has a scale of 1 inch = 1 yard. A playground slide is 9 feet tall. How tall is it on the model?

6. _____

7. On a blueprint, a roller coaster is 10 inches high. The actual height is 40 feet. Find the scale of the blueprint.

7. _____

8. The scale on a map of Illinois is 1 inch = 25 miles. Find the actual distance from Chicago to Cairo if the distance between them on the map is 15 inches.

8. _____

9. Express the ratio 8 to 24 as a percent.

9. _____

10. You correctly answered 12 out of 16 questions on a test. Express your grade as a percent.

10. _____

11. What percent of 90 is 99?

11. _____

12. Find 0.5% of 180.

12. _____

13. A T-shirt stand sells plain T-shirts for $9 and pocketed T-shirts for $12. In one day they sell 15 more plain shirts than shirts with pockets. If the income from the sales is $1710, how many of each type of shirt did they sell?

13. _____

14. How much interest will Josh earn if he invests $420 at an annual rate of 4.5% for 4 years?

14. _____

15. Lindell opens a savings account that earns 4.8% annual interest. After 5 years, he will earn $408 in interest. How much money did he deposit in the account?

15. _____

16. You are mixing a 10% acid solution and a 30% acid solution. How much of the 30% solution do you need to add to 240 milliliters of the 10% solution to make a 15% solution?

16. _____

Algebra: Concepts and Applications

Chapter 5 Quiz A
(Lessons 5–1 through 5–3)

1. Find the value of m that makes the proportion $\frac{m}{4} = \frac{m-6}{12}$ a true statement.

1. _____

2. Convert 4.8 kilograms to grams.

2. _____

3. A square city map is 24 inches on an edge. It shows a square area that is 12 miles on an edge. What is the scale of the map?

3. _____

4. A model of a cell must be much larger than the actual cell. If a cell model is 30 centimeters wide, and the scale of the model is 600 centimeters to 1 centimeter, how wide is the actual cell in millimeters?

4. _____

5. What percent of 125 is 75?

5. _____

6. Eighteen is 12% of what number?

6. _____

Chapter 5 Quiz B
(Lessons 5–4 through 5–7)

1. Bleach is typically 5.25% hypochlorite. How many ounces of hypochlorite are contained in a 128-ounce bottle of bleach?

1. _____

2. Mr. Jackson saved $1250 at an annual interest rate of 3.5% for 6 years. What was the amount of interest he earned?

2. _____

3. In 8 years, an account increases in value from $1200 to $2400. Find the percent of increase for the account.

3. _____

4. Five hundred fifty students out of 1250 went to a football playoff game. What is the experimental probability that a student chosen at random attended the game?

4. _____

5. A pair of dice is rolled. Find the probability that the sum of the numbers showing on the dice is 3 or less.

5. _____

6. A card is drawn from a deck of ten cards numbered 1 through 10. The card is replaced in the deck, and another card is drawn. Find the probability of drawing a 6 followed by an even number.

6. _____

5

Chapter 5 Cumulative Review

1. Evaluate $6 \times 9 - \frac{a}{b}$ if $a = 12$ and $b = -2$. (*Lesson 1–2*)

1. _____

In Questions 2–4, simplify each expression.

2. $3a + 4b + 3(2a + b)$ (*Lesson 1–4*)

2. _____

3. $-4n + (-2n) + n$ (*Lesson 2–3*)

3. _____

4. $-3(3x)(-5z)$ (*Lesson 2–5*)

4. _____

5. Over a 4-day period, the value of a share of stock rises $1\frac{3}{8}$, drops $\frac{3}{4}$, rises $1\frac{1}{2}$, and then drops $2\frac{7}{8}$. What is the net rise or drop of the stock over the period? (*Lesson 3–2*)

5. _____

6. Find the mean of the data below. (*Lesson 3–3*)

$$18, \ 24, \ 17, \ 42, \ 39, \ 19$$

6. _____

7. Solve $|x - 3| + 2 = 10$. (*Lesson 3–7*)

7. _____

8. Find the product of $\frac{4}{5}$, $-\frac{2}{3}$, and -1. (*Lesson 4–1*)

8. _____

9. An ice-cream shop offers 8 flavors of ice cream and 5 choices of toppings. You can have the ice cream in a cup, a plain cone, or a sugar cone. How many different combinations of a single flavor, a single topping, and a cup or one of the types of cone are there? (*Lesson 4–2*)

9. _____

In Questions 10–12, solve each equation or proportion.

10. $-8n + 12 = 4n + 36$ (*Lesson 4–6*)

10. _____

11. $6x - 3(x + 4) = 9$ (*Lesson 4–7*)

11. _____

12. $\frac{m}{4} = \frac{m + 12}{24}$ (*Lesson 5–1*)

12. _____

13. A scale model of a house is 2 feet wide. The actual house is 32 feet wide. Find the scale of the model. (*Lesson 5–2*)

13. _____

14. Twelve out of 25 students in a class are girls. Express this ratio as a percent. (*Lesson 5–3*)

14. _____

15. Find 24% of 2800. (*Lesson 5–3*)

15. _____

16. A card is drawn from a standard deck of 52 cards. What is the probability that the card is a 10 or a heart? (*Lesson 5–7*)

16. _____

Chapter 5 Standardized Test Practice
(Chapters 1–5)

Write the letter for the correct answer in the blank at the right of each problem.

1. Which expression is equivalent to $-2(x-1) + 4(x-1)$?
   A. $2x - 2$ **B.** $2x - 6$ **C.** $6x - 2$ **D.** $2x - 1$ 1. _____

2. Which of the following sampling methods is the best way to find the preferences of city citizens for what to do with a budget surplus?
   A. Every twentieth person who enters the municipal building is polled.
   B. Names are selected at random from a list of city homeowners.
   C. A call-in line is set up and advertised on the local news.
   D. Names of adults are selected at random from lists gathered from driver's license records, telephone directories, and voter registration.   2. _____

3. What relationship exists between the x- and y-coordinates of each of the points shown on the graph?
   A. They are opposites.
   B. They are equal.
   C. Their sum is 0.
   D. The y-coordinate is less than the x-coordinate.

   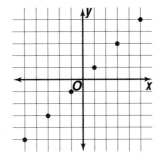

   3. _____

4. Evaluate $x + y - z$ if $x = -4$, $y = 12$, and $z = -14$.
   A. -30 **B.** -6 **C.** 20 **D.** 22 4. _____

5. Evaluate $\dfrac{8 - y}{w}$ if $y = -10$ and $w = -3$.

   A. -6 **B.** $-\dfrac{2}{3}$ **C.** $\dfrac{2}{3}$ **D.** 6 5. _____

6. Find the median of the quiz scores shown below.
   $$24, 19, 18, 22, 15, 20, 24, 18$$
   A. 18 **B.** 19 **C.** 19.5 **D.** 20 6. _____

7. What is the value of t if $-4.8 = -3.2 + t$?
   A. -8 **B.** -1.6 **C.** 1.5 **D.** 1.6 7. _____

8. What is the solution of $|x + 4| = 12$?
   A. -16 only   **B.** 8 and 16 **C.** -16 and 8 **D.** -16 and -8 8. _____

9. A restaurant menu offers 5 different main dishes, 2 salads, 3 vegetables, and 4 desserts. You choose one item of each type. How many different combinations are possible?
   A. 14 **B.** 70 **C.** 80 **D.** 120 9. _____

10. A pronghorn antelope runs at a rate of 72 feet per second for a distance of 360 yards. How long does it take?
    A. 5 s   **B.** 15 s   **C.** 25 s   **D.** 50 s   10. _____

11. For what value of n is $6n - 8 = -3n + 10$ true?
    A. -6 **B.** $\dfrac{2}{9}$ **C.** 2 **D.** 6 11. _____

Chapter 5 Standardized Test Practice
(Chapters 1–5) (continued)

12. What is the value of x in the trapezoid if its area is 96 square meters?

    A. 8   B. 10
    C. 12   D. 14

    12. _____

13. For what value of x is $\frac{x-5}{4} = \frac{x}{8}$ a true statement?

    A. −5   B. 0   C. $1\frac{1}{4}$ D. 10

    13. _____

14. A rectangular playground has dimensions of 170 feet by 220 feet. Find the scale that will allow you to draw the playground to cover a sheet of $8\frac{1}{2}$- by 11-inch paper exactly.

    A. 1 in. = 10 ft   B. 1 in. = 17 ft
    C. 1 in. = 20 ft   D. 1 in. = 34 ft

    14. _____

15. Which are equivalent amounts?

    I 20% of 75   II $\frac{20}{75}$ III 15   IV $\frac{1}{5}$ of 75

    A. I and II   B. I and III   C. I and IV   D. I, III, and IV

    15. _____

16. A pillow is stuffed with 20 ounces of a fill made of down and feathers. If the fill blend is to be 60% down, how many ounces of feathers are in the pillow?

    A. 8 oz   B. 9 oz   C. 10 oz   D. 12 oz

    16. _____

17. The sales tax rate in County A is 6.5%, and the sales tax rate in County B is 7.5%. How much less tax do you pay on $45 worth of groceries in County A?

    A. $0.45   B. $0.90   C. $1.00   D. $4.50

    17. _____

18. The price of a company's current best-selling 17-inch computer monitor is 40% less than the price of its best-selling 17-inch monitor three years ago, which sold for $800. What is the price of the current best-selling 17-inch monitor?

    A. $360   B. $420   C. $480   D. $580

    18. _____

19. The chance that it will rain is 20% today and 35% tomorrow. Find the probability that it will rain both today and tomorrow.

    A. 7%   B. 48%   C. 52%   D. 55%

    19. _____

20. A die are rolled twice. Find the probability that an odd number is rolled on the first roll and a number greater than 3 is rolled on the second.

    A. $\frac{1}{12}$ B. $\frac{1}{4}$ C. $\frac{1}{3}$ D. $\frac{1}{2}$

    20. _____

Chapter 5 Answer Key

Page 81   Page 82   Page 83   Page 84

Form 1A

Page 81

1. __C__

2. __C__

3. __D__

4. __C__

5. __B__

6. __C__

7. __D__

8. __B__

9. __C__

10. __C__

11. __B__

Page 82

12. __A__

13. __C__

14. __C__

15. __D__

16. __C__

17. __C__

18. __A__

19. __A__

20. __C__

Bonus __B__

Form 1B

Page 83

1. __C__

2. __C__

3. __B__

4. __B__

5. __B__

6. __B__

7. __D__

8. __C__

9. __B__

10. __C__

11. __D__

Page 84

12. __A__

13. __C__

14. __D__

15. __C__

16. __B__

17. __D__

18. __A__

19. __A__

20. __C__

Bonus __A__

Algebra: Concepts and Applications

Chapter 5 Answer Key
Form 2A

1. _____ 25 _____

2. _____ 8 _____

3. _____ 3 _____

4. _____ 1.25 gal _____

5. _____ 24 gal _____

6. _____ 1 : 16 _____

7. _____ 20 in. _____

8. _____ 144 mi _____

9. _____ 22.5% _____

10. _____ 700 _____

11. _____ 30,100,000 _____

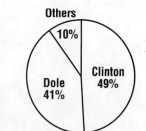

12. _____

13. _____ 3 yr _____

14. _____ at least $1000 _____

15. _____ 33 adult;
66 student _____

16. _____ 5% _____

17. _____ $33.60 _____

18. _____ $258.96 _____

19. _____ $\frac{1}{2}$ _____

20. _____ $\frac{5}{8}$ _____

21. _____ $\frac{2}{3}$ or $66\frac{2}{3}$% _____

22. _____ 3 : 4 _____

23. _____ $\frac{1}{16}$ _____

24. _____ $\frac{1}{9}$ _____

25. _____ $\frac{7}{13}$ _____

Bonus _____ $\frac{231}{256}$ or about
90.2% _____

Chapter 5 Answer Key
Form 2B

1. _____1.6_____

2. _____3_____

3. _____1_____

4. ___2200 mL___

5. ___5.5 gal___

6. _1 in. = 7.5 ft_

7. ___$3\frac{3}{8}$ in.___

8. ___12 in.___

9. ___87.5%___

10. ___175%___

11. ___20,000,000___

12.

13. ___$165___

14. ___$2000___

15. _64 CDs and 8 cassettes_

16. ___20%___

17. ___$28.80___

18. ___$17,160___

19. ___$\frac{3}{4}$___

20. ___$\frac{1}{4}$___

21. ___$\frac{7}{10}$ or 70%___

22. ___3:5___

23. ___$\frac{1}{12}$___

24. ___$\frac{19}{25}$___

25. ___$\frac{7}{13}$___

Bonus ___$\frac{15}{16}$ or 93.75%___

Chapter 5 Answer Key
Open-Ended Assessment
Sample Answers
Page 89

1. a. Think of a pint as one part. Since 6 pints of soft drink are needed, and 6 is twice 3 parts of soft drink, double the number of parts for the other ingredients. You then need 3.5 pints of orange juice and 6.5 pints of lemonade. This is the same as writing and solving a proportion. For the orange juice, the proportion is shown below.

$$\frac{6 \text{ pints soft drink}}{3 \text{ pints soft drink}} = \frac{x \text{ pints orange juice}}{1\frac{3}{4} \text{ pints orange juice}}$$

b. Multiply each ingredient by the least common denominator, 4. This gives 7 parts of orange juice, 12 parts of soda, and 11 parts of cranberry juice.

c. There are 7 + 12 + 11 or 30 parts in all. There are 8 pints in a gallon. Use the proportion below.

$$\frac{x \text{ pints soft drink}}{8 \text{ pints punch}} = \frac{12 \text{ parts soft drink}}{30 \text{ parts punch}}$$

Solving the proportion gives $x = 3\frac{1}{5}$ pt.

d. orange juice: $23\frac{1}{3}\%$, soda: 40%, cranberry juice: $36\frac{2}{3}\%$; For the circle graph, the section measures are orange juice: 84°, soft drink: 144°, and cranberry juice: 132°.

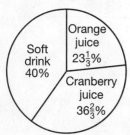

2. a. One possible size is 15 feet by 24 feet. To find the scale to make a drawing 18 inches wide, for example, use the proportion below.

$$\frac{18 \text{ inches}}{24 \text{ feet}} = \frac{1 \text{ inch}}{x \text{ feet}}$$

Solving gives $1\frac{1}{3}$ ft. So the scale is 1 in. = $1\frac{1}{3}$ ft, or 1 in. = 16 in.

b. The sketch below reflects the scale chosen in part 2a.

Recreation Room Plans

15 ft
(11.25 in.)

24 ft (18 in.)

c. Compared to the size of the paper, the room is narrower. So, if the 24-foot dimension is made to fit the 11-inch dimension of the paper, the 15-foot dimension will also fit. Using a proportion as in part 2a, but with 11 inches replacing 18 inches, gives a scale of about 1 in. = 2.2 ft, or 1 in. ≈ 26.2 in.

d. actual: 18 ft by 28.8 ft (about 28 ft, 10 in.); scale: 13.5 in. by 21.6 in.

e. original version: 360 sq ft; larger version: 518.4 sq ft; 44% increase

Chapter 5 Answer Key

Mid-Chapter Test
Page 90

1. _____ 10 _____

2. _____ 5 _____

3. _____ 28 qt _____

4. _____ 26 wk _____

5. _____ 2925 cal _____

6. _____ 3 in. _____

7. _____ 1 in. = 4 ft _____

8. _____ 375 mi _____

9. _____ $33\frac{1}{3}\%$ _____

10. _____ 75% _____

11. _____ 110% _____

12. _____ 0.9 _____

13. _____ 90 plain, 75 pocket _____

14. _____ $75.60 _____

15. _____ $1700 _____

16. _____ 80 mL _____

Quiz A
Page 91

1. _____ −3 _____

2. _____ 4800 g _____

3. _____ 1 in. = 0.5 mi _____

4. _____ 0.5 mm _____

5. _____ 60% _____

6. _____ 150 _____

Quiz B
Page 91

1. _____ 6.72 oz _____

2. _____ $262.50 _____

3. _____ 100% _____

4. _____ $\frac{11}{25}$ or 44% _____

5. _____ $\frac{1}{12}$ _____

6. _____ $\frac{1}{20}$ _____

Chapter 5 Answer Key

1. _____60_____

2. ___9a + 7b___

3. ___−5n___

4. ___45xz___

5. ___drop of $\frac{3}{4}$___

6. ___26.5___

7. ___11; −5___

8. ___$\frac{8}{15}$___

9. ___120___

10. ___−2___

11. ___7___

12. ___2.4___

13. ___1:16___

14. ___48%___

15. ___672___

16. ___$\frac{4}{13}$___

1. ___A___

2. ___D___

3. ___B___

4. ___D___

5. ___A___

6. ___C___

7. ___B___

8. ___C___

9. ___D___

10. ___B___

11. ___C___

12. ___B___

13. ___D___

14. ___C___

15. ___D___

16. ___A___

17. ___A___

18. ___C___

19. ___A___

20. ___B___

6

Chapter 6 Test, Form 1A

Write the letter for the correct answer in the blank at the right of each problem.

For Questions 1–3, refer to the graph at the right.

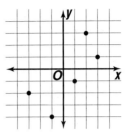

1. Express the relation shown on the graph as a set of ordered pairs.
   A. $\{(-2, -3), (-4, -1), (-1, 1), (3, 2), (1, 3)\}$
   B. $\{(-3, -2), (-1, -4), (1, -1), (2, 3), (3, 1)\}$
   C. $\{(-3, -2), (-1, -4), (-1, -1), (3, 2), (3, 1)\}$
   D. $\{(-2, -3), (-4, -1), (1, -1), (2, 3), (3, 1)\}$

   1. _____

2. What is the range of the relation?
   A. $\{-4, -3, -2, -1, 0, 1, 2, 3\}$ B. $\{-4, -2, -1, 1, 3\}$
   C. $\{-3, -1, 1, 2, 3\}$ D. $\{-3, -2, -1, 0, 1, 2, 3\}$

   2. _____

3. What is the domain of the relation?
   A. $\{-4, -2, -1, 1, 3\}$ B. $\{-4, -3, -2, -1, 0, 1, 2, 3\}$
   C. $\{-3, -2, -1, 0, 1, 2, 3\}$ D. $\{-3, -1, 1, 2, 3\}$

   3. _____

4. Jessie has eighteen straws, each four inches long. Suppose she uses some or all of the straws to form a square. Which relation shows the possible side lengths in inches and areas in square inches for the squares?
   A. $\{(1, 1), (2, 4), (3, 9), (4, 16)\}$
   B. $\{(4, 16), (8, 64), (12, 144), (16, 256), (20, 400)\}$
   C. $\{(4, 16), (8, 64), (12, 144), (16, 256)\}$
   D. $\{(4, 16), (8, 32), (12, 48), (16, 64)\}$

   4. _____

5. Solve $2x - y = -6$ if the domain is $\{-2, -1, 0, 1\}$.
   A. $\{(-2, 10), (-1, 8), (0, 6), (1, 4)\}$
   B. $\{(2, -2), (4, -1), (6, 0), (8, 1)\}$
   C. $\{(-2, -2), (-1, -4), (0, -6), (1, -8)\}$
   D. $\{(-2, 2), (-1, 4), (0, 6), (1, 8)\}$

   5. _____

6. Find the domain of $y = \frac{2}{3}x - 1$ if the range is $\{-3, -1, 7, 17\}$.
   A. $\{-3, 0, 12, 27\}$ B. $\{-3, -2, -1, 0\}$
   C. $\{-3, 0, 3, 6\}$ D. $\{-2, 0, 8, 18\}$

   6. _____

7. Which ordered pair (p, q) is a solution of $12 - 3p = -q$?
   A. $(1, 9)$ B. $(-3, -21)$ C. $(2, 6)$ D. $(3, 5)$

   7. _____

8. Which of the following is *not* a linear equation?
   A. $7y = 1 - \frac{14}{x}$ B. $-\frac{1}{2}x + \frac{3}{4}y - 18 = 6$
   C. $4y = -15$ D. $6x = 3y$

   8. _____

9. Identify A, B, and C when the linear equation $y = -2x + 3$ is written in standard form.
   A. A: 1, B: -2, C: 3   B. A: -2, B: 1, C: 3
   C. A: 2, B: -1, C: 3   D. A: 2, B: 1, C: 3

   9. _____

10. Which of the following describes the graph of $y + 4 = 0$?
    A. horizontal line through $(4, 0)$ B. horizontal line through $(0, -4)$
    C. vertical line through $(0, 4)$ D. vertical line through $(0, -4)$

    10. _____

11. Which relation is a function?

A.   B.   C.   D.

11. _____

12. Which relation is *not* a function?

A.

x	1	2	3	4	5
y	8	4	4	8	8

B.

x	0	1	−1	2	−2
y	4	4	4	4	4

C. $\{(1, 1), (2, 4), (-1, 1), (-2, 4)\}$ D. $\{(2, 5), (4, 4), (5, 2), (4, 8)\}$

12. _____

13. If $f(x) = 6x - 5$, find $f\left(\frac{7}{12}\right)$.

A. 9   B. $-\frac{3}{2}$ C. $-\frac{5}{2}$ D. $-4\frac{5}{12}$

13. _____

14. Which equation is *not* a direct variation?

A. $3x = 4y$ B. $6x - 5y = 0$ C. $\frac{x}{y} = \frac{6}{7}$ D. $4x - 7y = 2$

14. _____

15. Assume that y varies directly as x. If $y = 4.8$ when $x = 16$, find x when $y = 1.8$.

A. 4   B. 6   C. 9   D. 13

15. _____

16. If there are $5\frac{1}{2}$ yards in one rod, how many rods are there in 100 yards?

A. $17\frac{1}{2}$ B. $17\frac{3}{4}$ C. $18\frac{2}{11}$ D. $18\frac{1}{2}$

16. _____

17. Which situation represents an inverse variation?

A. Each student in the class needs 6 notebooks.
B. Six bushels of peaches are divided among a number of people.
C. Every runner in the relay runs 6 laps.
D. Joe works a number of hours for $6 per hour.

17. _____

18. Assume that y varies inversely as x. Find y when $x = 7$ if $y = 8.4$ when $x = 2.5$.

A. 2.08   B. 3   C. 12.9   D. 23.52

18. _____

19. Find the constant of variation if y varies inversely as x and $y = \frac{3}{4}$ when $x = 8$.

A. 6   B. $7\frac{1}{4}$ C. $8\frac{1}{2}$ D. $10\frac{2}{3}$

19. _____

20. The time spent to travel a certain distance varies inversely as a car's speed. If it takes $5\frac{1}{2}$ hours to travel a certain distance at 60 miles per hour, how long will it take to travel the same distance at 50 miles per hour?

A. 4.2 h   B. 4.6 h   C. 6.6 h   D. 6.9 h

20. _____

Bonus Assume that y varies directly as x, and z varies inversely as y. When $x = 20$, $y = 4$ and $z = 8$. Find z when $x = 50$. (*Hint:* First solve the direct variation for y.)

A. 3.2   B. 6.8   C. 12   D. 20

Bonus _____

Chapter 6 Test, Form 1B

Write the letter for the correct answer in the blank at the right of each problem.

For Questions 1–3, refer to the graph at the right.

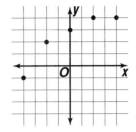

1. Express the relation shown on the graph as a set of ordered pairs.
   A. {(−4, −1), (−2, 2), (0, 3), (2, 4), (4, 4)}
   B. {(−4, 1), (−2, 2), (3, 0), (2, 4), (4, 4)}
   C. {(−1, 4), (2, −2), (0, 3), (2, 4), (4, 4)}
   D. {(−1, −4), (2, −2), (3, 0), (4, 2), (4, 4)}   1. _____

2. What is the domain of the relation?
   A. {−1, 2, 3, 4}   B. {−4, −3, −2, −1, 0, 1, 2, 3, 4}
   C. {−1, 0, 1, 2, 3, 4}   D. (−4, −2, 0, 2, 4}   2. _____

3. What is the range of the relation?
   A. {−4, −3, −2, −1, 0, 1, 2, 3, 4}   B. {−4, −2, 0, 2, 4}
   C. {−1, 0, 1, 2, 3, 4}   D. {−1, 2, 3, 4}   3. _____

4. Terence has $1.00 to spend on pencils, which cost $0.29 each. Which relation shows the possible numbers of pencils he can buy and amounts of change he will receive?
   A. {(0.29, 0.71), (0.58, 0.42), (0.87, 0.13)}
   B. {(1, 0.29), (2, 0.58), (3, 0.87)}
   C. {(1, 0.71), (2, 0.42), (3, 0.13)}
   D. {(0, 0), (1, 0.29), (2, 0.58), (3, 0.87)}   4. _____

5. Which ordered pair (a, b) is a solution of $4a − 5b = 7$?
   A. (3, 1)   B. (1, 3)   C. (2, 5)   D. (8, 25)   5. _____

6. Solve $y = 3x − 4$ if the domain is {−1, 1, 3, 5}.
   A. {(−1, 1), $\left(1, \frac{5}{3}\right)$, $\left(3, \frac{7}{3}\right)$, (5, 3)}
   B. {(−1, −7), (1, −1), (3, 5), (5, 11)}
   C. {(−1, −5), (1, −3), (3, −1), (5, 1)}
   D. {(−1, −7), (1, 3), (3, 9), (5, 15)}   6. _____

7. Find the domain of $y = 2x + 1$ if the range is {9, 13, 19, 23}.
   A. {4, 5, 6, 7}   B. {4, 6, 9, 11}
   C. {19, 27, 39, 47}   D. {5, 7, 10, 12}   7. _____

8. Identify A, B, and C when the linear equation $y = 4x − 3$ is written in standard form.
   A. A: 1, B: 4, C: −3   B. A: 4, B: 1, C: −3
   C. A: −4, B: 1, C: 3   D. A: −4, B: 1, C: −3   8. _____

9. Which of the following is *not* a linear equation?
   A. $2x = 0$ B. $8x − 5 = −y$
   C. $x + 2 = 4xy$ D. $\frac{1}{4}x − \frac{2}{5}y + 7 = 0$ 9. _____

10. Which of the following describes the graph of $2.5 = x$?
    A. horizontal line through (0, 2.5)   B. horizontal line through (2.5, 0)
    C. vertical line through (2.5, 0)   D. vertical line through (0, 2.5)   10. _____

11. Which relation is a function?

A.   B.   C.   D.

11. _____

12. Which relation is *not* a function?

A.
x	-1	-2	-3	1	2
y	8	4	4	8	8

B.
x	4	4	4	4	4
y	0	2	4	7	8

C. {(1, 7), (2, 11), (3, 15), (4, 19)}   D. {(2, 6), (3, 8), (4, 10), (5, 8)}

12. _____

13. If $g(x) = 3x + 2.4$, find $g(3.1)$.

A. 5.5   B. 11.5   C. 11.7   D. 11.9

13. _____

14. Assume that y varies directly as x. If $y = 108$ when $x = 27$, find y when $x = 12$.

A. 3   B. 45   C. 48   D. 93

14. _____

15. How many cups are in $2\frac{3}{8}$ gallons if there are 16 cups in one gallon?

A. 34   B. 36   C. 38   D. 40

15. _____

16. Which equation is a direct variation?

A. $\frac{x}{y} = \frac{5}{2}$ B. $5y - 2x = 4$ C. $xy = 18$ D. $\frac{x}{y} + x = 4$

16. _____

17. Which situation represents a direct variation?

A. The length times the width of a fenced yard is 200 square yards.
B. Party guests share the 200 pieces of candy in a piñata.
C. Mabel gets $200 for completing a job, regardless of the time it takes.
D. Each monitor in a computer lab costs $200.

17. _____

18. Find the constant of variation if y varies inversely as x, and $y = 15$ when $x = 5$.

A. $\frac{1}{3}$ B. 3   C. 25   D. 75

18. _____

19. Assume that y varies inversely as x. Find x when $y = 6$ if $y = 4.2$ when $x = 10$.

A. 6.5   B. 7   C. 8.8   D. 14.3

19. _____

20. The number of birthday presents you will get varies inversely as the average cost of the presents. If the present cost averages $12.50, you will get 8 presents. If you get 5 presents, what is the average cost per present?

A. $7.81   B. $18.50   C. $20   D. $22.50

20. _____

Bonus Assume that y varies inversely as x, and z varies directly as y. When $x = 5$, $y = 8$ and $z = 6$. Find z when $x = 10$. (*Hint:* First solve the inverse variation for y.)

A. 3   B. 6   C. 9   D. 12

Bonus _____

For Questions 1–3, refer to the relation given by the set of ordered pairs {(0, 4), (1, 3), (−1, −2), (2, −3), (−2, 0)}.

1. Express the relation as a graph.

1.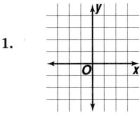

2. What is the range of the relation?

2. _____

3. What is the domain of the relation?

3. _____

4. There are eight students in a class. If at least as many of these eight students are boys as are girls, express a relation in a table for the possible numbers of girls x and boys y in the class.

4. _____

5. Solve $2y - x = 5$ if the domain is $\{-3, -1, 5, 9\}$.

5. _____

6. Find the domain of $20 - 4x = y$ if the range is $\{-8, -2, 0, 6\}$.

6. _____

7. A solution of the equation $5x + ay = -4$ is $(-2, -2)$. What is the value of a?

7. _____

8. If you are buying a pair of shoes for $39 and a number of pairs of socks for $4.50 each, the equation $c = 39 + 4.5n$ can be used to find your total cost c, where n represents the number of pairs of socks you buy. Determine the ordered pairs (c, n) that satisfy the cost equation if the domain is $\{1, 2, 3, 4\}$.

8. _____

Determine whether each equation is a linear equation. Explain. If an equation is linear, identify A, B, and C.

9. $\frac{y}{x} = y + 2$

9. _____

10. $3y = -2x + 12$

10. _____

11. $4x - 12 = y$

11. _____

Graph each equation.

12. $1 = 2x - y$

12.

13. $2x + 4y = 8$

13.

6

Chapter 6 Test, Form 2A (continued)

Determine whether each relation is a function.

14.

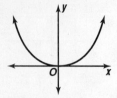

14. _____

15. $\{(0, 5), (1, 10), (2, 15), (1, 20)\}$

15. _____

For Questions 16–17, find each value if $p(x) = 4x + \frac{3}{2}$ and $q(x) = \frac{x}{5} - 4$.

16. $q(80)$

16. _____

17. $p\left(\frac{7}{2}\right)$

17. _____

18. You want to buy something that costs $3.00. You have a handful of dimes you would like to get rid of and a roll of quarters. The number of quarters q you will need depends on the number of dimes d according to the equation $25q = 300 - 10d$. Write this relation in functional notation.

18. _____

19. Determine whether $\frac{x}{y} = \frac{1}{2}$ is a direct variation.

19. _____

20. Assume that y varies directly as x. Find x when $y = 84$ if $y = 35$ when $x = 2.5$.

20. _____

21. One pound of corn will seed a row approximately 1240 feet long. How long a row will $\frac{3}{8}$ of a pound of corn seed?

21. _____

22. If one square foot equals 144 square inches, how many square inches are there in 2.3 square feet?

22. _____

23. Assume that y varies inversely as x. If $y = 21$ when $x = 6$, find x when $y = 9$.

23. _____

24. Marcus wants to save money to buy a mountain bike. The number of hours he will have to work to save the money varies inversely as the rate at which he is paid. At $6.50 per hour it will take him 90 hours. How long will it take him if he can find a job that pays $7.50 per hour?

24. _____

25. Assume that y varies inversely as x, and $y = 5$ when $x = 3.4$. Find the constant of variation. Then write an equation for the relation.

25. _____

Bonus Assume that y varies inversely as x, and z varies inversely as y. If $x = 8$, $y = 60$ and $z = 3$. Find z if $x = 15$. (*Hint:* First solve the inverse variation in x and y for y.)

Bonus _____

6

Chapter 6 Test, Form 2B

For Questions 1–3, refer to the relation given by the set of ordered pairs {(1, 4), (0, −2), (2, 3), (−1, 4), (−3, 0)}.

1. Express the relation as a graph.

1.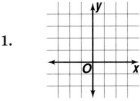

2. What is the domain of the relation?

2. _____

3. What is the range of the relation?

3. _____

4. Two dice are rolled. Express a relation in a table for the possible numbers showing on the first die x and the second die y if the outcome is two odd numbers whose sum is at least 8.

4. _____

5. Find the domain of $x - 2y = 1$ if the range is $\{-2, 0, 5, 8\}$.

5. _____

6. Solve $y = -2x + 7$ if the domain is $\{-2, 0, 4, 7\}$.

6. _____

7. A solution of the equation $4x = 10 - cy$ is $(5, -2)$. What is the value of c?

7. _____

8. A teacher wishes to schedule a quiz or exam during part of a two-hour class. The equation $\ell + e = 120$ can be used to find the available lecture time ℓ given that e minutes are planned for the quiz or exam. Determine the ordered pairs that satisfy the equation if the domain is $\{20, 30, 45, 60\}$.

8. _____

Determine whether each equation is a linear equation. Explain. If the equation is linear, identify A, B, and C.

9. $9y = 4x - 18$

9. _____

10. $xy = 4$

10. _____

11. $x^2 - 4 = y$

11. _____

Graph each equation.

12. $2 = x - y$

12.

13. $2y + x = -3$

13.

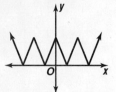
Determine whether each relation is a function.

14.

14. _____

15.

x	2	0	0	2
y	0	1	4	9

15. _____

For Questions 16–17, find each value if g(x) = 2x + 3 and
$h(x) = \frac{x}{2} - 7.$

16. $g(9)$

16. _____

17. $h(4)$

17. _____

18. The profits made by the boutique Happenin' Hats depend on the number of hats they sell. If the company's weekly expenses are $2250 and they charge $45 per hat, their profits p can be calculated by the equation $p = 45n - 2250$, where n is the number of hats sold. Write this relation in functional notation.

18. _____

19. Determine whether $1 - y = 2x$ is a direct variation.

19. _____

20. If there are 8 furlongs in a mile, how many miles are there in 30 furlongs?

20. _____

21. Assume that y varies directly as x. Find y when $x = 54$ if
$y = \frac{1}{4}$ when $x = 1\frac{1}{2}.$

21. _____

22. Erica can read 180 pages in 4 hours. At the same rate, how many pages can she read in 7 hours?

22. _____

23. Assume that y varies inversely as x, and $y = 18$ when $x = 3$. Find the constant of variation. Then write an equation for the relation.

23. _____

24. Assume that y varies inversely as x. If $y = 8$ when $x = 2.5$, find x when $y = 2$.

24. _____

25. Mr. Calvillo wants to enclose a rectangular area for a garden space of a given square footage. The length of the plot will vary inversely as the width. If he decides on a width of 18 feet, the garden will be 30 feet long. How long will a 45-foot wide garden be?

25. _____

Bonus Assume that y varies directly as x, and z varies directly as y. If $x = 12$, $y = 4$ and $z = 32$. Find z if $x = 15$. (*Hint:* First solve the direct variation in x and y for y.)

Bonus _____

6

Chapter 6 Open-Ended Assessment

Instructions: Demonstrate your knowledge by giving a clear, concise solution to each problem. Be sure to include all relevant drawings and to justify your answers. You may show your solution in more than one way or investigate beyond the requirements of the problem.

1. Suppose your family is driving on a cross-country vacation. The distance you cover in a day depends on your average speed. Your parents set the cruise control at 55 miles per hour, claiming that this speed gives the best gas mileage.

   a. Write an equation you can use to find the distance y traveled in x hours, assuming that you drive straight through without stops.

   b. Find the range of this relation if the domain is {2, 4, 6, 8}.

   c. Graph the ordered pairs from part b. Connect them to draw a line.

   d. Repeat parts a–c using 45 miles per hour and 65 miles per hour. Graph all three equations on the same set of axes.

   e. Describe the graphs. How does the speed affect the graph?

   f. Are the relations shown in the graph direct variations, inverse variations, or neither?

2. After the first day you are 440 miles from home. On the second day you continue driving. The equation $y = 440 + 55x$ represents your distance y from home the second day if you drive x hours at an average speed of 55 miles per hour.

   a. Find the range if the domain is {2, 4, 6, 8}.

   b. Graph the ordered pairs from part a. Connect them to draw a line. Compare this graph to the graph from Question 1, part c.

   c. Does this graph represent a direct variation? Explain.

3. Now suppose that you are going on a 600-mile trip. The time it will take to cover the 600 miles depends upon your speed.

   a. Write an equation using functional notation relating the time t required to travel the 600 miles to your average speed s.

   b. Find the range of this relation if the domain is {45, 55, 65}. Round to the nearest tenth.

   c. Graph the relation. Does this situation represent a direct variation? Explain.

   d. A racing cyclist rides at about 25 miles per hour, and a racing car driver travels at 150 miles per hour. How long would it take these individuals to cover 600 miles if they could maintain these speeds? Add points for these times and speeds to your graph in part c.

   e. Describe the shape of the graph. Does it appear to be linear?

   f. Is the relation shown in the graph a direct variation, inverse variation, or neither?

6

Chapter 6 Mid-Chapter Test
(Lessons 6–1 through 6–3)

1. Express the relation shown on the graph at the right as a set of ordered pairs.

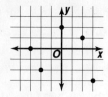

1. _____

2. Express the relation $\{(-6, -2), (-3, 0), (0, 5), (2, 3), (8, 9)\}$ as a table.

2. _____

3. What is the range of the relation in Question 1?

3. _____

4. What is the domain of the relation in Question 2?

4. _____

5. You have $0.80 in quarters and nickels. Write a relation that shows the possible combinations. Express the relation as a set of ordered pairs (number of quarters, number of nickels).

5. _____

For Questions 6–7, solve each equation for the domain given.

6. $2x + 3y = 24$; domain: $\{0, 3, 6, 9\}$

6. _____

7. $x - 8y = 0$; domain: $\{-8, 0, 8, 24\}$

7. _____

8. Graph the solution set of $x - y = 3$ if the domain is $\{-1, 1, 2, 4\}$.

8.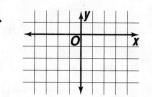

9. Find the domain of $y - 2x = 3$ if the range is $\{-3, 5, 9, 11\}$.

9. _____

10. Name an ordered pair that is a solution of $4x - 3y = 12$.

10. _____

For Questions 11–12, determine whether each equation is a linear equation. Explain. If an equation is linear, identify A, B, and C.

11. $2y = x - 12$

11. _____

12. $\frac{x}{y} + 2x = 8$

12. _____

13. Graph $3y - x = 5$.

13.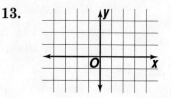

14. Describe the graph of $-3.1 - y = 0$.

14. _____

NAME _____ DATE _____ PERIOD _____

Chapter 6 Quiz A
(Lessons 6–1 and 6–2)

1. Express the relation given in the
table as a graph.

x	-4	-2	0	3
y	-1	0	3	2

1.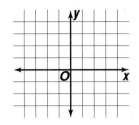

2. What is the range of the relation shown on
the graph?

2. _____

3. What is the domain of the relation $\{(2, 4), (3, 8), (8, 12), (15, 19)\}$?

3. _____

4. Solve $2x - y = 3$ if the domain is $\{-4, 0, 2, 5\}$.

4. _____

5. Find the domain of $y + 2x = 4$ if the range is $\{-8, 0, 6, 10\}$.

5. _____

6. Suppose a rectangle has a perimeter of 72 inches. Find the
possible widths of the rectangle given that the domain values
are the lengths $\{2, 6, 8, 24\}$.

6. _____

NAME _____ DATE _____ PERIOD _____

Chapter 6 Quiz B
(Lessons 6–3 through 6–6)

1. Graph $2x + y = 7$.

1.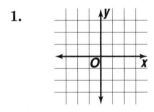

2. Is $\frac{4}{x} = \frac{9}{y}$ a linear equation? If so, identify A, B, and C.

2. _____

3. If $f(x) = \frac{2x - 7}{3}$, find $f(8)$.

3. _____

4. If it costs $1080 to have 24 yards of linoleum installed, how
much will it cost at the same rate to have 30 yards installed?

4. _____

5. Assume that y varies directly as x. Find x when $y = 243$ if
$x = 7$ when $y = 9$.

5. _____

6. Assume that y varies inversely as x. Find y when $x = 16$ if
$y = 6$ when $x = \frac{2}{3}$.

6. _____

Chapter 6 Cumulative Review

1. Simplify $6(a + 3b) - 4(2b - 5a)$. *(Lesson 1–4)*

1. _____

2. To study students' exercise habits, you choose 30 students at random from a list of those students involved in athletics at your school. Is this a good sample? Explain. *(Lesson 1–6)*

2. _____

3. Order $-2, 3, -7, 5$, and 0 from greatest to least. *(Lesson 2–1)*

3. _____

4. Evaluate $3xz - y + 2yz$ if $x = -1$, $y = 3$, and $z = -2$. *(Lesson 2–5)*

4. _____

5. Find $-\frac{7}{8} + \frac{1}{2} - \left(-\frac{3}{4}\right)$. *(Lesson 3–2)*

5. _____

6. Find the median of the data. *(Lesson 3–3)*
   26, 42, 35, 24, 60, 8

6. _____

7. At a wedding you may choose either a garden or Caesar salad, a steak, chicken, or fish entrée, broccoli or asparagus, and chocolate cake or apple pie for dessert. How many dinners are possible? *(Lesson 4–2)*

7. _____

8. Fifteen less than six times a number b is equal to seven more than four times b. Find b. *(Lesson 4–6)*

8. _____

For Questions 9–11, solve each equation or proportion.

9. $|-k - 2| + 2 = 3$ *(Lesson 3–7)*

9. _____

10. $-\frac{3}{5}m = -45$ *(Lesson 4–4)*

10. _____

11. $\frac{b + 10}{6} = \frac{b - 6}{2}$ *(Lesson 5–1)*

11. _____

12. 49 is 35% of what number? *(Lesson 5–3)*

12. _____

13. If you pick one letter from the word MATHEMATICS, what is the probability that it will be either M or a vowel? *(Lesson 5–6)*

13. _____

14. Find the range of $x - 3y = 10$ if the domain is $\{-5, -2, 7, 13\}$. *(Lesson 6–2)*

14. _____

15. Graph $2x - 3y = 1$. *(Lesson 6–3)*

15.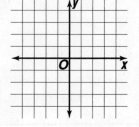

16. If y varies directly as x, and $y = 54$ when $x = 12$, find y when $x = 20$. *(Lesson 6–5)*

16. _____

Algebra: Concepts and Applications

Write the letter for the correct answer in the blank at the right of each problem.

1. Which equation corresponds to the sentence below?

    The sum of five times k and 12 equals -4.

    A. $5 + k + 12 = -4$ **B.** $5k + 12 = -4$

    C. $5(k + 12) = -4$ **D.** $5k - 12 = 4$ 1. _____

2. Find the value of $16 + 12 \div 4 \cdot 2$.

    A. $3\frac{1}{2}$ **B.** 14 **C.** $17\frac{1}{2}$ **D.** 22 2. _____

3. Which of the following sentences is true?

    A. $-|-8| < |-4|$ **B.** $|5| > |-6|$

    C. $|-3| > |-5|$ **D.** $|7| < -|-7|$ 3. _____

4. Evaluate $-14 - (-5) + (-3) + 6$.

    A. -18 **B.** -9 **C.** -6 **D.** 0 4. _____

5. Evaluate $(-8ab) \div (2bc)$ if $a = 4$, $b = -1$, and $c = -2$.

    A. 8 **B.** 4 **C.** -4 **D.** -8 5. _____

6. Which of the following rational numbers is the smallest?

    A. $\frac{5}{9}$ **B.** $\frac{4}{11}$ **C.** $\frac{3}{8}$ **D.** $\frac{2}{5}$ 6. _____

7. Refer to the stem-and-leaf plot. Which of the statements below is *not* true?

    A. The median is 26.   **B.** The mode is 32.

    C. The range is 27.   **D.** The mean is $24\frac{1}{3}$.

Stem	Leaf
1	2 5 9
2	0 6 8
3	2 2 5 1|2 = 12

    7. _____

8. Twenty-seven less than some number is -11. What is the number?

    A. 38 **B.** 16 **C.** -16 **D.** -38 8. _____

9. Solve $|y - 6| = 2$.

    A. $\varnothing$ **B.** $\{-8, 8\}$ **C.** $\{2, 8\}$ **D.** $\{4, 8\}$ 9. _____

10. Evaluate $4ac - b$ if $a = \frac{3}{8}$, $b = -\frac{1}{2}$, and $c = -\frac{2}{5}$.

    A. $\frac{11}{10}$ **B.** $\frac{1}{10}$ **C.** $-\frac{1}{10}$ **D.** $-\frac{11}{10}$ 10. _____

11. Two friends plan an evening of dinner followed by a movie. There are four movies they are interested in seeing and three restaurants near the theater. From how many possibilities of a movie and a restaurant do they have to choose?

    A. 4 **B.** 7 **C.** 12 **D.** 14 11. _____

12. There are 16 cups in one gallon. How many $\frac{2}{3}$-cup servings can be poured from a one-gallon container of juice?

    A. $10\frac{2}{3}$　　　　**B.** 20　　　　**C.** 24　　　　**D.** 26

    12. _____

13. What is the solution of $4x - 5 = -7$?

    A. 3　　　　**B.** $-\frac{1}{2}$　　　　**C.** -2　　　　**D.** -3

    13. _____

14. The Peachtree Center in Atlanta is 264 meters tall. If a model of the Peachtree Center uses a scale of 1 centimeter = 8 meters, how tall is the model?

    A. 32 cm　　　　**B.** 33 cm　　　　**C.** 34 cm　　　　**D.** 35 cm

    14. _____

15. What number is 42% of 250?

    A. 105　　　　**B.** 115　　　　**C.** 155　　　　**D.** 595

    15. _____

16. Find the percent of increase for a stock that rises from 45 to 62. Round to the nearest percent.

    A. 17%　　　　**B.** 27%　　　　**C.** 38%　　　　**D.** 40%

    16. _____

17. Find the probability that you will get a 5 on the first spinner and a number less than 8 on the second spinner.

    A. $\frac{14}{15}$　　　　**B.** $\frac{8}{15}$

    C. $\frac{1}{3}$　　　　**D.** $\frac{1}{5}$

    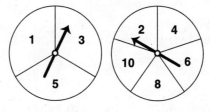

    17. _____

18. Find the domain of $y = 2x + 1$ if the range is $\{-5, 1, 3, 9\}$.

    A. $\{-9, 3, 7, 19\}$　　　　　　**B.** $\{-3, 0, 1, 4\}$
    C. $\{-3, 1, 3, 5\}$　　　　　　**D.** $\{-2, 0, 3, 5\}$

    18. _____

19. Which of the following is the graph of $2x - 3y = 3$?

    A.　　　　　　　　　　　**B.**

    C.　　　　　　　　　　　**D.**

    19. _____

20. Assume that y varies inversely as x. If $y = 14$ when $x = 3.5$, find x when $y = 10$.

    A. 2.5　　　　**B.** 3.6　　　　**C.** 4.9　　　　**D.** 5.2

    20. _____

Chapter 6 Answer Key

Form 1A

11. C

1. B

12. D

2. B

13. B

3. D

14. D

15. B

4. C

16. C

5. D

17. B

6. A

18. B

7. B

19. A

8. A

9. D

20. C

10. B   Bonus A

Form 1B

11. D

1. A

12. B

2. D

13. C

3. D

14. C

15. C

4. C

16. A

5. A

17. D

6. B

18. D

7. B

19. B

8. D

9. C

20. C

10. C   Bonus A

Chapter 6 Answer Key

Form 2A

1.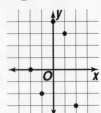

2. $\{-3, -2, 0, 3, 4\}$

3. $\{-2, -1, 0, 1, 2\}$

4.

Girls, x	4	3	2	1	0
Boys, y	4	5	6	7	8

5. $\{(-3, 1), (-1, 2),$ $(5, 5), (9, 7)\}$

6. $\left\{7, 5\frac{1}{2}, 5, 3\frac{1}{2}\right\}$

7. -3

8. $\{(1, 43.50), (2, 48),$ $(3, 52.50), (4, 57)\}$

9. No; the term $\frac{y}{x}$ has two variables. The equation cannot be written in the form $Ax + By = C$.

10. yes; $A = 2, B = 3,$ $C = 12$ or $A = -2,$ $B = -3, C = -12$

11. yes; $A = 4, B = -1,$ $C = 12$ or $A = -4,$ $B = 1, C = -12$

12.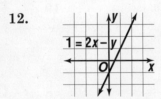

13.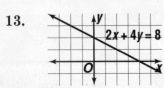

14. yes

15. no

16. 12

17. $15\frac{1}{2}$

18. $q(d) = 12 - \frac{2}{5}d$

19. yes

20. 6

21. 465 ft

22. 331.2

23. 14

24. 78 h

25. $17; xy = 17$ or $y = \frac{17}{x}$

Bonus $5\frac{5}{8}$

                   Algebra: Concepts and Applications

Chapter 6 Answer Key
Form 2B

Page 107

1.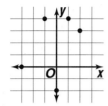

2. $\{-3, -1, 0, 1, 2\}$

3. $\{-2, 0, 3, 4\}$

4.

First die, x	3	5	5
Second die, y	5	3	5

5. $\{-3, 1, 11, 17\}$

6. $\{(-2, 11), (0, 7), (4, -1), (7, -7)\}$

7. 5

8. $\{(20, 100), (30, 90), (45, 75), (60, 60)\}$

9. yes; $A = 4$, $B = -9$, $C = 18$ or $A = -4$, $B = 9$, $C = -18$

10. No; the term xy has two variables. The equation cannot be written in the form $Ax + By = C$.

11. No; the term has a variable to a power other than 1. The term x^2 cannot be written in the form Ax.

12.

13.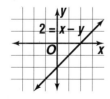

Page 108

14. yes

15. no

16. 21

17. -5

18. $p(n) = 45n - 2250$

19. no

20. $3\frac{3}{4}$

21. 9

22. 315

23. 54; $xy = 54$ or $y = \frac{54}{x}$

24. 10

25. 12 ft

Bonus   40

Chapter 6 Answer Key

Open-Ended Assessment
Sample Answers
Page 109

1. a. $y = 55x$

b. {110, 220, 330, 440}

c.

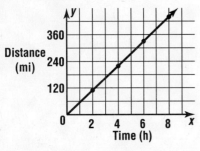

d. 45 mph: $y = 45x$;
range: {90, 180, 270, 360}
65 mph: $y = 65x$;
range: {130, 260, 390, 520}

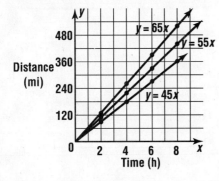

e. The graphs of distance traveled versus speed are lines passing through the origin. The greater the speed, the steeper the line.

f. direct variations

2. a. {550, 660, 770, 880}

b.

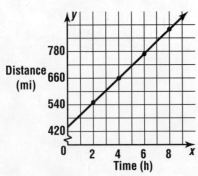

The graphs appear to have the same steepness, but the graph for the distance from home the second day is shifted upward.

c. No; the graph is not a straight line passing through the origin.

3. a. $t(s) = \dfrac{600}{s}$

b. {13.3, 10.9, 9.2}

c.

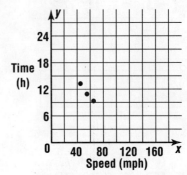

No; the points do not lie on a straight line through the origin.

d. cyclist: 24 h, racing car driver: 4 h

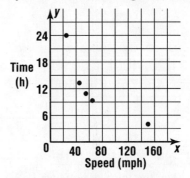

e. The graph appears to curve in towards the origin. It is not linear.

f. inverse

Chapter 6 Answer Key

1. {(−3, 0), (−2, −2), (0, 2), (2, 1), (3, −3)}

2.

x	−6	−3	0	2	8
y	−2	0	5	3	9

3. {−3, −2, 0, 1, 2}

4. {−6, −3, 0, 2, 8}

5. {(0, 16), (1, 11), (2, 6), (3, 1)}

6. {(0, 8), (3, 6), (6, 4), (9, 2)}

7. {(−8, −1), (0, 0), (8, 1), (24, 3)}

8.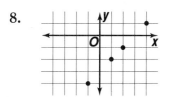

9. {−3, 1, 3, 4}

10. Sample answer: (6, 4)

11. yes; $A = 1, B = −2, C = 12$ or $A = −1, B = 2, C = −12$

12. No; the term $\frac{x}{y}$ has two variables. The equation cannot be written in the form $Ax + By = C$.

13.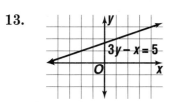

14. a horizontal line passing through (0, −3.1)

1.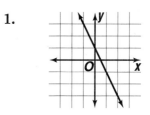

2. {−1, 0, 2, 3}

3. {2, 3, 8, 15}

4. {(−4, −11), (0, −3), (2, 1), (5, 7)}

5. {−3, −1, 2, 6}

6. {34, 30, 28, 12}

1.

2. yes; $A = 9, B = −4, C = 0$ or $A = −9, B = 4, C = 0$

3. 3

4. $1350

5. 189

6. $\frac{1}{4}$

Chapter 6 Answer Key

1. $26a + 10b$

2. No; the exercise habits of those involved in athletics will not accurately reflect those of students in general.

3. $5, 3, 0, -2, -7$

4. -9

5. $\dfrac{3}{8}$

6. 36.5

7. 24

8. 11

9. $\{-3, -1\}$

10. 75

11. 14

12. 140

13. $\dfrac{6}{11}$

14. $\{-5, -4, -1, 1\}$

15.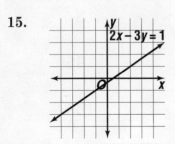

16. 90

1. B

2. D

3. A

4. C

5. A

6. B

7. C

8. B

9. D

10. C

11. C

12. C

13. B

14. B

15. A

16. C

17. D

18. B

19. C

20. C

Write the letter for the correct answer in the blank at the right of each problem.

For Questions 1–2, determine the slope of the line passing through the points whose coordinates are given.

1. $(6, 2)$ and $(4, -8)$

   A. $\frac{1}{5}$ **B.** $\frac{1}{3}$ **C.** 3 **D.** 5

   1. _____

2. $(8, -5)$ and $(3, -5)$

   A. -2 **B.** 0 **C.** 2 **D.** undefined

   2. _____

3. Determine the slope of the line shown at the right.

   A. 2 **B.** $\frac{1}{2}$

   C. $-\frac{1}{2}$ **D.** -2

   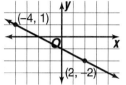

   3. _____

For Questions 4–5, write the point-slope form of an equation for each line.

4. the line passing through the point at $(3, -2)$ with slope 4

   A. $y - 2 = 4(x - 3)$ **B.** $y + 2 = 4(x - 3)$
   C. $y - 2 = 4(x + 3)$ **D.** $y - 3 = 4(x + 2)$

   4. _____

5. the line through points at $(-3, 6)$ and $(2, -9)$

   A. $y - 6 = -\frac{1}{3}(x + 3)$ **B.** $y - 6 = -3(x + 3)$

   C. $y + 9 = -\frac{1}{3}(x - 2)$ **D.** $y - 9 = -3(x - 3)$

   5. _____

6. Which is the point-slope form of an equation for the line shown at the right?

   A. $y - 4 = \frac{6}{5}(x + 1)$

   B. $y - 4 = -\frac{6}{5}(x + 1)$

   C. $y - 4 = \frac{5}{6}(x + 1)$

   D. $y - 4 = -\frac{5}{6}(x + 1)$

   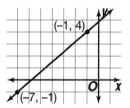

   6. _____

Write an equation in slope-intercept form for each line.

7. the line passing through the point at $(-3, 4)$ with slope -2

   A. $y = 2x + 10$ **B.** $y = -2x + 3$
   C. $y = -2x + 10$ **D.** $y = -2x - 2$

   7. _____

8. the line through points at $(4, -2)$ and $(6, 1)$

   A. $y = \frac{3}{2}x + 8$ **B.** $y = \frac{3}{2}x - 8$ **C.** $y = \frac{2}{3}x - 3$ **D.** $y = \frac{2}{3}x - 4\frac{2}{3}$

   8. _____

9. the line through points at $(5, 3)$ and $(0, -4)$

   A. $y = -\frac{5}{7}x - 4$ **B.** $y = \frac{7}{5}x - 4$ **C.** $y = -\frac{7}{5}x - 4$ **D.** $y = -\frac{7}{5}x + 10$

   9. _____

10. Which statement best describes the relationship shown by the scatter plot at the right?

   A. positive relationship   B. negative relationship
   C. no relationship   D. cannot be determined

   10. _____

Determine what kind of relationship a scatter plot would show between the variables.

11. the width of a tree trunk versus its age
   A. positive relationship   B. negative relationship
   C. no relationship   D. cannot be determined

   11. _____

12. the amount of fat versus the number of calories in a dessert
   A. positive relationship   B. negative relationship
   C. no relationship   D. cannot be determined

   12. _____

For Questions 13–14, determine the x-intercept and y-intercept of the graph of each equation.

13. $-3x + 2y = 6$
   A. x: 2, y: 3   B. x: -3, y: -2 C. x: -2, y: 3   D. x: 3, y: -2

   13. _____

14. $2x - 5y = 10$
   A. x: $\frac{2}{5}$, y: -2 B. x: 2, y: 5   C. x: 5, y: 2   D. x: 5, y: -2

   14. _____

15. Determine the slope and y-intercept of the graph of $-3x - 2y = 6$.
   A. $m = \frac{3}{2}$, $b = -3$ B. $m = \frac{2}{3}$, $b = -3$

   C. $m = -\frac{3}{2}$, $b = -3$ D. $m = -\frac{3}{2}$, $b = 3$

   15. _____

16. Which of the following statements is true about the graphs of $y = 2x - 4$ and $y = 2x + 3$?
   A. They have the same slope.   B. They intersect.
   C. They have different slopes.   D. They have the same y-intercept.

   16. _____

17. Which of the following pairs forms a family of graphs?
   A. $y = x + 2$ and $y = -5x - 2$ B. $y = 3x - 5$ and $y = -3x + 1$
   C. $y = -x - 1$ and $y = x + 1$ D. $y = -4x + 3$ and $y = -4x - 2$

   17. _____

18. For which of the following pairs are the graphs perpendicular?
   A. $y = 3x + 5$ and $y = -\frac{1}{3}x + 2$ B. $y = \frac{1}{2}x + 5$ and $y = -\frac{1}{2}x - 6$

   C. $y = x - 5$ and $y = x + 5$ C. $y = 3x - 2$ and $y = -3x + 1$

   18. _____

19. Which of the following has a graph that is perpendicular to the graph of $x - 2y = 8$?
   A. $x + 2y = 6$ B. $-x - 2y = 6$ C. $2x - 2y = 6$ D. $2x + y = 6$

   19. _____

20. Which of the following has a graph that is parallel to the graph of $2x - y = 6$ and passes through the point at $(3, -2)$?
   A. $2x + y = 4$ B. $2x - y = -8$ C. $x + 2y = 16$ D. $-2x + y = -8$

   20. _____

Bonus The graph of which equation does *not* form a family of graphs with the graph of $x - y = 3$?
   A. $y = -x - 3$ B. $-2x + 2y = 0$ C. $y + x = 3$ D. $3y = 2x - 9$ **Bonus** _____

For Questions 1–2, determine the slope of the line passing through the points whose coordinates are given.

1. $(-4, 2)$ and $(6, 8)$

   A. $\dfrac{1}{4}$ B. $\dfrac{3}{5}$ C. $\dfrac{5}{3}$ D. 3

   1. _____

2. $(-3, 3)$ and $(-3, -3)$

   A. 6 B. 0 C. -1 D. undefined

   2. _____

3. Determine the slope of the line shown at the right.

   A. $\dfrac{3}{2}$ B. $\dfrac{2}{3}$

   C. $-\dfrac{2}{3}$ D. $-\dfrac{3}{2}$

   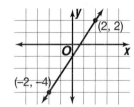

   3. _____

For Questions 4–5, write the point-slope form of an equation for each line.

4. the line passing through the point at $(-3, 4)$ with slope 2

   A. $y - 3 = 2(x - 4)$ B. $y + 3 = 2(x - 4)$
   C. $y - 4 = 2(x + 3)$ D. $y - 4 = 2(x - 3)$

   4. _____

5. the line through points at $(-2, 4)$ and $(3, 6)$

   A. $y - 6 = -\dfrac{2}{5}(x - 3)$ B. $y - 4 = -\dfrac{5}{2}(x + 2)$

   C. $y - 6 = \dfrac{2}{5}(x - 3)$ D. $y - 4 = \dfrac{2}{5}(x - 2)$

   5. _____

6. Which is the point-slope form of an equation for the line shown at the right?

   A. $y - 2 = -\dfrac{1}{3}(x - 3)$

   B. $y - 2 = -\dfrac{1}{3}(x + 3)$

   C. $y - 2 = \dfrac{1}{3}(x - 3)$

   D. $y - 2 = \dfrac{1}{3}(x + 3)$

   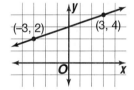

   6. _____

Write an equation in slope-intercept form for each line.

7. the line passing through through the point at $(-2, 3)$ with slope 6

   A. $y = 6x + 15$ B. $y = 6x - 9$ C. $y = 6x - 15$ D. $y = 6(x + 2)$

   7. _____

8. the line through points at $(1, -4)$ and $(2, 6)$

   A. $y = \dfrac{1}{10}x - 4\dfrac{1}{10}$ B. $y = 10x - 14$
   C. $y = -10x + 26$ D. $y = -10x + 6$

   8. _____

9. the line through points at $(0, -2)$ and $(2, 6)$

   A. $y = 4x - 2$ B. $y = 4x + 2$ C. $y = 2x - 2$ D. $y = \dfrac{1}{4}x - 2$

   9. _____

10. Which statement best describes the relationship shown by the scatter plot at the right?
    A. positive relationship   B. negative relationship
    C. no relationship   D. cannot be determined

10. _____

Determine what kind of relationship a scatter plot would show between the variables.

11. the age of an infant versus its weight
    A. positive relationship   B. negative relationship
    C. no relationship   D. cannot be determined

11. _____

12. the number of students attending a baseball game versus the score
    A. positive relationship   B. negative relationship
    C. no relationship   D. cannot be determined

12. _____

For Questions 13–14, determine the x-intercept and y-intercept of the graph of each equation.

13. $-2x - 4y = 8$
    A. x: -4, y: 2   B. x: -4, y: -2 C. x: 2 y: -4 D. x: 4, y: -2

13. _____

14. $x + 3y = -3$
    A. x: -1, y: -3 B. x: -3, y: 1   C. x: 1, y: -3 D. x: -3, y: -1

14. _____

15. Determine the slope and y-intercept of the graph of $-3x - y = 6$.
    A. $m = 3, b = 6$ B. $m = -3, b = -6$
    C. $m = 3, b = -6$ D. $m = -3, b = 6$

15. _____

16. Which of the following statements is true about the graphs of $y = -4x - 2$ and $y = 4x - 2$?
    A. They have the same slope.   B. The graphs do not intersect.
    C. They have different slopes.   D. They have the same y-intercept.

16. _____

17. Which of the following pairs forms a family of graphs?
    A. $y = -x + 1$ and $y = -4x - 1$ B. $y = -2x - 5$ and $y = 7x + 5$
    C. $y = -x - 3$ and $y = -2x - 3$ D. $y = 6x + 1$ and $y = -6x - 2$

17. _____

18. For which of the following pairs are the graphs perpendicular?
    A. $y = -3x + 2$ and $y = -\frac{1}{3}x + 4$ B. $y = -2x - 4$ and $y = -\frac{1}{2}x + 1$

    C. $y = -x - 5$ and $y = -x + 1$ D. $y = -2x + 2$ and $y = \frac{1}{2}x - 4$

18. _____

19. Which of the following has a graph that is parallel to the graph of $x - 2y = 8$?
    A. $x + 2y = 6$ B. $-x - 2y = 6$ C. $3x - 6y = 6$ D. $3x + 6y = 6$

19. _____

20. Which of the following has a graph that is perpendicular to the graph of $2x - y = 6$ and passes through the point at $(4, -2)$?
    A. $x + 2y = 0$ B. $x + 2y = 8$ C. $2x - y = -6$ D. $-2x + y = -6$

20. _____

Bonus The graph of which equation does *not* form a family of graphs with the graph of $y = 4x - 3$?
    A. $x + 2y = -6$ B. $-4x - y = -3$
    C. $8x - 2y = 0$ D. $5x - 11y = 33$

Bonus _____

Chapter 7 Test, Form 2A

For Questions 1–4, determine the slope of each line.

1. the line through points at $(-4, -8)$ and $(-4, 2)$

1. _____

2. the line through points at $(3, 6)$ and $(1, -4)$

2. _____

3.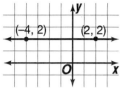

3. _____

4.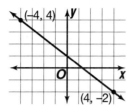

4. _____

For Questions 5–6, write the point-slope form of an equation for each line.

5. the line passing through the point at $(4, -1)$ with slope 2

5. _____

6. the line through points at $(3, -3)$ and $(5, 1)$

6. _____

7. Write the point-slope form of an equation for the line shown at the right.

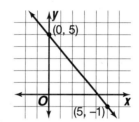

7. _____

Write an equation in slope-intercept form of the line having the given slope and passing through the given point.

8. $m = -3, (4, -1)$

8. _____

9. $m = 0, (0, -3)$

9. _____

For Questions 10–11, write an equation in slope-intercept form of the line passing through each pair of points.

10. $(6, -2)$ and $(3, -4)$

10. _____

11. $(-8, 2)$ and $(0, 6)$

11. _____

12. Determine whether the scatter plot shows a *positive* relationship, a *negative* relationship, or *no* relationship. If there is a relationship, describe it.

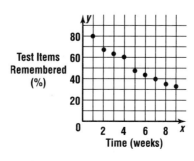

12. _____

Determine whether a scatter plot of the data would show positive, negative, *or* no relationship *between the variables.*

13. the distance from an object versus its apparent size

13. _____

14. the number of students attending a basketball game versus the noise level in the arena

14. _____

For Questions 15–16, determine the x-intercept and y-intercept of the graph of each equation.

15. $2x + 4y = 8$

15. _____

16. $-3x - 5y = 15$

16. _____

17. Determine the slope and y-intercept of the graph of $3x + y = 8$.

17. _____

18. Determine the slope and y-intercept of the graph of $-x + 2y = 4$. Then graph the equation.

18. _____

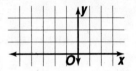

19. Compare and contrast the graphs of $y = 3x - 2$ and $y = -2x + 1$. Verify by graphing the equations.

19. _____

20. Explain why the graphs of $y = -2x + 3$ and $y = 2x + 3$ are a family of graphs.

20. _____

21. Change $y = x - 3$ so that the graph of the new equation has a steeper, negative slope and the same y-intercept.

21. _____

Write an equation in slope-intercept form of a line with the following characteristics.

22. perpendicular to the graph of $y = \frac{3}{2}x - 3$

22. _____

23. parallel to the graph of $-4x + 3y = 12$

23. _____

24. parallel to the graph of $x + y = 6$ and passing through the point at $(1, -4)$

24. _____

25. perpendicular to the graph of $2x - 3y = 12$ and passing through the point at $(4, 3)$.

25. _____

Bonus The line through points at $(4, 6)$ and $(x, -4)$ has a slope of $-\frac{2}{3}$. What is x?

Bonus _____

7 Chapter 7 Test, Form 2B

For Questions 1–4, determine the slope of each line.

1. the line through points at $(-3, 6)$ and $(7, 2)$

1. _____

2. the line through points at $(5, -2)$ and $(5, 4)$

2. _____

3.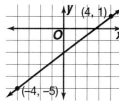

4.

3. _____

4. _____

For Questions 5–6, write the point-slope form of an equation for each line.

5. the line passing through the point at $(-2, 5)$ with slope 3

5. _____

6. the line through points at $(4, 1)$ and $(1, -5)$

6. _____

7. Write the point-slope form of an equation for the line shown at the right.

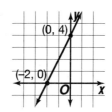

7. _____

Write an equation in slope-intercept form of the line having the given slope and passing through the given point.

8. $m = -4$, $(3, -5)$

8. _____

9. $m = 0$, $(-5, 1)$

9. _____

For Questions 10–11, write an equation in slope-intercept form of the line passing through each pair of points.

10. $(-4, 1)$ and $(-6, -2)$

10. _____

11. $(3, -2)$ and $(0, -4)$

11. _____

12. Determine whether the scatter plot shows a *positive* relationship, a *negative* relationship, or *no* relationship. If there is a relationship, describe it.

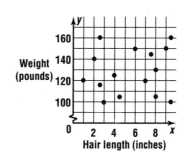

12. _____

Algebra: Concepts and Applications

7

Determine whether a scatter plot of the data would show
positive, negative, or no relationship between the variables.

13. the number of calories burned versus hours of exercise done

13. _____

14. the number of students attending a football game versus the
    number of seats left available in the stadium

14. _____

For Questions 15–16, determine the x-intercept and y-intercept
of the graph of each equation.

15. $2x - 4y = 8$

15. _____

16. $2x + y = 10$

16. _____

17. Determine the slope and y-intercept of the graph of
    $-2x - y = 4$.

17. _____

18. Determine the slope and y-intercept of the graph of $y = -3$.
    Then graph the equation.

18. _____

19. Compare and contrast the graphs of $y = -3x - 2$ and
    $y = x - 2$. Verify by graphing the equations.

19. _____

20. Explain why $y = 3x + 1$ and $y = 3x - 2$ are a family of graphs.

20. _____

21. Change $y = -3x + 2$ so that the graph of the new equation
    has the same slope, but is shifted down 4 units.

21. _____

Write an equation in slope-intercept form of a line with the
following characteristics.

22. _____

22. parallel to the graph of $y = \frac{3}{2}x - 3$

23. perpendicular to the graph of $-x + 4y = 2$

23. _____

24. parallel to the graph of $-x + y = 4$ and passing through the
    point $(2, -1)$

24. _____

25. perpendicular to the graph of $4x - 2y = 8$ and passing
    through the point at $(0, 3)$

25. _____

Bonus The line through points at $(3, y)$ and $(-5, 4)$ has a slope of
3. What is y?

Bonus _____

7

Chapter 7 Open-Ended Assessment

Instructions: Demonstrate your knowledge by giving a clear, concise solution for each problem. Be sure to include all relevant graphs and to justify your answers. You may show your solutions in more than one way or investigate beyond the requirements of the problem.

1. Katherine has sold 50 candy bars for a fundraiser. She expects to sell an additional 12 candy bars each day.

   a. Make a table showing Katherine's total sales for the next 7 days. Use the sales of 50 candy bars so far as the results for day 0.

   b. Graph the data from the table. Connect the points.

   c. Write an equation in point-slope form that describes the data in the table.

   d. Write an equation in slope-intercept form that describes the data in the table.

   e. What do the slope and *y*-intercept of the graph represent?

   f. Use the equation in part d to predict Katherine's total sales after 4 weeks.

   g. What would a steeper slope to the graph but the same *y*-intercept represent? What would the same slope but a greater *y*-intercept represent?

2. The table at the right represents the number of women in the U.S. work force at various times in the past century.

   a. Make a scatter plot of the data.

   b. Determine if there is a *positive*, *negative*, or *no* relationship in the data. If there is a relationship, describe it.

   c. Describe any trends you notice in the data.

   d. Based on the scatter plot, estimate the number of women in the U.S. work force in the year 2000.

Year	Number (millions)
1900	5
1920	8
1930	10
1950	16
1970	31
1990	57

Chapter 7 Mid-Chapter Test
(Lessons 7–1 through 7–4)

7

For Questions 1–3, determine the slope of each line.

1.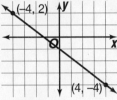

2.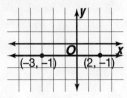

1. _____

2. _____

3. the line through points at $(-3, -3)$ and $(-6, 3)$

3. _____

4. In the linear equation $y - y_1 = m(x - x_1)$, what does m represent?

4. _____

5. Write an equation in point-slope form for the line through points at $(2, -4)$ and $(-5, 3)$.

5. _____

6. Write the point-slope form of an equation for the line shown at the right.

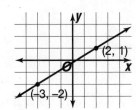

6. _____

For Questions 7–9, write an equation in slope-intercept form for each line.

7. the line through points at $(4, 5)$ and $(2, -1)$

7. _____

8. the line through points at $(-3, 5)$ and $(0, 5)$

8. _____

9. the line passing through the point at $(2, -6)$ with slope 0

9. _____

10. Determine whether the scatter plot shows a *positive* relationship, a *negative* relationship, or *no* relationship. If there is a relationship, describe it.

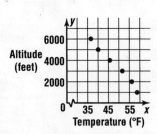

10. _____

Determine whether a scatter plot of the data would show positive, negative, or no relationship between the variables.

11. the number of hours a student watches television versus how many hours he or she spends on homework

11. _____

12. the height of a person versus her or his shoe size

12. _____

NAME _____ DATE _____ PERIOD _____

Chapter 7 Quiz A
(Lessons 7–1 through 7–3)

1. Determine the slope of the line shown at the right.

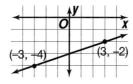

1. _____

2. Write the point-slope form of an equation for a line passing through the point at $(-5, 6)$ with slope $\frac{2}{3}$.

2. _____

3. Write an equation in point-slope form for the line through points at $(4, 3)$ and $(-5, 2)$.

3. _____

4. Write an equation in slope-intercept form for the line passing through the point at $(-3, 6)$ with slope $-\frac{4}{3}$.

4. _____

5. Write an equation in slope-intercept form of the line shown at the right.

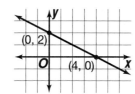

5. _____

NAME _____ DATE _____ PERIOD _____

Chapter 7 Quiz B
(Lessons 7–4 through 7–7)

1. Determine whether the scatter plot shows a *positive* relationship, a *negative* relationship, or *no* relationship. If there is a relationship, describe it.

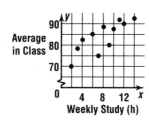

1. _____

2. Determine the x-intercept and y-intercept of the graph of $4x + 3y = -12$.

2. _____

3. Determine the slope and y-intercept of the graph of $-x + 3y = 6$.

3. _____

4. Compare and contrast the graphs of $y = -\frac{1}{2}x + 4$ and $y = \frac{1}{2}x - 3$.

4. _____

5. Determine whether the graphs of $y = \frac{2}{3}x$ and $6x + 4y = 12$ are *parallel, perpendicular,* or *neither.*

5. _____

1. Write an equation for the sentence below. *(Lesson 1–1)*

   The difference of twice a number and 16 is equal to the quotient of three times the number and 8.

   1. _____

2. Yoshi's grade will be attending a brand new school next year. Students who will be attending the school are going to vote on the mascot for the school. To predict which mascot students will choose, Yoshi asks all of the students at her lunch table for their preferences. Is this a representative sample? Why or why not? *(Lesson 1–6)*

   2. _____

For Questions 3–5, evaluate each expression.

3. $6 - (-11)$ *(Lesson 2–4)*

   3. _____

4. $-48 \div (-12)$ *(Lesson 2–6)*

   4. _____

5. $-1.8 - 3.2 + 2.4$ *(Lesson 3–2)*

   5. _____

6. Find the solution of $x = 16 \div 2 + 2 \cdot 5$. *(Lesson 3–4)*

   6. _____

For Questions 7–8, solve each equation.

7. $-8.2n = -41$ *(Lesson 4–4)*

   7. _____

8. $6 + 4(x + 2) = 18$ *(Lesson 4–7)*

   8. _____

9. A scale model of a house is 18 inches wide. The actual house is 48 feet wide. Find the scale of the model. *(Lesson 5–2)*

   9. _____

10. 80% of what number is 33.6? *(Lesson 5–3)*

    10. _____

11. Determine whether the relation $\{(3, 2), (4, 5), (-3, 5), (-4, 2)\}$ is a function. *(Lesson 6–4)*

    11. _____

12. Suppose y varies directly as x and $y = 27$ when $x = 3$. Find x when $y = 45$. *(Lesson 6–5)*

    12. _____

13. Suppose y varies inversely as x and $y = 24$ when $x = 3$. Find x when $y = 36$. *(Lesson 6–6)*

    13. _____

14. Write the point-slope form of an equation for the line passing through the point at $(3, -6)$ with slope $-\frac{4}{3}$. *(Lesson 7–2)*

    14. _____

15. Write an equation in slope-intercept form for the line through points at $(2, -4)$ and $(6, -2)$. *(Lesson 7–3)*

    15. _____

16. Determine the slope and y-intercept of the graph of $12 + 3y = -2x$. *(Lesson 7–5)*

    16. _____

7

Chapter 7 Standardized Test Practice
(Chapters 1–7)

Write the letter for the correct answer in the blank at the right of each problem.

1. Which of the following is an example of the Associative Property of Addition?
   A. $(h + 2) + 3 = h + (2 + 3)$ **B.** $(h \cdot 2) \cdot 3 = h \cdot (2 \cdot 3)$
   C. $h + 2 = 2 + h$ **D.** $2(h + 2) = 2h + 4$

   1. _____

2. How many ways are there to make a sum of 12 using the numbers 1, 2, and 5?
   A. 5   **B.** 8   **C.** 12   **D.** 13

   2. _____

3. Jerome's middle school has 280 students. Which is the best way to display data of the heights to the nearest centimeter of all the students in the school?
   A. line graph   **B.** stem-and-leaf plot
   C. histogram   **D.** frequency table

   3. _____

4. Evaluate $x - z + w$ if $x = -4$, $z = -6$, and $w = -8$.
   A. -18 **B.** -10 **C.** -6 **D.** -2

   4. _____

5. Evaluate $\frac{xy}{-4}$ if $x = -2$ and $y = 12$.
   A. -6 **B.** $-\frac{5}{2}$ **C.** $\frac{5}{2}$ **D.** 6

   5. _____

6. Find $-2\frac{1}{3} - 3\frac{1}{6} + 1\frac{5}{6}$.
   A. -4 **B.** $-3\frac{2}{3}$ **C.** $-3\frac{1}{2}$ **D.** -1

   6. _____

7. Find the mean of the data below, which give the number of days with precipitation recorded in a town over a 10-month period.
   $$10, 12, 7, 4, 6, 8, 10, 14, 9, 10$$
   A. 9   **B.** 9.5   **C.** 10   **D.** 12

   7. _____

8. For what value of x is the equation $\frac{4}{5} = x - \left(-\frac{1}{5}\right)$ true?
   A. $-\frac{3}{5}$ **B.** $\frac{4}{25}$ **C.** $\frac{3}{5}$ **D.** 1

   8. _____

9. Evaluate $\frac{x}{3}$ if $x = \frac{2}{5}$.
   A. $\frac{2}{15}$ **B.** $\frac{1}{3}$ **C.** 1   **D.** $1\frac{1}{5}$

   9. _____

10. Find the value of s if the perimeter of the square is 36 inches.
    A. 2   **B.** 4
    C. 5   **D.** 6

    $(s + 4)$ m

    10. _____

11. For what value of n is the equation $3(n - 2) - 4(n + 1) = 11$ true?

    A. -21 **B.** -12 **C.** -1 **D.** 21 11. _____

12. Find the value of x that makes $\frac{x-6}{8} = \frac{x}{16}$ a proportion.

    A. -12 **B.** 0 **C.** $\frac{3}{4}$ **D.** 12 12. _____

13. The scale of a model of a cruise ship is 1 to 180. If the model is 28 inches long, how long is the actual ship?

    A. 360 ft   **B.** 420 ft   **C.** 480 ft   **D.** 640 ft   13. _____

14. Janelle bought a new purse that was on sale for 15% off. If the original cost was $42, find the sale price.

    A. $6.30   **B.** $35.70   **C.** $36.30   **D.** $48.30   14. _____

15. Find the domain of $y = 3x - 4$ if the range is $\{-10, -7, -1, 2\}$.

    A. $\{-34\}$ **B.** $\{-34, -25, -7, 2\}$

    C. $\{-2\}$ **D.** $\{-2, -1, 1, 2\}$ 15. _____

16. Which of the following equations is *not* a linear equation?

    A. $y = 4$ **B.** $\frac{3}{4}x - \frac{2}{3}y = 0$

    C. $y + 2xy = 3$ **D.** $0.42x - 16.3 = -5.1y$ 16. _____

17. The function $f(x) = 25x + 400$ represents Jason's total savings after x weeks. How much has he saved after 8 weeks?

    A. $550   **B.** $560   **C.** $600   **D.** $3225   17. _____

18. Determine the slope of the line through points at $(4, -8)$ and $(3, -6)$.

    A. -14 **B.** -2 **C.** 2 **D.** $\frac{2}{7}$ 18. _____

19. Find an equation in slope-intercept form for the line.

    A. $y = -\frac{1}{4}x - 11$ **B.** $y = -x - 13$

    C. $y = -4x - 11$ **D.** $y = -4x - 13$

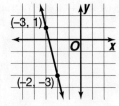

     19. _____

20. Which of the following has a graph that is perpendicular to the graph of $y = -\frac{1}{2}x + 4$?

    A. $y = -\frac{1}{2}x - 4$ **B.** $y = 2x + 4$

    C. $y = -\frac{1}{2}x + 3$ **D.** $y = -2x + 4$ 20. _____

Chapter 7 Answer Key

Form 1A

Page 121

1. __D__
2. __B__
3. __C__
4. __B__
5. __B__
6. __C__
7. __D__
8. __B__
9. __B__

Page 122

10. __B__
11. __A__
12. __A__
13. __C__
14. __D__
15. __C__
16. __A__
17. __D__
18. __A__
19. __D__
20. __D__
Bonus __C__

Form 1B

Page 123

1. __B__
2. __D__
3. __A__
4. __C__
5. __C__
6. __D__
7. __A__
8. __B__
9. __A__

Page 124

10. __C__
11. __A__
12. __C__
13. __B__
14. __D__
15. __B__
16. __D__
17. __C__
18. __D__
19. __C__
20. __A__
Bonus __B__

Chapter 7 Answer Key
Form 2A

1. __undefined__

2. __5__

3. __0__

4. $-\dfrac{3}{4}$

5. $y + 1 = 2(x - 4)$

6. $y - 1 = 2(x - 5)$ or $y + 3 = 2(x - 3)$

7. $y - 5 = -\dfrac{6}{5}x$ or $y + 1 = -\dfrac{6}{5}(x - 5)$

8. $y = -3x + 11$

9. $y = -3$

10. $y = \dfrac{2}{3}x - 6$

11. $y = \dfrac{1}{2}x + 6$

12. __Negative; the more time that passes, the fewer test items that are remembered.__

13. __negative__

14. __positive__

15. $x{:}\ 4,\ y{:}\ 2$

16. $x{:}\ {-5},\ y{:}\ {-3}$

17. $m = -3,\ b = 8$

18. $m = \dfrac{1}{2};\ b = 2;$

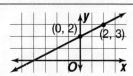

19. __The graphs have different slopes and different y-intercepts; they are not a family of graphs.__

20. __They have the same y-intercept.__

21. Sample answer: $y = -2x - 3$

22. Sample answer: $y = -\dfrac{2}{3}x - 4$

23. Sample answer: $y = \dfrac{4}{3}x$

24. $y = -x - 3$

25. $y = -\dfrac{3}{2}x + 9$

Bonus __19__

Chapter 7 Answer Key
Form 2B

1. $-\dfrac{2}{5}$

2. undefined

3. $\dfrac{3}{4}$

4. -1

5. $y - 5 = 3(x + 2)$

6. $y - 1 = 2(x - 4)$ or $y + 5 = 2(x - 1)$

7. $y - 4 = 2x$ or $y = 2(x + 2)$

8. $y = -4x + 7$

9. $y = 1$

10. $y = \dfrac{3}{2}x + 7$

11. $y = \dfrac{2}{3}x - 4$

12. no

13. positive

14. negative

15. $x: 4, y: -2$

16. $x: 5, y: 10$

17. $m = -2, b = -4$

18. $m = 0, b = -3;$

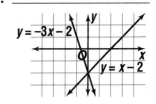

19. They are a family of graphs with the same y-intercept but different slopes.

$y = -3x - 2$ $y = x - 2$

20. They have the same slope.

21. $y = -3x - 2$

22. Sample answer: $y = \dfrac{3}{2}x + 1$

23. Sample answer: $y = -4x + 1$

24. $y = x - 3$

25. $y = -\dfrac{1}{2}x + 3$

Bonus ____ 28

Chapter 7 Answer Key

Open-Ended Assessment
Sample Answers
Page 129

1. a.

Day	Sales
0	50
1	62
2	74
3	86
4	98
5	110
6	122
7	134

b.

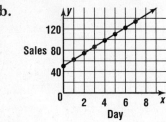

c. $y - 62 = 12(x - 1)$

d. $y = 12x + 50$

e. The slope represents the daily sales. The y-intercept represents the number of candy bars sold initially.

f. 386 candy bars

g. the same initial sales, but higher daily sales; higher initial sales, but the same daily sales

2. a.

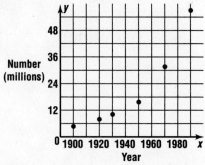

b. Positive; as the years increase, the number of women in the work force increases.

c. The data appear to curve upward, meaning that the number of women in the work force has increased more rapidly as time has passed.

d. 80 million

Chapter 7 Answer Key

Mid-Chapter Test
Page 130

1. $-\dfrac{3}{4}$

2. 0

3. -2

4. the slope

5. $y + 4 = -(x - 2)$ or $y - 3 = -(x + 5)$

6. $y + 2 = \dfrac{3}{5}(x + 3)$ or $y - 1 = \dfrac{3}{5}(x - 2)$

7. $y = 3x - 7$

8. $y = 5$

9. $y = -6$

10. Negative; the higher the temperature, the lower the altitude.

11. negative

12. positive

Quiz A
Page 131

1. $\dfrac{1}{3}$

2. $y - 6 = \dfrac{2}{3}(x + 5)$

3. $y - 2 = \dfrac{1}{9}(x + 5)$ or $y - 3 = \dfrac{1}{9}(x - 4)$

4. $y = -\dfrac{4}{3}x + 2$

5. $y = -\dfrac{1}{2}x + 2$

Quiz B
Page 131

1. Positive; in general, the more hours of study, the higher the average in class.

2. $x: -3; y: -4$

3. $m = \dfrac{1}{3}, b = 2$

4. The lines are not a family of graphs. The graphs have the same steepness, but one has a positive slope and the other a negative slope. The graphs have different y-intercepts.

5. perpendicular

Chapter 7 Answer Key

Cumulative Review
Page 132

1. $2n - 16 = \frac{3n}{8}$

2. Sample answer: No; students at the same table may have similar interests, so their opinions may not represent the views of students as a whole.

3. 17

4. 4

5. −2.6

6. 18

7. 5

8. 1

9. 1 in. = $2\frac{2}{3}$ ft or 1:32

10. 42

11. yes

12. 5

13. 2

14. $y + 6 = -\frac{4}{3}(x - 3)$

15. $y = \frac{1}{2}x - 5$

16. $m = -\frac{2}{3}; b = -4$

Standardized Test Practice
Page 133

1. A

2. D

3. C

4. C

5. D

6. B

7. A

8. C

9. A

10. C

Page 134

11. A

12. D

13. B

14. B

15. D

16. C

17. C

18. B

19. C

20. B

8

Chapter 8 Test, Form 1A

Write the letter for the correct answer in the blank at the right of each problem.

1. Write the expression $2 \cdot x \cdot x \cdot x \cdot x \cdot x \cdot x$ using exponents.
   A. $2x^2$ B. $2x^6$ C. $64x^6$ D. $(2x)^6$ 1. _____

2. Which expression is equivalent to $-3y^6$?
   A. $(-3y)(-3y)(-3y)(-3y)(-3y)(-3y)$
   B. $-729y^6$
   C. $-3 \cdot y \cdot y \cdot y \cdot y \cdot y \cdot y$
   D. $729y^6$ 2. _____

3. Evaluate $-2x^5y$ if $x = -2$ and $y = 4$.
   A. -256 B. 128 C. 256 D. 4096 3. _____

For Questions 4–9, simplify each expression.

4. $x^4 \cdot x^2 \cdot x$
   A. x^6 B. x^7 C. x^8 D. $8x^7$ 4. _____

5. $(3x^3y)(2x^2y)$
   A. $5x^6y$ B. $5x^5y^2$ C. $6x^5y^2$ D. $6x^6y$ 5. _____

6. $\dfrac{24w^3y^5}{-12w^2y^4}$
   A. $-12wy$ B. $-2w^5y^9$ C. $2wy$ D. $-2wy$ 6. _____

7. $a^5(a^{-3})$
   A. a^8 B. $\dfrac{1}{a^{15}}$ C. $-a^{15}$ D. a^2 7. _____

8. $\dfrac{k^{-3}}{k^6}$
   A. $\dfrac{1}{k^9}$ B. $\dfrac{1}{k^3}$ C. $\dfrac{1}{k^{18}}$ D. $-k^9$ 8. _____

9. $\dfrac{4w^3y^5}{-16w^{-2}y^4}$
   A. $-4w^5y$ B. $-\dfrac{y}{4w^5}$ C. $-\dfrac{w^5y^9}{4}$ D. $-\dfrac{w^5y}{4}$ 9. _____

10. Express 48 kilobytes in standard form.
    A. 0.00048 bytes   B. 480 bytes
    C. 4800 bytes   D. 48,000 bytes   10. _____

11. Express 0.00025 meters in scientific notation.
    A. 2.5×10^{-5} m   B. 2.5×10^{-4} m
    C. 2.5×10^4 m   D. 2.5×10^5 m   11. _____

12. Evaluate $(3.1 \times 10^2)(3 \times 10^6)$. Express the answer in scientific notation.
    A. 6.1×10^8 B. 9.3×10^{12} C. 9.3×10^8 D. 9.3×10^9
         12. _____

13. Pluto is about 5.9×10^9 kilometers from the sun, or about 39.5 times farther from the sun than Earth is. About how far is Earth from the sun?
    A. 1.5×10^8 km   B. 2.3×10^{11} km
    C. 3.36×10^9 km   D. 1.5×10^7 km   13. _____

NAME ______________________ DATE __________ PERIOD ______

Chapter 8 Test, Form 1A *(continued)*

Simplify each expression.

14. $\sqrt{256}$

A. 128 **B.** 18 **C.** 16 **D.** −16 **14.** ______

15. $-\sqrt{324}$

A. −162 **B.** −18 **C.** −16 **D.** 18 **15.** ______

16. $\frac{\sqrt{144}}{\sqrt{64}}$

A. 2.25 **B.** $\sqrt{\frac{3}{2}}$ **C.** $\frac{3}{2}$ **D.** 4 **16.** ______

17. $-\sqrt{\frac{64}{225}}$

A. $\frac{8}{15}$ **B.** $\frac{8}{25}$ **C.** $-\frac{8}{25}$ **D.** $-\frac{8}{15}$ **17.** ______

For Questions 18–20, estimate each square root to the nearest integer.

18. $\sqrt{163}$

A. 11 **B.** 12 **C.** 13 **D.** 14 **18.** ______

19. $\sqrt{0.45}$

A. 0 **B.** 1 **C.** 2 **D.** 7 **19.** ______

20. $\sqrt{1500}$

A. 30 **B.** 35 **C.** 37 **D.** 39 **20.** ______

21. The formula $t = \sqrt{\frac{d}{4.9}}$ gives the time t in seconds for an object to fall d meters. About how long will it take an object to fall 500 meters?

A. 10 s **B.** 11 s **C.** 15 s **D.** 22 s **21.** ______

22. Find the length of the hypotenuse of the right triangle shown at the right.

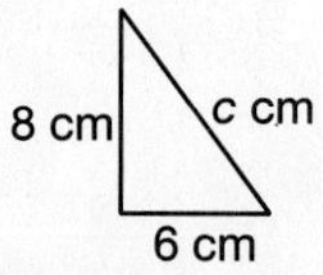

A. 9 cm **B.** 10 cm
C. 12 cm **D.** 14 cm **22.** ______

23. Find the missing measure b in the right triangle shown at the right.

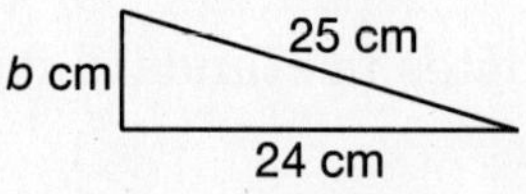

A. 1 cm **B.** 5 cm
C. 7 cm **D.** 10 cm **23.** ______

24. A side view of a roof is shown at the right. Find the height h to the nearest foot.

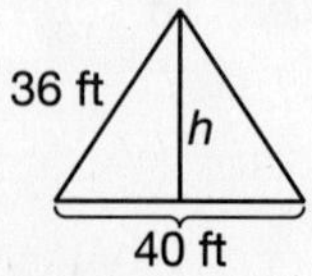

A. 17 ft **B.** 28 ft
C. 30 ft **D.** 32 ft **24.** ______

25. Which triangle with side lengths given below is *not* a right triangle?

A. 3, 4, 5 **B.** 7, 8, 9 **C.** 9, 40, 41 **D.** 10, 24, 26 **25.** ______

Bonus A right triangle has sides of 6 inches and 8 inches. What is the measure of the third side?

A. 5.3 only **B.** 10 only **C.** 5.3 or 10 **D.** 14 only **Bonus** ______

8 Chapter 8 Test, Form 2B

1. Write $-4 \cdot y \cdot y \cdot y$ using exponents.

1. _____

2. Write $3cd^3$ as a multiplication expression.

2. _____

3. Evaluate $-5x^4z$ if $x = -2$ and $z = 3$.

3. _____

4. The prime factorization of 200 is $2 \cdot 2 \cdot 2 \cdot 5 \cdot 5$. Rewrite the prime factorization using exponents.

4. _____

For Questions 5–12, simplify each expression.

5. $5^2 \cdot 5^4$

5. _____

6. $(3x^4y)(xy^2)$

6. _____

7. $(11cd)(2c^2d)(d)$

7. _____

8. $\dfrac{n^5}{n^3}$

8. _____

9. $\dfrac{-14m^2n}{7m^2}$

9. _____

10. $5c^{-5}d^{-1}$

10. _____

11. $\dfrac{f^3g^4}{f^4g^6}$

11. _____

12. $\dfrac{-18m^5n^2}{6m^{-4}n^3}$

12. _____

13. Evaluate $2x^{-1}y^3$ if $x = 2$ and $y = -1$.

13. _____

For Questions 14–17, express each number in scientific notation.

14. 0.0049

14. _____

15. 7,200,000,000

15. _____

16. $(1.4 \times 10^7)(2.5 \times 10^2)$

16. _____

17. $\dfrac{8 \times 10^6}{4 \times 10^2}$

17. _____

18. Express 480 kilotons in standard form as tons.

18. _____

Simplify each expression.

19. $\sqrt{289}$

19. _____

20. $-\sqrt{576}$

20. _____

21. $\sqrt{\dfrac{36}{225}}$

21. _____

22. Simplify $-\sqrt{\dfrac{0.01}{0.25}}$.

22. _____

23. If $x = \sqrt{0.04}$, what is the value of x?

23. _____

Estimate the square root to the nearest whole number.

24. $\sqrt{220}$

24. _____

25. $\sqrt{0.85}$

25. _____

26. $\sqrt{500}$

26. _____

27. $\sqrt{120.2}$

27. _____

For Questions 28–31, find the missing measure *x* of the right triangle. Round to the nearest tenth if necessary.

28.

29.

28. _____

29. _____

30.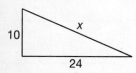

31.

30. _____

31. _____

32. A telephone pole is supported by a wire of length x as shown. Find x to the nearest whole number.

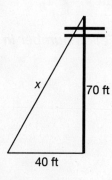

32. _____

33. A rectangle has side length 30 millimeters and diagonal length 34 millimeters. Find the length of the third side. Round to the nearest tenth if necessary.

33. _____

Bonus A box has sides of length 5, 12, and 10 inches. Find the length d of a diagonal of the box. Round to the nearest tenth.

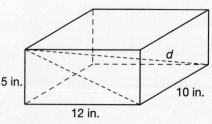

Bonus _____

8 Chapter 8 Open-Ended Assessment

Instructions: Demonstrate your knowledge by giving a clear, concise solution for each problem. Be sure to include all relevant diagrams and to justify your answers. You may show your solutions in more than one way or investigate beyond the requirements of the problem.

1. You have found products such as $(2 \times 10^3)(3 \times 10^2) =$ $(2 \times 3)(10^3 \times 10^2)$ or 6×10^5. Often, however, the product of the integer parts will not be between 1 and 10.

   a. Rewrite the product $(5 \times 10^{-3})(6 \times 10^9)$ using the Associative and Commutative Properties as the product of an integer and a power of 10.

   b. Is the result in part a in scientific notation? Explain.

   c. Rewrite the product of the integers from part a in scientific notation. Then write the power of 10 from part a in scientific notation.

   d. Find the product of the two expressions in part c, giving the result in scientific notation. What does this tell you about the product of 5×10^{-3} and 6×10^9?

   e. Use the process in parts a–d to find $(4.5 \times 10^4)(8 \times 10^5)$. Write the result in scientific notation.

   f. Use the process in parts a–d to find $\frac{3 \times 10^4}{6 \times 10^{-2}}$. Write the result in scientific notation.

2. A triangle with three equal sides is called *equilateral*.

   a. Draw three equilateral triangles. Use side lengths of 1, 2, and 4 centimeters. Label each triangle with its side lengths.

   b. Draw a line segment dividing each triangle into two equal right triangles. These are known as 30°-60°-90° right triangles because of the measures of the angles. Find the length of the hypotenuse of each right triangle.

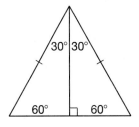

   c. Find the length of each side of each right triangle. Use the facts that $\sqrt{\frac{3}{4}} = \frac{\sqrt{3}}{2}$ and $\sqrt{12} = 2\sqrt{3}$ to label the triangles with the side lengths.

   d. Use your results to describe the relationships between the length of the sides and hypotenuse of a 30°-60°-90° right triangle.

NAME _____ DATE _____ PERIOD _____

Chapter 8 Mid-Chapter Test
(Lessons 8–1 through 8–4)

Write each expression using exponents.

1. $5 \cdot 5 \cdot 5 \cdot 7 \cdot 7$

1. _____

2. $4 \cdot x \cdot x \cdot x \cdot x \cdot x \cdot y \cdot y \cdot y$

2. _____

Write each power as a multiplication expression.

3. $3 \cdot 4^5$

3. _____

4. $6a^4 b^5$

4. _____

Evaluate each expression if x = −3 and y = 2.

5. $2x^3 y^3$

5. _____

6. $-4(x^2 - y^2)$

6. _____

Simplify each expression.

7. $3^5 \cdot 3^4$

7. _____

8. $x^3 \cdot x^5$

8. _____

9. $(x^3 y^4)(x^2 y^5)$

9. _____

10. $\dfrac{a^5}{a^2}$

10. _____

11. $-\dfrac{24h^7}{4h^3}$

11. _____

12. $\dfrac{14m^5 n^4}{7m^2 n^2}$

12. _____

13. $d^2 e^{-4}$

13. _____

14. $\dfrac{k^{-3}}{k^4}$

14. _____

15. $\dfrac{a^{-4} b^2}{a^3 b^5}$

15. _____

16. $\dfrac{4a^3 b^4}{-24a^{-2} b^2}$

16. _____

For Questions 17–19, express each number in scientific notation.

17. 48,000,000

17. _____

18. 0.0000068

18. _____

19. $(6.5 \times 10^{-3})(1.2 \times 10^5)$

19. _____

20. Express 9.4 nanoseconds in standard form as seconds.

20. _____

Algebra: Concepts and Applications

NAME _____ DATE _____ PERIOD _____

Chapter 8 Quiz A
(Lessons 8–1 through 8–3)

Write each expression using exponents.

1. $4 \cdot 4 \cdot 4 \cdot 8 \cdot 8 \cdot 8 \cdot 8$

1. _____

2. $-3 \cdot x \cdot x \cdot x \cdot x \cdot y \cdot y$

2. _____

3. $(-5)(-5)(-5)(-5)$

3. _____

Simplify each expression.

4. $x^5 \cdot x^2$

4. _____

5. $(x^4y^2)(x^3y^5)$

5. _____

6. $\dfrac{a^7}{a^5}$

6. _____

7. $\dfrac{27x^8}{9x^{-3}}$

7. _____

8. $\dfrac{18m^3n^4}{-6m^{-2}n^5}$

8. _____

NAME _____ DATE _____ PERIOD _____

Chapter 8 Quiz B
(Lessons 8–4 through 8–7)

For Questions 1–2, express each number in scientific notation.

1. 0.000047

1. _____

2. $(1.5 \times 10^5)(5.2 \times 10^2)$

2. _____

3. A typical grain of pollen weighs 0.000004 milligrams. Express
   this measure in scientific notation.

3. _____

For Questions 4–5, simplify each expression.

4. $\sqrt{361}$

4. _____

5. $\sqrt{\dfrac{144}{49}}$

5. _____

6. Estimate $\sqrt{142.8}$ to the nearest whole number.

6. _____

**Find the value of x in each right triangle. Round to the nearest
tenth if necessary.**

7.

8.

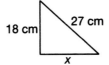

7. _____

8. _____

1. Write an equation for the sentence below. *(Lesson 1–1)*
   Seven more than three times a number is twenty-eight.

   1. _____

2. Simplify $4(3n + 1)$. *(Lesson 1–4)*

   2. _____

3. Evaluate $|4 - (-8)|$. *(Lesson 2–1)*

   3. _____

4. Simplify $-3 - (-6)$. *(Lesson 2–4)*

   4. _____

5. Find the mean of the data 18, 24, 45, 36, 12, and 24.
   (Lesson 3–3)

   5. _____

6. Solve $x + 16.5 = -5.2$. *(Lesson 3–6)*

   6. _____

7. Find the quotient of $\frac{3}{4}$ and $1\frac{1}{2}$. *(Lesson 4–3)*

   7. _____

8. Solve $-6 - 0.2n = 4.8$. *(Lesson 4–5)*

   8. _____

9. A sweater that originally cost $68 is on sale for $47.60. Find
   the percent of decrease in the price. *(Lesson 5–5)*

   9. _____

10. If there is a 30% chance that it will rain on Friday and a 40%
    chance that it will rain on Saturday, find the probability that
    it will rain on either Friday or Saturday. *(Lesson 5–7)*

    10. _____

11. Find the domain of the relation $\{(0, -2), (4, 1), (-3, 5),$ and
    $(0, 4)\}$. *(Lesson 6–1)*

    11. _____

12. What range value corresponds to a domain value of 4 on the
    graph of $2x + 4y = 8$? *(Lesson 6–3)*

    12. _____

13. Suppose y varies inversely as x and $y = 12$ when $x = 3$. Find
    x when $y = 18$. *(Lesson 6–6)*

    13. _____

14. Write the slope-intercept form of an equation for the line
    passing through points at $(4, -4)$ and $(8, -2)$. *(Lesson 7–3)*

    14. _____

15. Why are the graphs of $y = -3x + 4$ and $y = -3x - 2$ a family
    of graphs? Give the equation of a line whose graph forms a
    family with one, but not both, of these graphs. *(Lesson 7–6)*

    15. _____

16. Determine whether the graphs of $y = -\frac{2}{3}x + 2$ and
    $3x + 2y = -8$ are perpendicular. *(Lesson 7–7)*

    16. _____

17. Evaluate $4x + y^3$ if $x = -3$ and $y = -2$. *(Lesson 8–1)*

    17. _____

18. Simplify $(a^2b^2)(a^4b^5)$. *(Lesson 8–2)*

    18. _____

19. Write $2^{-1}m^2n^{-4}$ using positive exponents. *(Lesson 8–3)*

    19. _____

20. Simplify $\frac{8.4 \times 10^6}{2.1 \times 10^4}$. *(Lesson 8–4)*

    20. _____

8

Chapter 8 Standardized Test Practice
(Chapters 1–8)

Write the letter for the correct answer in the blank at the right of each problem.

1. Which property is illustrated below?

   $x + (2y + 3z) = (2y + 3z) + x$

   A. Associative Property of Addition
   B. Commutative Property of Addition
   C. Distributive Property
   D. Commutative Property of Multiplication

   1. _____

2. A puppy is 3 years younger than its mother. The puppy's father is 2 years older than its mother. The sum of the ages of the puppy, one of its litter mates, and its parents is 12 years. How old is the father?

   A. 4 yr   **B.** 5 yr   **C.** 6 yr   **D.** 8 yr

   2. _____

3. During a very cold night, the temperature dropped 2 degrees every hour after midnight. If the temperature at midnight was 3 degrees, what was the temperature at 6 A.M.?

   A. $-15°$ **B.** $-9°$ **C.** $-7°$ **D.** $15°$

   3. _____

4. Evaluate $a - b + c$ if $a = -8$, $b = -3$, and $c = 14$.

   A. -25 **B.** -9 **C.** -3 **D.** 9

   4. _____

5. Write the numbers below from least to greatest.

   $$-\frac{5}{12}, \ -0.5, \ -\frac{3}{8}, \ -\frac{6}{13}$$

   A. $-\frac{3}{8}, \ -\frac{5}{12}, \ -\frac{6}{13}, \ -0.5$ **B.** $-0.5, \ -\frac{6}{13}, \ -\frac{5}{12}, \ -\frac{3}{8}$

   C. $-0.5, \ -\frac{5}{12}, \ -\frac{6}{13}, \ -\frac{3}{8}$ **D.** $-\frac{6}{13}, \ -0.5, \ -\frac{5}{12}, \ -\frac{3}{8}$

   5. _____

6. For what value of x is $20 - 2 \cdot 2 - 12 = x$ true?

   A. -4 **B.** 0   **C.** 4   **D.** 24

   6. _____

7. Solve $|x + 6| + 4 = 18$.

   A. -28 and 12   **B.** -20 only   **C.** 8 only   **D.** -20 and 8

   7. _____

8. For what value of x is $\frac{x}{4} + 12 = 36$ true?

   A. 6   **B.** 12   **C.** 96   **D.** 192

   8. _____

9. For what value of x is $24 = 4(3x + 2) + 2(x - 6)$ true?

   A. -2 **B.** $\frac{2}{7}$ **C.** $\frac{11}{7}$ **D.** 2

   9. _____

10. Of the points you have made for your basketball team so far this season, 30% have been from free throws. If you have made 24 points from free throws, how many points have you made in all?

    A. 72   **B.** 80   **C.** 96   **D.** 125

    10. _____

11. A bag of 80 marbles contains 12 green marbles. If you draw a green marble at random, you win a free fountain drink. What are the odds that you will win a drink?

  A. 3:17 **B.** 3:18 **C.** 3:20 **D.** 17:20

  11. _____

12. Which of the following ordered pairs is *not* a solution of the equation $3x + y = 12$?

  A. (3, 3) **B.** (1, 9) **C.** (2, 6) **D.** (0, 4)

  12. _____

13. Which of the following relations is *not* a function?
  A. {(0, 0), (1, 1), (2, 2), (3, 3)}
  B. {(1, 1), (2, 1), (3, 1), (4, 1)}
  C. {(−3, 1), (−2, 5), (6, 4), (−3, 7)}
  D. {(−1, 4), (0, 0), (2, 4), (1, 4)}

  13. _____

14. Boyle's law states that the pressure of a gas varies inversely as the volume. If the volume of a gas is 100 milliliters when the pressure is 150 kPa, find the volume when the pressure is 50 kPa.

  A. 30 mL **B.** $33\frac{1}{3}$ mL **C.** 75 mL **D.** 300 mL

  14. _____

15. Determine the slope of the line shown at the right.

  A. −2 **B.** $-\frac{1}{2}$

  C. $\frac{1}{2}$ **D.** 2

  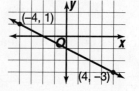

  15. _____

16. What is the point-slope form of an equation for the line passing through points at (2, −6) and (−2, −3)?

  A. $y - 6 = \frac{3}{4}(x - 2)$ **B.** $y + 3 = -\frac{3}{4}(x + 2)$

  C. $y - 3 = -\frac{3}{4}(x - 2)$ **D.** $y + 6 = \frac{3}{4}(x - 2)$

  16. _____

17. For what value of k are the graphs of $y = kx + 4$ and $y = \frac{1}{2}x - 3$ perpendicular?

  A. −2 **B.** $\frac{1}{3}$ **C.** $\frac{1}{2}$ **D.** 2

  17. _____

18. What is the product of $-4x^2y$, $-2xy^3$, and $-y^3$?
  A. $-6x^3y^7$ **B.** $-8x^3y^6$ **C.** $8x^3y$ **D.** $-8x^3y^7$

  18. _____

19. Simplify $\frac{20h^3k^4}{30h^{-3}k^5}$.

  A. $\frac{2}{3k}$ **B.** $\frac{2h^6}{3k}$ **C.** $\frac{2}{3h^6k}$ **D.** $\frac{2}{3h^6k^9}$

  19. _____

20. Which triangle with side lengths given below is *not* a right triangle?
  A. 7, 7, 7 **B.** 9, 12, 15 **C.** 14, 48, 50 **D.** 18, 80, 82

  20. _____

Chapter 8 Answer Key

Form 1A

Page 141

1. __B__

2. __C__

3. __C__

4. __B__

5. __C__

6. __D__

7. __D__

8. __A__

9. __D__

10. __D__

11. __B__

12. __C__

13. __A__

Page 142

14. __C__

15. __B__

16. __C__

17. __D__

18. __C__

19. __B__

20. __D__

21. __A__

22. __B__

23. __C__

24. __C__

25. __B__

Bonus __C__

Form 1B

Page 143

1. __B__

2. __C__

3. __D__

4. __B__

5. __C__

6. __D__

7. __A__

8. __B__

9. __D__

10. __C__

11. __B__

12. __B__

13. __C__

Page 144

14. __B__

15. __B__

16. __C__

17. __B__

18. __C__

19. __A__

20. __B__

21. __C__

22. __B__

23. __C__

24. __C__

25. __D__

Bonus __C__

Chapter 8 Answer Key
Form 2A

1. $6h^4$

2. $2 \cdot a \cdot a \cdot a \cdot b \cdot b \cdot b \cdot b$

3. 24

4. $(2^3)(3)(5^2)$

5. $8x^4y^2$

6. a^8b^6

7. $-6x^4y^4$

8. m^6

9. $4n^3p^3$

10. $\dfrac{6b^2}{a^5c^3}$

11. $\dfrac{2c^8}{3}$

12. $-\dfrac{2r^8}{s^2}$

13. $\dfrac{1}{8}$

14. 6.2×10^{-4}

15. 4.8×10^9

16. 6.12×10^{11}

17. 3×10^2

18. 0.0000125 g

19. 27

20. -36

21. $-\dfrac{4}{3}$

22. 0.5 or $\dfrac{1}{2}$

23. 0.08

24. 14

25. 0

26. 25

27. 29

28. 24

29. 44.7

30. 24

31. 7.2

32. 35.8 ft

33. 15 ft

Bonus 7.1 ft

Chapter 8 Answer Key

Form 2B

1. $-4y^3$

2. $3 \cdot c \cdot d \cdot d \cdot d$

3. -240

4. $2^3 5^2$

5. 5^6

6. $3x^5 y^3$

7. $22c^3 d^3$

8. n^2

9. $-2n$

10. $\dfrac{5}{c^5 d}$

11. $\dfrac{1}{fg^2}$

12. $-\dfrac{3m^9}{n}$

13. -1

14. 4.9×10^{-3}

15. 7.2×10^9

16. 3.5×10^9

17. 2×10^4

18. $480{,}000$ tons

19. 17

20. -24

21. $\dfrac{2}{5}$

22. -0.2 or $-\dfrac{1}{5}$

23. 0.2

24. 15

25. 1

26. 22

27. 11

28. 12.5

29. 18.0

30. 26

31. 25 ft

32. 81 ft

33. 16 mm

Bonus 16.4 in.

Chapter 8 Answer Key
Open-Ended Assessment
Sample Answers
Page 149

1. **a.** 30×10^6

   b. No; the integer part is greater than 10.

   c. 3×10^1; 1×10^6

   d. 3×10^7; (5×10^{-3}) and $(6 \times 10^9) = 3 \times 10^7$

   e. 3.6×10^{10}

   f. 5×10^5

2. **a.**

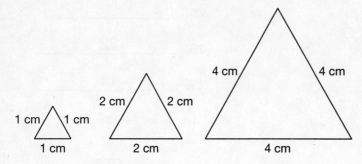

   b.

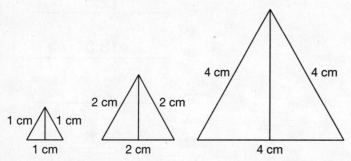

   The length of the hypotenuse of each right triangle is the side length of the equilateral triangle of which it is a part.

   c. 1-cm triangle: $1, \frac{1}{2}, \frac{\sqrt{3}}{2}$; 2-cm triangle: $2, 1$; $\sqrt{3}$;

   3-cm triangle: $4, 2, 2\sqrt{3}$

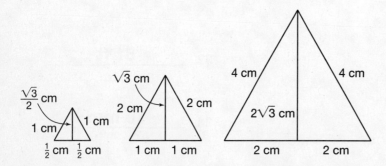

   d. The hypotenuse is twice the shortest side of a 30°-60°-90° triangle. The other side is $\sqrt{3}$ times one half the hypotenuse, or $\sqrt{3}$ times the shorter side.

Chapter 8 Answer Key

Mid-Chapter Test
Page 150

1. $5^3 7^2$

2. $4x^5 y^3$

3. $\dfrac{3 \cdot 4 \cdot 4 \cdot 4 \cdot 4 \cdot 4}{6 \cdot a \cdot a \cdot a \cdot a \cdot}$

4. $b \cdot b \cdot b \cdot b \cdot b$

5. -432

6. -20

7. 3^9

8. x^8

9. $x^5 y^9$

10. a^3

11. $-6h^4$

12. $2m^3 n^2$

13. $\dfrac{d^2}{e^4}$

14. $\dfrac{1}{k^7}$

15. $\dfrac{1}{a^7 b^3}$

16. $\dfrac{-a^5 b^2}{6}$

17. 4.8×10^7

18. 6.8×10^{-6}

19. 7.8×10^2

20. 0.0000000094 s

Quiz A
Page 151

1. $4^3 8^4$

2. $-3x^4 y^2$

3. $(-5)^4$

4. x^7

5. $x^7 y^7$

6. a^2

7. $3x^{11}$

8. $-\dfrac{3m^5}{n}$

Quiz B
Page 151

1. 4.7×10^{-5}

2. 7.8×10^7

3. 4×10^{-6} mg

4. 19

5. $\dfrac{12}{7}$

6. 12

7. 30

8. 20.1 cm

Chapter 8 Answer Key

Cumulative Review
Page 152

1. $3n + 7 = 28$
2. $12n + 4$
3. 12
4. 3
5. 26.5
6. -21.7
7. $\dfrac{1}{2}$
8. -54
9. 30%
10. 58%
11. $\{-3, 0, 4\}$
12. 0
13. 2
14. $y = \dfrac{1}{2}x - 6$
15. They have the same slope; Sample answer: Any equation in slope-intercept form that has a y-intercept of -2 or 4 and a slope not equal to -3.
16. no
17. -20
18. $a^6 b^7$
19. $\dfrac{m^2}{2n^4}$
20. 4×10^2

Standardized Test Practice
Page 153

1. B
2. C
3. B
4. D
5. B
6. C
7. D
8. C
9. D
10. B

Page 154

11. A
12. D
13. C
14. D
15. B
16. B
17. A
18. D
19. B
20. A

9 Chapter 9 Test, Form 1A

Write the letter for the correct answer in the blank at the right of each problem.

1. Which of the following is a monomial?

   A. $5x + 2$ **B.** $x - y$ **C.** $\frac{1}{2}xy$ **D.** b^{-2}

   1. _____

Find the degree of each polynomial.

2. $3x^4 + 2x^3$

   A. 3   **B.** 4   **C.** 6   **D.** 7

   2. _____

3. $2a^2b^3 + 4ab^2$

   A. 2   **B.** 3   **C.** 4   **D.** 5

   3. _____

Arrange the terms of each polynomial so that the powers of x are in descending order.

4. $3x + 2x^3 + x^2$

   A. $3x + 2x^3 + x^2$

   C. $3x + x^2 + 2x^3$

   B. $2x^3 + x^2 + 3x$

   D. $x^2 + 2x^3 + 3x$

   4. _____

5. $5x + x^3 + x^2y + x^4y^2$

   A. $x^4y^2 + x^3 + x^2y + 5x$

   C. $x^4y^2 + x^2y + 5x + x^3$

   B. $5x + x^2y + x^3 + x^4y^2$

   D. $5x + x^3 + x^2y + x^4y^2$

   5. _____

Find each sum or difference.

6. $(3x^2 - 4x) + (2x^2 + 2x)$

   A. $x^2 + 6x$ **B.** $x^2 - 6x$ **C.** $5x^2 - 2x$ **D.** $5x^2 + 2x$

   6. _____

7. $(-6y + 3x) + (2y + 8x)$

   A. $-4y + 11x$ **B.** $-8y + 11x$ **C.** $4y + 10x$ **D.** $8y - 11x$

   7. _____

8. $(5x^2 + 7x - 4) + (x^2 + 6x - 1)$

   A. $5x^2 + 12x - 5$

   C. $6x^2 + 12x - 3$

   B. $4x^2 + 13x - 5$

   D. $6x^2 + 13x - 5$

   8. _____

9. $(7a + 7) - (3a - 2)$

   A. $10a + 5$ **B.** $4a + 9$ **C.** $4a + 5$ **D.** $4a - 5$

   9. _____

10. $(3x^2 + 9x + 2) - (-3 + 7x^2)$

    A. $10x^2 + 9x$

    C. $10x^2 - 1$

    B. $-4x^2 + 9x + 5$

    D. $10x^2 + 9x + 5$

    10. _____

Find each product.

11. $-5(m + 10)$

    A. $-5m + 10$ **B.** $-5m - 15$ **C.** $-5m + 5$ **D.** $-5m - 50$

    11. _____

12. $b(3b - 12)$

    A. $3b^2 - 12b$ **B.** $3b - 12b$ **C.** $3b - 12$ **D.** $3b^2 + 12b$

    12. _____

13. $-x^2(5x^2 - x + 2)$

    A. $5x^4 - x^3 - 2x^2$

    C. $-5x^4 + x^3 - 2x^2$

    B. $-5x^4 - x^3 - 2x^2$

    D. $-5x^4 + x^3 - x^2$

    13. _____

Solve each equation.

14. $2(y + 3) = -2$
  A. -4 B. -1 C. 0 D. 4 14. _____

15. $2(x - 2) + 5 = -1(2x - 9) + 4$
  A. 0 B. 3 C. 5 D. 8 15. _____

Find each product.

16. $(g + 3)(g + 4)$
  A. $g^2 + 7g + 12$ B. $g^2 + 3g + 7$
  C. $g^2 + 12g + 7$ D. $g^2 + 7g + 7$ 16. _____

17. $(s + 2)(s - 6)$
  A. $s^2 + 4s - 12$ B. $s^2 - 4s - 8$
  C. $s^2 - 4s + 12$ D. $s^2 - 4s - 12$ 17. _____

18. $(2x + 1)(x - 9)$
  A. $2x^2 - 10x - 9$ B. $2x^2 - 18x - 9$
  C. $2x^2 + 17x + 9$ D. $2x^2 - 17x - 9$ 18. _____

19. $(x + y)(8x - 7y)$
  A. $8x^2 + xy - 7y^2$ B. $x^2 + 15xy + 7y^2$
  C. $8x^2 + 15xy + 7y^2$ D. $9x + xy + 6y$ 19. _____

20. $(x^2 + 1)(x^2 + 2)$
  A. $x^4 + 3x^2 + 2$ B. $x^2 + 3x + 2$
  C. $x^4 + 3 + 2x^2$ D. $x^4 + x^2 + 3$ 20. _____

21. $(x + 7)^2$
  A. $x^2 + 7x + 49$ B. $x^2 + 7x + 14$
  C. $x^2 + 14x + 49$ D. $x^2 + 7x + 35$ 21. _____

22. $(2a - b)^2$
  A. $2a^2 - 4ab + b^2$ B. $4a^2 - 4ab + b^2$
  C. $4a^2 - 2ab - b^2$ D. $2a^2 - 4ab - b^2$ 22. _____

23. $(x + 9y)(x - 9y)$
  A. $x^2 + 81y^2$ B. $x^2 - 90y^2$
  C. $x^2 - 81y^2$ D. $x^2 - 18xy - 81y^2$ 23. _____

24. $(7x - 5y)^2$
  A. $14x^2 - 35xy + 25y^2$ B. $14x^2 - 70xy - 25y^2$
  C. $49x^2 - 70xy + 25y^2$ D. $49x^2 - 35xy + 25y^2$ 24. _____

25. $(9c + 10d)(9c - 10d)$
  A. $81c^2 + 100d^2$ B. $9c^2 - 10d^2$
  C. $18c^2 - 20d^2$ D. $81c^2 - 100d^2$ 25. _____

Bonus Find the product of $(2x + a)$ and $(2x + d)$.
  A. $4x^2 + 2ax + 2dx + ad$ B. $4x^2 + 2adx + ad$
  C. $4x^2 + 2adx + ad^2$ D. $2x^2 + 2ax + 2dx + d^2$ **Bonus** _____

Algebra: Concepts and Applications

9

Chapter 9 Test, Form 1B

Write the letter for the correct answer in the blank at the right of each problem.

1. Which of the following is a monomial?

   A. $\frac{1}{y}$ **B.** $2xy$ **C.** $x + 1$ **D.** $\frac{a}{b}$

   1. _____

Find the degree of each polynomial.

2. $x^3 + 4x$

   A. 1   **B.** 3   **C.** 4   **D.** 5

   2. _____

3. $a^2b + 5b^2$

   A. 3   **B.** 4   **C.** 5   **D.** 7

   3. _____

Arrange the terms of each polynomial so that the powers of x are in descending order.

4. $x + 4x^2 + 2x^4$

   A. $x + 4x^2 + 2x^4$ **B.** $x + 2x^4 + 4x^2$

   C. $2x^4 + 4x^2 + x$ **D.** $4x^2 + 2x^4 + x$

   4. _____

5. $3x^3y + 2x + 5x^2y$

   A. $3x^3y + 5x^2y + 2x$ **B.** $2x + 5x^2y + 3x^3y$

   C. $2x + 3x^3y + 5x^2y$ **D.** $3x^3y + 2x + 5x^2y$

   5. _____

Find each sum or difference.

6. $(2x - 5) + (x + 3)$

   A. $x + 8$ **B.** $x - 2$ **C.** $3x - 2$ **D.** $3x + 2$

   6. _____

7. $(4y + 3x) + (y - 2x)$

   A. $4y + x$ **B.** $5y + 5x$ **C.** $5y - x$ **D.** $5y + x$

   7. _____

8. $(3x^2 + 4x) + (2x^2 + 9x - 1)$

   A. $5x^2 + 13x - 1$ **B.** $7x^2 + 11x + 3$

   C. $5x^2 + 12x$ **D.** $5x^2 + 14x + 1$

   8. _____

9. $(8a + 5) - (3a + 4)$

   A. $11a + 9$ **B.** $5a + 9$

   C. $5a - 1$ **D.** $5a + 1$

   9. _____

10. $(7x^2 - 2x) - (3x^2 - x)$

    A. $10x^2 - 3x$ **B.** $4x^2 - x$

    C. $10x^2 - 1$ **D.** $4x^2 - 3x$

    10. _____

Find each product.

11. $2(m + 10)$

    A. $2m + 10$ **B.** $2m + 20$ **C.** $2m + 12$ **D.** $m + 20$

    11. _____

12. $b(b + 12)$

    A. $b^2 + 12$ **B.** $b^2 + 12b$ **C.** $2b + 12$ **D.** $2b + 12b$

    12. _____

13. $3x(x^2 + 4)$

    A. $3x^3 + 12x$ **B.** $3x^2 + 12x$ **C.** $3x + 7$ **D.** $3x^3 + 12$

    13. _____

Solve each equation.

14. $2(y + 3) = 4$

    A. -4 **B.** -1 **C.** 0 **D.** 4 14. _____

15. $7(d - 5) + 8 = (3d - 8) + 1$

    A. 0 **B.** 3 **C.** 5 **D.** 8 15. _____

Find each product.

16. $(g + 6)(g + 4)$

    A. $g^2 + 6g + 10$ **B.** $g^2 + 2g + 10$

    C. $g^2 + 24g + 10$ **D.** $g^2 + 10g + 24$ 16. _____

17. $(a + 3)(a - 7)$

    A. $a^2 + 3a - 49$ **B.** $a^2 + 4a - 4$

    C. $a^2 - 4a - 21$ **D.** $a^2 - 10a - 21$ 17. _____

18. $(3x + 6)(x - 6)$

    A. $3x^2 + 12x - 36$ **B.** $3x^2 - 12x + 36$

    C. $3x^2 - 12x - 36$ **D.** $3x^2 + 24x - 6$ 18. _____

19. $(x + y)(3x + 8y)$

    A. $3x^2 + 11xy + 8y^2$ **B.** $x^2 + 11xy + 8y^2$

    C. $3x^2 + 12xy + 9y^2$ **D.** $3x + 11xy + 8y$ 19. _____

20. $(4b - 5)(9b - 2)$

    A. $13b^2 - 14b + 10$ **B.** $36b^2 - 37b + 10$

    C. $36b^2 + 53b - 10$ **D.** $36b^2 - 53b + 10$ 20. _____

21. $(t + 1)^2$

    A. $t^2 + t + 1$ **B.** $t^2 + 2t$

    C. $t^2 + 2t + 2$ **D.** $t^2 + 2t + 1$ 21. _____

22. $(a - 4)^2$

    A. $a^2 - 8a + 16$ **B.** $a^2 - 4a + 16$

    C. $a^2 - 2a + 8$ **D.** $2a + 8a - 16$ 22. _____

23. $(x + 6)(x - 6)$

    A. $x^2 - 36$ **B.** $x^2 - 12$

    C. $x^2 + 36$ **D.** $x^2 - 36x$ 23. _____

24. $(2x - 3y)(2x + 3y)$

    A. $4x^2 - 12xy + 9y^2$ **B.** $4x^2 - 6y^2$

    C. $4x^2 - 9y^2$ **D.** $4x^2 + 9y^2$ 24. _____

25. $(9 + 6d)^2$

    A. $81 + 36d^2$ **B.** $18 + 12d^2$

    C. $81 + 15d + 36d^2$ **D.** $81 + 108d + 36d^2$ 25. _____

Bonus Find the product of $(x + a)$ and $(x + d)$.

    A. $x^2 + ax + dx + ad$ **B.** $x^2 + ax + ad$

    C. $2x + ax + ad$ **D.** $x^2 + 2adx + ad$ **Bonus** _____

9

Chapter 9 Test, Form 2A

State whether each expression is a polynomial. If it is a
polynomial, identify it as a **monomial, binomial, or trinomial.**

1. $x^2 + \frac{1}{3}x$

1. _____

2. $\frac{x^2}{y}$

2. _____

3. $-a^2b^3c^2d^4$

3. _____

Find the degree of each polynomial.

4. $x^4 + x^2 - x^3$

4. _____

5. $a^3 + 7a^2 + 9a$

5. _____

Arrange the terms of each polynomial so that the powers of x
are in ascending order.

6. $5 + x^5 + 2x^3 + 4x$

6. _____

7. $x^2y^4 + x^5y^3 + xy^2 + x^3y$

7. _____

Find each sum or difference.

8. $(3x^2 + 7x - 2) + (2x^2 - 3x + 4)$

8. _____

9. $(4x + 8y) + (-7y + 3x)$

9. _____

10. $(x^2 + 4x - 1) + (9x^2 - 8x + 9)$

10. _____

11. $(8x + 6) - (2x - 1)$

11. _____

12. $(4x^2 + 9x - 1) - (5 - x^2)$

12. _____

13. $(8 + 7a + 10a^2) - (a^2 - 3a - 2)$

13. _____

Find each product.

14. $-7(y + 3)$

14. _____

15. $a(4a - 1)$

15. _____

16. $-2x^2(x^2 - 4x + 2)$

16. _____

Solve each equation.

17. $3(x - 2) = 6$

17. _____

18. $y(y + 2) - y(y - 4) - 10 = 20$

18. _____

Simplify.

19. $6x(2x^2 + 8x - 3) - 6(3 - 4x^2)$

19. _____

20. $4a(a^2 + 7a) - a(2a - 9a^2)$

20. _____

Find each product.

21. $(b + 4)(b + 8)$

21. _____

22. $(s - 5)(s + 10)$

22. _____

23. $(x + 6)(2x + 2)$

23. _____

24. $(7a + 3b)(9a + 4b)$

24. _____

25. $(5x + 7y)(9x - 8y)$

25. _____

26. $(x^2 + 4)(4x^2 - 9)$

26. _____

27. $(x + 4)^2$

27. _____

28. $(2s - 10)^2$

28. _____

29. $(x + 6y)(x - 6y)$

29. _____

30. $(7a + 8b)^2$

30. _____

31. $(2x + 7y)(2x - 7y)$

31. _____

32. $(9a - 8b)(9a + 8b)$

32. _____

33. $(g - 10h)(g - 10h)$

33. _____

Bonus Find the product of x, $(5x + 1)$, and $(x - 8)$.

Bonus _____

9

Chapter 9 Test, Form 2B

State whether each expression is a polynomial. If it is a polynomial, identify it as a monomial, binomial, or trinomial.

1. $2x^2 + x + \frac{1}{3}$

1. _____

2. $a^4 - 3a$

2. _____

3. $\frac{2}{y}$

3. _____

Find the degree of each polynomial.

4. $x^3 - x$

4. _____

5. $a^3 + a^2 + a$

5. _____

Arrange the terms of each polynomial so that the powers of x are in ascending order.

6. $2 + x^5 + 4x^3 + 6x$

6. _____

7. $4x^2 + 3x^5 + 2x + 4$

7. _____

Find each sum or difference.

8. $(6x - 2) + (2x + 4)$

8. _____

9. $(2x + y) + (x - 4y)$

9. _____

10. $(f^2 + 4f - 1) + (2f^2 - 3f + 2)$

10. _____

11. $(9x + 5) - (2x - 4)$

11. _____

12. $(6x - 1) - (2x - 6)$

12. _____

13. $(5 + 2a + 3a^2) - (a^2 + a - 6)$

13. _____

Find each product.

14. $8(y + 2)$

14. _____

15. $2a(2a - 3)$

15. _____

16. $4x(x^2 + 5)$

16. _____

Solve each equation.

17. $4(x - 2) = 0$

17. _____

18. $7(y + 3) - 30 = 40$

18. _____

Simplify.

19. $x(4x^2 + 3x - 5) - 2(4 - x^2)$

19. _____

20. $5(a^2 + 2a) - a(6a - 9)$

20. _____

Find each product.

21. $(b + 2)(b + 6)$

21. _____

22. $(s - 3)(s - 1)$

22. _____

23. $(x + 5)(2x + 1)$

23. _____

24. $(a - 3)(2a - 8)$

24. _____

25. $(2x + 6)(x - 10)$

25. _____

26. $(7x + 1)(x^2 + 1)$

26. _____

27. $(x + 1)^2$

27. _____

28. $(s - 4)^2$

28. _____

29. $(x + 2)(x - 2)$

29. _____

30. $(a + b)^2$

30. _____

31. $(x + 3y)(x - 3y)$

31. _____

32. $(a - 2b)(a + 2b)$

32. _____

33. $(g - 6h)(g + 6h)$

33. _____

Bonus Find the product of x, $(x + 1)$, and $(x - 1)$.

Bonus _____

Chapter 9 Open-Ended Assessment

9

Instructions: Demonstrate your knowledge by giving a clear, concise solution for each problem. Be sure to include all relevant drawings and to justify your answers. You may show your solution in more than one way or investigate beyond the requirements of the problem.

1. In the chart below, write at least three examples of each type of polynomial.

Monomial	Binomial	Trinomial	Polynomial

2. Use the figure at the right of a right triangle, a square, and a rectangle to answer the questions below.

   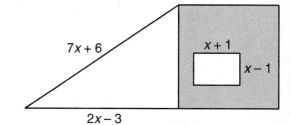

   a. Find the sum of the measures of the two given sides of the triangle.

   b. The measure of the perimeter of the triangle is $11x + 6$. Find the measure of the third side of the triangle.

   c. Find the perimeter of the square.

   d. Find the area of the square.

   e. Find the area of the small rectangle.

   f. Find the area of the shaded region.

   g. The area of a triangle is given by the expression $\frac{1}{2}bh$, where b represents the length of the base and h represents the height for that base. Find the area of the triangle.

3. Is the product of two binomials always a trinomial? Explain your reasoning.

Chapter 9 Mid-Chapter Test
(Lessons 9–1 through 9–3)

Determine whether each expression is a monomial. Explain why or why not.

1. $9k$

1. _____

2. x^{-4}

2. _____

State whether each expression is a polynomial. If it is a polynomial, identify it as a monomial, binomial, or trinomial.

3. b^3

3. _____

4. $5x^2 + 2x$

4. _____

5. $x^{-4} - 8$

5. _____

Find the degree of each polynomial.

6. $3b^2 + 2b$

6. _____

7. $4x^3 + 2x^2 + x$

7. _____

Find each sum or difference.

8. $(2x + 5) + (x - 6)$

8. _____

9. $(15x + 12y) + (3x - y)$

9. _____

10. $(b^2 + 4b + 8) + (3b^2 - 2b)$

10. _____

11. $(6m^2 + 8m) - (3m^2 + 2m)$

11. _____

12. $(6x - 8) - (2x + 10)$

12. _____

13. $(4x^2 + 5x + 8) - (x^2 - 2x - 4)$

13. _____

Find each product.

14. $8(x + 8)$

14. _____

15. $-2(2x + 9)$

15. _____

16. $3x(5 + 6x)$

16. _____

17. $a(8a - 4)$

17. _____

Solve each equation.

18. $3(x + 5) = 12$

18. _____

19. $2(4y - 10) - 1 = 9 - 2y$

19. _____

20. $5(p + 8) - 20 = 20(1 + p)$

20. _____

NAME _____ DATE _____ PERIOD _____

Chapter 9 Quiz A
(Lessons 9–1 and 9–2)

State whether each expression is a polynomial. If it is a polynomial, identify it as a monomial, binomial, *or* trinomial.

1. $x^2 + \frac{1}{4}x$

1. _____

2. $\frac{2x}{3y}$

2. _____

Arrange the terms of each polynomial so that the powers of x are in ascending order.

3. $x^4 + 2x^2 + 4x$

3. _____

4. $x + 8x^3 + 6x^2$

4. _____

5. $ax^2 + bx^3 + 4cx$

5. _____

Find each sum or difference.

6. $(5x + 1) + (x + 12)$

6. _____

7. $(6x + 7y) + (4x + 9y)$

7. _____

8. $(3x + 2) + (-x - 8)$

8. _____

9. $(x^2 + 5x - 2) - (x^2 - 3x + 8)$

9. _____

10. $(7x + 2) - (x - 11)$

10. _____

NAME _____ DATE _____ PERIOD _____

Chapter 9 Quiz B
(Lessons 9–3 through 9–5)

Find each product.

1. $12(x + 2)$

1. _____

2. $-4(y + 5)$

2. _____

Solve each equation.

3. $3(x + 3) = 6$

3. _____

4. $4(d - 4) = d - 1$

4. _____

Find each product.

5. $(x + 7)(x + 9)$

5. _____

6. $(a - 5)(a + 4)$

6. _____

7. $(y + 8)(y - 3)$

7. _____

8. $(x + 8)^2$

8. _____

9. $(3g - h)^2$

9. _____

10. $(j + 9)(j - 9)$

10. _____

9 Chapter 9 Cumulative Review

1. Write an equation for the sentence below. *(Lesson 1–1)*

   Fifteen is equal to a number b multiplied by 7.

   1. _____

Simplify each expression. *(Lesson 2–3)*

2. $8x + (-7x)$

   2. _____

3. $-4y + (-3y)$

   3. _____

Solve each equation. *(Lesson 3–5)*

4. $p + (-8) = 10$

   4. _____

5. $12 = 20 - z$

   5. _____

Solve each equation. Check your solution. *(Lesson 4–6)*

6. $3r + 8 = 4r + 3$

   6. _____

7. $9q + 2 = 13 + 9q$

   7. _____

On a map, the scale is 2 inches = 5 miles. Find the actual distance for each map distance. *(Lesson 5–2)*

8. 6 inches

   8. _____

9. 15 inches

   9. _____

Solve. Assume that y varies directly as x. *(Lesson 6–5)*

10. Find y when $x = 18$ if $y = 21$ when $x = 14$.

    10. _____

11. If $y = 45$ when $x = 9$, find x when $y = 10$.

    11. _____

Determine whether the graphs of each pair of equations are parallel, perpendicular, or neither. *(Lesson 7–7)*

12. $y = 8x + 4$
    $y = -8x - 4$

    12. _____

13. $2y = 3x + 4$
    $y = -\frac{2}{3}x$

    13. _____

For Questions 14–15, simplify. *(Lesson 8–5)*

14. $\sqrt{\frac{1}{4}}$

    14. _____

15. $-\sqrt{\frac{100}{81}}$

    15. _____

16. Find the product of $(4x + 2y)$ and $(x + y)$. *(Lesson 9–4)*

    16. _____

9

Chapter 9 Standardized Test Practice
(Chapters 1–9)

Write the letter for the correct answer in the blank at the right of each problem.

1. Which is the equation for the sentence below?

   Eleven more than five divided into a number n is 19.

   A. $11 + \frac{n}{5} = 19$ **B.** $19 + \frac{n}{5} = 11$

   C. $11 + \frac{5}{n} = 19$ **D.** $11 - \frac{n}{5} = 19$ 1. _____

2. Find the value of $9 - 3 \div (1 + 2) - 5$.

   A. 3   **B.** $\frac{8}{5}$ **C.** 0   **D.** -3 2. _____

3. Name the property shown by the statement below.

   $$(m + n) + 2n = m + (n + 2n)$$

   A. Associative Property of Addition
   B. Associative Property of Multiplication
   C. Commutative Property of Addition
   D. Commutative Property of Multiplication   3. _____

4. Order the integers below from least to greatest.

   $65, -32, -21, 58, 3, -8, -12$

   A. $3, -8, -12, -21, -32, 58, 65$ **B.** $65, 58, 3, -8, -12, -21, -32$
   C. $65, 58, -32, -21, -12, -8, 3$ **D.** $-32, -21, -12, -8, 3, 58, 65$ 4. _____

5. Name the quadrant in which the point at $(-7, 17)$ is located.

   A. I   **B.** II   **C.** III   **D.** IV   5. _____

6. Evaluate $a - b$ if $a = 5$ and $b = -3$.

   A. -8 **B.** -2 **C.** 2   **D.** 8   6. _____

7. For the data set below, the value 12 is which of the following?

   $10, 12, 12, 14, 14, 14, 15, 22$

   A. mean   **B.** median   **C.** mode   **D.** range   7. _____

8. Solve $|x + 2| = 5$.

   A. 3   **B.** 7 or -7 **C.** 3 or -7 **D.** 3 or -3 8. _____

9. Which equation has the solution $x = -2$?

   A. $2x = -2 + x$ **B.** $x - 2 = 0$
   C. $-4 + x = -2$ **D.** $3(x + 1) = -6$ 9. _____

10. If $5b = -15$, then $b + 9$ equals

    A. -6.   **B.** 6.   **C.** 12.   **D.** $b + 1$.   10. _____

11. On a map, the scale is 1 centimeter = 10 kilometers. Find the actual distance for a map distance of 4.2 centimeters.

    A. 42 cm   **B.** 420 cm   **C.** 4.2 km   **D.** 42 km   11. _____

12. What number is 22% of 90?

    A. 11   **B.** 19.8   **C.** 22   **D.** 24.4   **12.** _____

13. One letter from the word PRACTICE is chosen at random. Which of the following is P(vowel)?

    A. 0.25   **B.** 0.3   **C.** 0.33   **D.** $\frac{3}{8}$ **13.** _____

14. Which of the following is a linear equation?

    A. $y = \frac{1}{x}$ **B.** $xy = 5$ **C.** $y = w + x$ **D.** $y - x = 2$ **14.** _____

15. Which of the following relations is *not* a function?

    A. $\{(1, 3), (2, 4), (0, 5), (4, 3)\}$ **B.** $\{(0, 3.1), (1, 3.2), (2, 3.3)\}$

    C. $\{(1, 5), (3, 7), (1, 9), (7, -2)\}$ **D.** $\{(5, -1), (4, -2), (3, -1)\}$ **15.** _____

16. Assume y varies directly as x. If $y = 45$ when $x = 36$, find y when x is 12.

    A. 21   **B.** 15   **C.** 10   **D.** 8   **16.** _____

17. A line through the points at $(-3, -7)$ and $(-3, -1)$ has slope

    A. 0.   **B.** 2.   **C.** 6.   **D.** undefined.   **17.** _____

18. The point-slope form of an equation for a line passing through the point at $(0, 4)$ with slope 2 is

    A. $y = 2x - 4$.   **B.** $y - 4 = 2x$.

    C. $y = 2(x - 4)$.   **D.** $2x + y = 4$.   **18.** _____

19. Determine which of the following equations is of a line that is perpendicular to the graph of $y = \frac{3}{4}x + 5$.

    A. $x = \frac{3}{4}y + 5$ **B.** $y = -\frac{3}{4}x - 5$

    C. $y = -\frac{4}{3}x$ **D.** $y = -\frac{3}{4}x + 5$ **19.** _____

20. Simplify $(3a^2b^3)(-a^3b)$.

    A. $3a^6b^4$ **B.** $3ab^2$ **C.** $-3a^5b^4$ **D.** $3a^6b^3$ **20.** _____

21. Express 3.9×10^5 in standard form.

    A. 3,900   **B.** 39,000   **C.** 390,000   **D.** 3,900,000   **21.** _____

22. Estimate $\sqrt{75}$ to the nearest whole number.

    A. 10   **B.** 9   **C.** 8   **D.** 7   **22.** _____

23. Which of the following is *not* a monomial?

    A. x^3 **B.** 27   **C.** h^{-2} **D.** ab^2c^3 **23.** _____

24. Solve $x(3 + x) = x^2 - 15$.

    A. -5 **B.** -3 **C.** 3   **D.** 5   **24.** _____

25. Which expression is equivalent to $a^2 - 4$?

    A. $(a - 2)(a - 2)$ **B.** $(a - 2)^2$

    C. $(a + 16)(a - 16)$ **D.** $(a + 2)(a - 2)$ **25.** _____

Chapter 9 Answer Key

Form 1A

Page 161

1. C

2. B

3. D

4. B

5. A

6. C

7. A

8. D

9. B

10. B

11. D

12. A

13. C

Page 162

14. A

15. B

16. A

17. D

18. D

19. A

20. A

21. C

22. B

23. C

24. C

25. D

Bonus A

Form 1B

Page 163

1. B

2. B

3. A

4. C

5. A

6. C

7. D

8. A

9. D

10. B

11. B

12. B

13. A

Page 164

14. B

15. C

16. D

17. C

18. C

19. A

20. D

21. D

22. A

23. A

24. C

25. D

Bonus A

Chapter 9 Answer Key
Form 2A

1. __yes, binomial__

2. __no__

3. __yes, monomial__

4. __4__

5. __3__

6. $5 + 4x + 2x^3 + x^5$

7. $xy^2 + x^2y^4 + x^3y + x^5y^3$

8. $5x^2 + 4x + 2$

9. $7x + y$

10. $10x^2 - 4x + 8$

11. $6x + 7$

12. $5x^2 + 9x - 6$

13. $9a^2 + 10a + 10$

14. $-7y - 21$

15. $4a^2 - a$

16. $-2x^4 + 8x^3 - 4x^2$

17. __4__

18. __5__

19. $12x^3 + 72x^2 - 18x - 18$

20. $13a^3 + 26a^2$

21. $b^2 + 12b + 32$

22. $s^2 + 5s - 50$

23. $2x^2 + 14x + 12$

24. $63a^2 + 55ab + 12b^2$

25. $45x^2 + 23xy - 56y^2$

26. $4x^4 + 7x^2 - 36$

27. $x^2 + 8x + 16$

28. $4s^2 - 40s + 100$

29. $x^2 - 36y^2$

30. $49a^2 + 112ab + 64b^2$

31. $4x^2 - 49y^2$

32. $81a^2 - 64b^2$

33. $g^2 - 20gh + 100h^2$

Bonus $5x^3 - 39x^2 - 8x$

Chapter 9 Answer Key
Form 2B

Page 167

1. yes, trinomial

2. yes, binomial

3. no

4. 3

5. 3

6. $2 + 6x + 4x^3 + x^5$

7. $4 + 2x + 4x^2 + 3x^5$

8. $8x + 2$

9. $3x - 3y$

10. $3f^2 + f + 1$

11. $7x + 9$

12. $4x + 5$

13. $11 + a + 2a^2$

14. $8y + 16$

15. $4a^2 - 6a$

16. $4x^3 + 20x$

17. 2

18. 7

Page 168

19. $4x^3 + 14x^2 - 5x - 8$

20. $-a^2 + 19a$

21. $b^2 + 8b + 12$

22. $s^2 - 4s + 3$

23. $2x^2 + 11x + 5$

24. $2a^2 - 14a + 24$

25. $2x^2 - 14x - 60$

26. $7x^3 + x^2 + 7x + 1$

27. $x^2 + 2x + 1$

28. $s^2 - 8s + 16$

29. $x^2 - 4$

30. $a^2 + 2ab + b^2$

31. $x^2 - 9y^2$

32. $a^2 - 4b^2$

33. $g^2 - 36h^2$

Bonus $x^3 - x$

Chapter 9 Answer Key

Open-Ended Assessment
Sample Answers
Page 169

1.

Monomial	Binomial	Trinomial	Polynomial
8.2	$x + 1$	$x^2 + x + 3$	$x + 1$
$3x$	$2x + 5$	$x + y + z$	y^4
$5a^2$	$3x^2 - x$	$y + y^2 + y^3$	$3 + 2x$

2. a. $9x + 3$

   b. $2x + 3$

   c. $8x + 12$

   d. $4x^2 + 12x + 9$

   e. $x^2 - 1$

   f. $3x^2 + 12x + 10$

   g. $2x^2 - \dfrac{9}{2}$

3. No. A product of a sum and a difference such as $(x + y)(x - y)$ is a binomial, and the product of two binomials such as $(x + a)(y + b)$ has four terms.

Chapter 9 Answer Key

1. It is a product of a number and a variable so it is a monomial.

2. It is not a monomial because the exponent is negative.

3. yes; monomial

4. yes, binomial

5. no

6. 2

7. 3

8. $3x - 1$

9. $18x + 11y$

10. $4b^2 + 2b + 8$

11. $3m^2 + 6m$

12. $4x - 18$

13. $3x^2 + 7x + 12$

14. $8x + 64$

15. $-4x - 18$

16. $15x + 18x^2$

17. $8a^2 - 4a$

18. -1

19. 3

20. 0

1. yes, binomial

2. no

3. $4x + 2x^2 + x^4$

4. $x + 6x^2 + 8x^3$

5. $4cx + ax^2 + bx^3$

6. $6x + 13$

7. $10x + 16y$

8. $2x - 6$

9. $8x - 10$

10. $6x + 13$

1. $12x + 24$

2. $-4y - 20$

3. -1

4. 5

5. $x^2 + 16x + 63$

6. $a^2 - a - 20$

7. $y^2 + 5y - 24$

8. $x^2 + 16x + 64$

9. $9g^2 - 6gh + h^2$

10. $j^2 - 81$

Chapter 9 Answer Key

Cumulative Review
Page 172

1. $15 = 7b$

2. x

3. $-7y$

4. 18

5. 8

6. 5

7. no solution

8. 15 miles

9. 37.5 miles

10. 27

11. 2

12. neither

13. perpendicular

14. $\frac{1}{2}$

15. $-\frac{10}{9}$

16. $4x^2 + 6xy + 2y^2$

Standardized Test Practice
Page 173

1. A

2. A

3. A

4. D

5. B

6. D

7. D

8. C

9. A

10. B

11. D

Page 174

12. B

13. D

14. D

15. C

16. B

17. D

18. B

19. C

20. C

21. C

22. B

23. C

24. A

25. D

10

Chapter 10 Test, Form 1A

Write the letter for the correct answer in the blank at the right of each problem.

For Questions 1–2, find the factors of each number and classify the number as **prime** *or* **composite.**

1. 37

   A. 1, 3, 7; composite   **B.** 1, 37; prime

   C. 1, 19; composite   **D.** 1, 7; prime   1. _____

2. 36

   A. 1, 2, 3, 4, 6, 9, 12, 18, 36; composite

   B. 1, 2, 4, 6, 12, 18; composite

   C. 1, 3, 6, 9, 12, 16; composite

   D. 1, 3, 36; prime   2. _____

3. The area of a rectangle is 48 square inches. Find the length and width so that the rectangle has the least perimeter. Assume that the length and width are both whole numbers.

   A. 3 in., 16 in.   **B.** 4 in., 12 in.   **C.** 2 in., 24 in.   **D.** 6 in., 8 in.   3. _____

Find the greatest common factor of each set of numbers or monomials.

4. 28, 40

   A. 2   **B.** 4   **C.** 7   **D.** 14   4. _____

5. $48a^2b$, $36ab$

   A. $3a$ **B.** $4ab$ **C.** $12ab$ **D.** $24b$ 5. _____

Factor each polynomial. If the polynomial cannot be factored, write **prime.**

6. $12x + 16x^2y$

   A. $4x(3 + 4xy)$ **B.** $4(3 + 4xy)$ **C.** $12x(1 + 4x)$ **D.** $4xy(3 + 4x)$ 6. _____

7. $9a - 4b$

   A. prime   **B.** $4(5a - b)$ **C.** $a(9 - 4b)$ **D.** $3(3a - 2b)$ 7. _____

8. $5c^2 + 10cd + 25cd^2$

   A. $5cd(c + 2 + 5d)$ **B.** $5(c^2 + 2d + 5d^2)$

   C. $5c(c + 2d + 5d)$ **D.** $5c(c + 2d + 5d^2)$ 8. _____

Find each quotient.

9. $(21xy + 35y) \div 7y$

   A. $3x + 5y$ **B.** $3x + 5$ **C.** $3 + 5y$ **D.** $3xy + 5$ 9. _____

10. $(42a^2b + 18b^3) \div 6b$

   A. $8a^2 + 3b^2$ **B.** $8a + 3b^2$ **C.** $7a^2 + 3b^2$ **D.** $7a^2 + 3b^3$ 10. _____

Factor each trinomial. If the trinomial cannot be factored, write **prime.**

11. $x^2 + 3x + 2$

   A. $(x + 1)(x + 2)$ **B.** $(x + 3)(x + 2)$ **C.** prime   **D.** $(x + 4)(x - 1)$ 11. _____

12. $y^2 + y - 6$

   A. $(y + 5)(y - 1)$ **B.** $(y + 3)(y - 2)$ **C.** prime   **D.** $(y + 7)(y - 1)$ 12. _____

Factor each trinomial. If the trinomial cannot be factored, write **prime.**

13. $a^2 - 3a - 4$

    A. $(a + 1)(a - 4)$ **B.** prime

    C. $(a - 1)(a + 4)$ **D.** $(a - 1)(a - 4)$ **13.** _____

14. $x^3 + 4x^2 + 3x$

    A. prime   **B.** $(x^2 + 1)(x + 3)$

    C. $(x + 1)(x^2 + 3)$ **D.** $x(x + 1)(x + 3)$ **14.** _____

15. $3a^3 - 3a^2 - 6a$

    A. $3(a + 1)(a - 2)$ **B.** $a(a - 1)(a - 6)$

    C. $(3a + 1)(a^2 - 2)$ **D.** $3a(a + 1)(a - 2)$ **15.** _____

16. $6r^2 + 5r + 6$

    A. prime   **B.** $(3r + 2)(3r + 3)$

    C. $(3r + 2)(2r + 3)$ **D.** $(2r + 3)(3r + 3)$ **16.** _____

17. $8x^2 + 6x + 1$

    A. $(8x + 1)(x + 1)$ **B.** $(2x + 1)(4x + 1)$

    C. $(4x + 1)(4x + 1)$ **D.** prime   **17.** _____

18. $3y^2 + 5y - 2$

    A. $(3y - 1)(y - 2)$ **B.** $(3y + 1)(y + 2)$

    C. $(3y + 1)(y - 4)$ **D.** $(3y - 1)(y + 2)$ **18.** _____

19. $3d^2 - 4d + 1$

    A. $(3d - 1)(d - 1)$ **B.** $(3d + 1)(d - 1)$

    C. prime   **D.** $(2d - 1)(d - 2)$ **19.** _____

20. $6x^2 + 16x - 6$

    A. $3(2x + 1)(x - 2)$ **B.** prime

    C. $2(x + 3)(3x - 1)$ **D.** $(5x + 3)(x - 2)$ **20.** _____

21. $a^2 - 25$

    A. prime   **B.** $(a - 5)^2$

    C. $(a - 5)(a + 5)$ **D.** $(a - 5)(a + 10)$ **21.** _____

22. $g^2 + 12g + 36$

    A. $(g + 4)^2$ **B.** $(g + 6)^2$

    C. $(g + 6)(g - 6)$ **D.** $(g + 9)(g + 3)$ **22.** _____

23. $x^2 - 49$

    A. $(x - 7)^2$ **B.** prime

    C. $(x + 7)^2$ **D.** $(x - 7)(x + 7)$ **23.** _____

24. $4y^2 + 12y + 9$

    A. $(2y + 3)(2y - 3)$ **B.** $(2y - 3)^2$

    C. $(2y + 3)^2$ **D.** $(2y + 6)(2y + 2)$ **24.** _____

25. $9k^2 - 4$

    A. $(3k - 2)^2$ **B.** $(3k + 2)^2$

    C. $(3k - 2)(3k + 2)$ **D.** prime   **25.** _____

Bonus Find all values of b so that the trinomial $x^2 + bx + 6$ can be factored.

    A. 2, 3   **B.** 5, 7   **C.** 5, −5, 7, −7   **D.** 1, 2, 3, 6   **Bonus** _____

10

Chapter 10 Test, Form 1B

Write the letter for the correct answer in the blank at the right of each problem.

*For Questions 1–2, find the factors of each number and classify the number as **prime** or **composite**.*

1. 17
   A. 1, 3, 17; composite
   C. 1, 17; composite
   B. 1, 17; prime
   D. 1, 7; prime

   1. _____

2. 32
   A. 1, 2, 4, 8, 16, 32; composite
   B. 1, 2, 4, 6, 12, 32; composite
   C. 1, 2, 3, 4, 16, 32; composite
   D. 1, 2, 32; prime

   2. _____

3. The area of a rectangle is 54 square centimeters. Find the length and width so that the rectangle has the greatest perimeter. Assume that the length and width are both whole numbers.
   A. 6 cm, 9 cm   **B.** 3 cm, 18 cm   **C.** 2 cm, 27 cm   **D.** 1 cm, 54 cm

   3. _____

Find the greatest common factor of each set of numbers or monomials.

4. 21, 24
   A. 2   **B.** 3   **C.** 4   **D.** 7

   4. _____

5. $25a^2$, $15ab$
   A. $3a$ **B.** $5a$ **C.** $15ab$ **D.** $5a^2$

   5. _____

*Factor each polynomial. If the polynomial cannot be factored, write **prime**.*

6. $4x + 20$
   A. $4x(1 + 5)$ **B.** $4x(x + 5)$ **C.** $4(x + 5)$ **D.** $2(2x + 5)$

   6. _____

7. $7a - 9b$
   A. prime   **B.** $7(a - 2b)$ **C.** $a(7 - 9b)$ **D.** $3(4a - 6b)$

   7. _____

8. $3c^2 + 12c + 15d$
   A. $3(c + 4)(c + 1)$
   C. $3c(c + 4c + 5d)$
   B. $3c(c + 4 + 5d)$
   D. $3(c^2 + 4c + 5d)$

   8. _____

Find each quotient.

9. $(18xy + 24x) \div 6x$
   A. $3y + 4x$ **B.** $3xy + 4$ **C.** $3y + 4$ **D.** $4y + 4$

   9. _____

10. $(20a^2 - 16bc) \div 4$
   A. $6a^2 - 4bc$ **B.** $5a^2 - 4bc$ **C.** $5a - 4bc$ **D.** $5a^2 - 4b$

   10. _____

*Factor each trinomial. If the trinomial cannot be factored, write **prime**.*

11. $x^2 + 4x + 3$
   A. $(x + 1)(x + 3)$ **B.** $(x + 2)(x + 2)$ **C.** prime   **D.** $(x + 4)(x - 1)$

   11. _____

12. $y^2 + y - 12$
   A. $(y + 6)(y - 2)$ **B.** $(y + 3)(y - 4)$ **C.** $(y + 4)(y - 3)$ **D.** prime

   12. _____

   Algebra: Concepts and Applications

Factor each trinomial. If the trinomial cannot be factored, write prime.

13. $a^2 - 2a - 3$

    A. $(a + 1)(a - 3)$ **B.** prime

    C. $(a - 3)(a + 1)$ **D.** $(a - 2)(a - 3)$ 13. _____

14. $x^3 + x^2 + 3$

    A. prime   **B.** $(x^2 + 1)(x + 3)$

    C. $(x + 1)(x^2 + 3)$ **D.** $x(x + 1)(x + 3)$ 14. _____

15. $2a^2 - 2a - 4$

    A. $2(a + 2)(a - 2)$ **B.** $a(a + 1)(a - 2)$

    C. $(2a + 1)(a - 2)$ **D.** $2(a + 1)(a - 2)$ 15. _____

16. $8r^2 + 6r + 2$

    A. $(2r + 1)(4r + 1)$ **B.** $2(4r^2 + 3r + 1)$

    C. $(4r + 1)(2r + 2)$ **D.** $(2r + 3)(2r + 1)$ 16. _____

17. $6x^2 + 11x + 3$

    A. $(2x + 1)(3x + 4)$ **B.** $(3x + 1)(2x + 3)$

    C. $(x + 5)(6x + 1)$ **D.** prime   17. _____

18. $4y^2 + 2y - 2$

    A. $(3y - 1)(y - 2)$ **B.** $2(2y - 1)(y - 1)$

    C. $2(2y - 1)(y + 1)$ **D.** $(4y + 1)(y - 2)$ 18. _____

19. $2d^2 - 7d + 6$

    A. $(2d - 3)(d - 2)$ **B.** $(2d + 7)(d - 1)$

    C. prime   **D.** $(2d - 6)(d - 1)$ 19. _____

20. $12x^2 + 2x - 2$

    A. $2(2x + 1)(3x - 1)$ **B.** prime

    C. $4(x + 1)(3x - 1)$ **D.** $(4x + 3)(3x - 1)$ 20. _____

21. $a^2 - 9$

    A. prime   **B.** $(a - 3)^2$

    C. $(a - 9)(a + 9)$ **D.** $(a - 3)(a + 3)$ 21. _____

22. $g^2 + 10g + 25$

    A. $(g + 5)(g + 2)$ **B.** $(g + 10)^2$

    C. $(g + 5)(g - 5)$ **D.** $(g + 5)^2$ 22. _____

23. $x^2 - 36$

    A. $(x - 6)^2$ **B.** prime

    C. $(x + 6)^2$ **D.** $(x - 6)(x + 6)$ 23. _____

24. $9y^2 + 12y + 4$

    A. $(3y + 2)(3y - 2)$ **B.** $(2y - 3)^2$

    C. $(3y + 2)^2$ **D.** $(3y + 6)(3y - 2)$ 24. _____

25. $25k^2 - 4$

    A. $(5k - 2)^2$ **B.** $(5k + 2)^2$

    C. $(5k - 2)(5k + 2)$ **D.** prime   25. _____

Bonus Find all values of b so that the trinomial $x^2 + bx + 4$ can be factored.

    A. 2, 3, 4   **B.** 1, 2, 4   **C.** $-4, 4, -5, 5$ **D.** 3, 4, 5   **Bonus** _____

10 Chapter 10 Test, Form 2A

Find the factors of each number and classify the number as prime *or* composite.

1. 19

1. _____

2. 48

2. _____

Factor each monomial.

3. $15x^2$

3. _____

4. $-18b^2c$

4. _____

Find the greatest common factor of each set of numbers or monomials.

5. 18, 21

5. _____

6. $11x, 22x^2$

6. _____

7. $6ax, 18ax^2, 30ax$

7. _____

Factor each polynomial. If the polynomial cannot be factored, write prime.

8. $9x + 12x^2$

8. _____

9. $17ab + 23c$

9. _____

10. $4xy^2 - 2yz$

10. _____

For Questions 11–13, find each quotient.

11. $(5x^2 - 10y^2) \div 5$

11. _____

12. $(4abc + 2bc) \div 2c$

12. _____

13. $(8g^2h^3j - 12g^3hj^2) \div 4g$

13. _____

14. The area of a rectangle is $(10x + 15y)$ square meters. If the length is 5 meters, find the width.

14. _____

Factor each trinomial. If the trinomial cannot be factored, write prime.

15. $s^2 + 10s + 9$

15. _____

16. $x^2 - 3x - 10$

16. _____

Factor each trinomial. If the trinomial cannot be factored, write
prime.

17. $y^2 + y - 20$

17. _____

18. $b^2 - 6b + 8$

18. _____

19. $3a^2 + 18a + 15$

19. _____

20. $x^3 - x^2 - 12x$

20. _____

21. $6d^2 + 5d + 1$

21. _____

22. $10f^2 + 7f + 1$

22. _____

23. $2x^2 + 11x + 12$

23. _____

24. $8w^2 + 8w - 6$

24. _____

25. $6y^2 - 13y + 6$

25. _____

26. $24m^2 - 38m + 15$

26. _____

27. $-x^2 - x - 2$

27. _____

28. $g^2 + 10g + 25$

28. _____

29. $4k^2 + 12k + 9$

29. _____

30. $36z^2 - 25$

30. _____

31. $16e^2 - 24e + 9$

31. _____

32. $4x^2 - 28x + 49$

32. _____

33. $9y^2 - 4$

33. _____

Bonus The difference of two positive numbers is 2. The
difference of their squares is 20. Find the numbers.

Bonus _____

10

Chapter 10 Test, Form 2B

Find the factors of each number and classify the number as prime *or* composite.

1. 11

1. _____

2. 50

2. _____

Factor each monomial.

3. $9ab$

3. _____

4. $-16xy^2$

4. _____

Find the greatest common factor of each set of numbers or monomials.

5. 20, 24

5. _____

6. $10x$, $15x^2$

6. _____

7. $7x$, $14ax^2$, $28ax$

7. _____

Factor each polynomial. If the polynomial cannot be factored, write prime.

8. $3 + 12x$

8. _____

9. $7ab + 13c$

9. _____

10. $6y^2 - 2yz$

10. _____

For Questions 11–13, find each quotient.

11. $(15x - 10y^2) \div 5$

11. _____

12. $(6ac + 2bc) \div 2c$

12. _____

13. $(8g^2j - 12g^3hj) \div 4g$

13. _____

14. The area of a rectangle is $(36xy + 24y)$ square inches. If the width is $12y$ inches, find the length.

14. _____

Factor each trinomial. If the trinomial cannot be factored, write prime.

15. $s^2 + 7s + 10$

15. _____

16. $x^2 - x - 6$

16. _____

Factor each trinomial. If the trinomial cannot be factored, write prime.

17. $y^2 - 4y - 5$

17. _____

18. $b^2 - b + 8$

18. _____

19. $3a^2 + 9a + 6$

19. _____

20. $x^3 + 3x^2 - 10x$

20. _____

21. $4d^2 + 6d + 2$

21. _____

22. $6f^2 + 5f + 1$

22. _____

23. $6x^2 + 10x + 4$

23. _____

24. $12w^2 + 10w - 8$

24. _____

25. $20y^2 - 33y + 10$

25. _____

26. $8m^2 - 34m + 30$

26. _____

27. $-x^2 - x - 6$

27. _____

28. $g^2 + 8g + 16$

28. _____

29. $4k^2 + 20k + 25$

29. _____

30. $25z^2 - 16$

30. _____

31. $16e^2 - 4$

31. _____

32. $4x^2 - 24x + 36$

32. _____

33. $49y^2 - 25$

33. _____

Bonus The area of a square is $(9x^2 + 36x + 36)$ square feet. Find the length of one side of the square.

Bonus _____

Chapter 10 Open-Ended Assessment

Instructions: Demonstrate your knowledge by giving a clear, concise solution for each problem. Be sure to include all relevant drawings and to justify your answers. You may show your solution in more than one way or investigate beyond the requirements of the problem.

1. The area of a rectangle is 36 square inches. Find the length and width so that the rectangle has the least perimeter. Assume that the length and width are both whole numbers.

2. A walkway is built around a rectangular garden. If this walkway is 2 meters wide, write an expression that represents the area of the walkway.

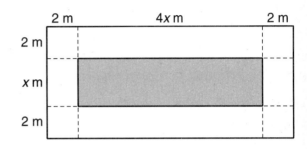

3. The width of this rectangle is 1 foot more than the length. If a 5-foot by 6-foot rectangle is removed from the corner, how much of the original rectangle remains?

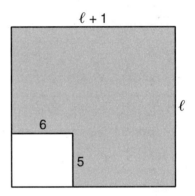

4. The volume of a rectangular shipping crate is $12x^3 + 10x^2 + 2x$. Find possible dimensions for the crate.

5. A square and its area are shown at the right. Find the perimeter of the square. Express the answer in factored form.

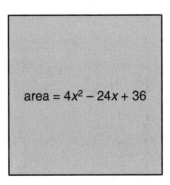

area = $4x^2 - 24x + 36$

Chapter 10 Mid-Chapter Test
(Lessons 10–1 through 10–3)

1. The area of a rectangle is 90 square inches. Find the length and width so that the rectangle has the least perimeter. Assume that the length and width are both whole numbers.

1. _____

Factor each monomial.

2. 60

2. _____

3. $6b^3$

3. _____

4. $8x^2$

4. _____

5. $-4m^2n$

5. _____

Find the greatest common factor of each set of monomials.

6. $7ax, 21ax^2, 35ax^3$

6. _____

7. $6p, 3p^2, 33px$

7. _____

Find each quotient.

8. $(10ab + 2bc) \div 2$

8. _____

9. $(30cd^2 - 10bc^3d) \div 5c$

9. _____

10. $(30f^2g^2h + 21gh^2) \div 3gh$

10. _____

11. $(64z - 80z^3) \div 8z$

11. _____

Factor each polynomial. If the polynomial cannot be factored, write prime.

12. $6x - 8$

12. _____

13. $4a^2 + 8a$

13. _____

14. $18x + 19y^2$

14. _____

15. $x^2 + 7x + 6$

15. _____

16. $a^2 + 5a + 6$

16. _____

17. $g^2 + 2g - 15$

17. _____

18. $z^2 + 3z - 10$

18. _____

19. $y^2 - y - 20$

19. _____

20. $2k^3 + 4k^2 - 16k$

20. _____

NAME _____ DATE _____ PERIOD _____

Chapter 10 Quiz A
(Lessons 10–1 and 10–2)

Find the factors of each number and classify the number as prime *or* composite.

1. 28

2. 31

Find the greatest common factor of each set of numbers or monomials.

3. 40, 42

4. $18x$, $30xy$

5. ad^2, bd^3, $4d$

Find each quotient.

6. $(18y + 45y^2) \div 9y$

7. $(55a^2 - 33ay^2) \div 11a$

Factor each polynomial. If the polynomial cannot be factored, write prime.

8. $6x + 24x^2$

9. $17a - 20bc$

10. $8c^2 + 40c^2d + 56cd^3$

1. _____

2. _____

3. _____

4. _____

5. _____

6. _____

7. _____

8. _____

9. _____

10. _____

NAME _____ DATE _____ PERIOD _____

Chapter 10 Quiz B
(Lessons 10–3 through 10–5)

Factor each polynomial. If the polynomial cannot be factored, write prime.

1. $x^2 + 8x + 7$

2. $a^2 - 2a - 8$

3. $2m^2 + 18m + 16$

4. $5b^2 + 11b + 2$

5. $3y^2 - 11y + 6$

6. $5c^2 - 4c - 1$

7. $x^2 + 22x + 121$

8. $4y^2 - 4y + 1$

9. $a^2 - 81$

10. $36b^2 - 169$

1. _____

2. _____

3. _____

4. _____

5. _____

6. _____

7. _____

8. _____

9. _____

10. _____

Algebra: Concepts and Applications

1. Write an equation for the sentence below. *(Lesson 1–1)*

Twenty-four is equal to twice the product of numbers x and z.

1. _____

2. Simplify $-9y + (-4y)$. *(Lesson 2–3)*

2. _____

3. Solve $-4 = g + (-2)$. *(Lesson 3–5)*

3. _____

4. Find $8(4.1)$. *(Lesson 4–1)*

4. _____

Use the percent equation to find each number. *(Lesson 5–4)*

5. Find 45% of 36.

5. _____

6. 40 is 5% of what number?

6. _____

Solve. Assume that y varies directly as x. *(Lesson 6–5)*

7. Find y when $x = 18$ if $y = 33$ when $x = 11$.

7. _____

8. If $y = 40$ when $x = 32$, find x when $y = 30$.

8. _____

Determine whether the graphs of each pair of equations are parallel, perpendicular, or neither. *(Lesson 7–7)*

9. $y = -7x + 5$
$y = -7x - 5$

9. _____

10. $3y = 4x$

$y = -\dfrac{3}{4}x$

10. _____

Write each expression using exponents. *(Lesson 8–1)*

11. 7 squared

11. _____

12. $(-3)(x)(x)(x)(y)(y)$

12. _____

Find each product. *(Lesson 9–3)*

13. $4(x - 2)$

13. _____

14. $7y(y - y^2)$

14. _____

Find the greatest common factor of each set of numbers.
(Lesson 10–1)

15. 17, 18, 19

15. _____

16. 32, 36, 44

16. _____

10 Chapter 10 Standardized Test Practice
(Chapters 1–10)

Write the letter for the correct answer in the blank at the right of each problem.

1. Which is the equation for the sentence below?

   Thirteen less than six multiplied by a number n is four.
   - **A.** $6n - 13 = 4$
   - **B.** $13 - 6n = 4$
   - **C.** $13 - (6 \times 4) = n$
   - **D.** $(13 - 6)n - 4 = 0$

   1. _____

2. Find the value of $13 - 20 \div (2 + 8) - 4$.
   - **A.** 8
   - **B.** 7
   - **C.** $\frac{1}{2}$
   - **D.** -7.5

   2. _____

3. Evaluate $2m - n$ if $m = 3$ and $n = -2$.
   - **A.** 8
   - **B.** 5
   - **C.** 2
   - **D.** -1

   3. _____

4. Order the integers below from least to greatest.

   $$73, -51, -19, 62, 3, -8, -15$$
   - **A.** $3, -8, -15, -19, -51, 62, 73$
   - **B.** $73, 62, 3, -8, -15, -19, -51$
   - **C.** $73, 62, -51, -19, -15, -8, 3$
   - **D.** $-51, -19, -15, -8, 3, 62, 73$

   4. _____

5. For the data set below, the value 14 is which of the following?

   $$12, 12, 12, 14, 14, 15, 15, 22$$
   - **A.** mean
   - **B.** median
   - **C.** mode
   - **D.** range

   5. _____

6. Solve $|x + 5| = 11$.
   - **A.** 6
   - **B.** 16
   - **C.** 6 or -16
   - **D.** -6 or 16

   6. _____

7. Simplify $-4.7(23x)$.
   - **A.** 108.1
   - **B.** $18.3x$
   - **C.** $-108.1x$
   - **D.** $-18.3x$

   7. _____

8. Solve $-9y = 72$.
   - **A.** 81
   - **B.** 63
   - **C.** 8
   - **D.** -8

   8. _____

9. 15 is 3% of what number?
   - **A.** 500
   - **B.** 45
   - **C.** 20
   - **D.** 5

   9. _____

10. On a map, the scale is 1 centimeter = 5 kilometers. Find the actual distance if the map distance is 9.2 centimeters.
    - **A.** 46 kilometers
    - **B.** 9.2 kilometers
    - **C.** 4.6 kilometers
    - **D.** 46 centimeters

    10. _____

11. Which of the following is *not* a linear equation?
    - **A.** $y = -x$
    - **B.** $y = x^2$
    - **C.** $y = 5$
    - **D.** $y - x = 2$

    11. _____

12. If $g(x) = -2x + 6$, find $g(0)$.
    - **A.** 0
    - **B.** g
    - **C.** 3
    - **D.** 6

    12. _____

13. Assume that y varies directly as x. If $y = 33$ when $x = 22$, y is which of the following when x is 18?

   A. 7   **B.** 11   **C.** 12   **D.** 27   **13.** _____

14. A line passing through points at $(-2, -7)$ and $(3, -7)$ has slope

   A. 0.   **B.** 2.   **C.** 5.   **D.** undefined.   **14.** _____

15. The point-slope form of an equation for a line with slope 5 passing through the point at $(0, -1)$ is

   A. $y + 1 = 5x$.   **B.** $y = 5x - 1$.

   C. $y = 5(x - 1)$.   **D.** $5x + y = 1$.   **15.** _____

16. Which of the following is the equation of a line parallel to the graph of $y = -7x + 1$?

   A. $x = 7y + 1$ **B.** $y = -7x - 5$

   C. $y = 7x - 1$ **D.** $y = \frac{1}{2}x + 5$ **16.** _____

17. Simplify the expression $(g^3)(g^3)(g^2)$.

   A. g^6 **B.** g^8

   C. g^9 **D.** g^{18} **17.** _____

18. Write x^{-4} using positive exponents.

   A. $4x^2$ **B.** $\frac{1}{x^4}$ **C.** x^4 **D.** $\frac{1}{4x}$ **18.** _____

19. Express 4.5×10^{-2} in standard form.

   A. 0.045   **B.** 0.45

   C. 4.5   **D.** 45   **19.** _____

20. Which of the following is a binomial?

   A. x^2 **B.** $2x$

   C. h^{-2} **D.** $a + b$ **20.** _____

21. Which of the following is equivalent to $5x + 8y$?

   A. $(2x + 7y) + (2x + y)$ **B.** $(2x + 3y) + (6x + 2y)$

   C. $(5x + 8y)(x + y)$ **D.** $(7x + 9y) - (2x + y)$ **21.** _____

22. Find the product of $5a$ and $10a + 5a^2$.

   A. $15a + 5a^2$ **B.** $10a + 10a^2$

   C. $50a^2 + 25a^3$ **D.** $2 + a$ **22.** _____

23. Four is the greatest common factor of which pair of numbers?

   A. 48, 52   **B.** 2, 4

   C. 4, 6   **D.** 8, 16   **23.** _____

24. Which of the following is prime?

   A. $f + 4g$ **B.** $2a + 3a$

   C. 21   **D.** 39   **24.** _____

25. Which of the following is *not* a perfect square?

   A. x^2 **B.** $x^2 - 25$

   C. 9   **D.** $x^2 + 2x + 1$ **25.** _____

Chapter 10 Answer Key

13. **A**

1. **B**   14. **D**

15. **D**

2. **A**   16. **A**

3. **D**   17. **B**

18. **D**

4. **B**

5. **C**   19. **A**

20. **C**

6. **A**

7. **A**   21. **C**

8. **D**   22. **B**

9. **B**   23. **D**

10. **C**   24. **C**

11. **A**   25. **C**

12. **B**   Bonus **C**

13. **A**

1. **B**   14. **A**

15. **D**

2. **A**   16. **B**

3. **D**   17. **B**

18. **C**

4. **B**

5. **B**   19. **A**

20. **A**

6. **C**

7. **A**   21. **D**

8. **D**   22. **D**

9. **C**   23. **D**

10. **B**   24. **C**

11. **A**   25. **C**

12. **C**   Bonus **C**

195

Algebra: Concepts and Applications

Chapter 10 Answer Key

Form 2A

1. __1, 19; prime__

2. __1, 2, 3, 4, 6, 8, 12, 16, 24, 48; composite__

3. $3 \cdot 5 \cdot x \cdot x$

4. $-1 \cdot 2 \cdot 3 \cdot 3 \cdot b \cdot b \cdot c$

5. 3

6. $11x$

7. $6ax$

8. $3x(3 + 4x)$

9. __prime__

10. $2y(2xy - z)$

11. $x^2 - 2y^2$

12. $2ab + b$

13. $2gh^3j - 3g^2hj^2$

14. $(2x + 3y)\,m$

15. $(s + 1)(s + 9)$

16. $(x + 2)(x - 5)$

17. $(y + 5)(y - 4)$

18. $(b - 2)(b - 4)$

19. $3(a + 1)(a + 5)$

20. $x(x + 3)(x - 4)$

21. $(2d + 1)(3d + 1)$

22. $(5f + 1)(2f + 1)$

23. $(2x + 3)(x + 4)$

24. $2(2w - 1)(2w + 3)$

25. $(2y - 3)(3y - 2)$

26. $(6m - 5)(4m - 3)$

27. __prime__

28. $(g + 5)^2$

29. $(2k + 3)^2$

30. $(6z + 5)(6z - 5)$

31. $(4e - 3)^2$

32. $(2x - 7)^2$

33. $(3y - 2)(3y + 2)$

Bonus __4, 6__

Chapter 10 Answer Key
Form 2B

1. __1, 11; prime__

2. __1, 2, 5, 10, 25, 50; composite__

3. __$3 \cdot 3 \cdot a \cdot b$__

4. __$-1 \cdot 2 \cdot 2 \cdot 2 \cdot 2 \cdot x \cdot y \cdot y$__

5. __4__

6. __$5x$__

7. __$7x$__

8. __$3(1 + 4x)$__

9. __prime__

10. __$2y(3y - z)$__

11. __$3x - 2y^2$__

12. __$3a + b$__

13. __$2gj - 3g^2hj$__

14. __$(3x + 2)$ in.__

15. __$(s + 2)(s + 5)$__

16. __$(x + 2)(x - 3)$__

17. __$(y + 1)(y - 5)$__

18. __prime__

19. __$3(a + 1)(a + 2)$__

20. __$x(x + 5)(x - 2)$__

21. __$2(2d + 1)(d + 1)$__

22. __$(3f + 1)(2f + 1)$__

23. __$2(x + 1)(3x + 2)$__

24. __$2(2w - 1)(3w + 4)$__

25. __$(5y - 2)(4y - 5)$__

26. __$2(4m - 5)(m - 3)$__

27. __prime__

28. __$(g + 4)^2$__

29. __$(2k + 5)^2$__

30. __$(5z + 4)(5z - 4)$__

31. __$(4e - 2)(4e + 2)$__

32. __$(2x - 6)^2$ or $4(x - 3)^2$__

33. __$(7y - 5)(7y + 5)$__

Bonus __$(3x + 6)$ or $3(x + 2)$ feet__

     Algebra: Concepts and Applications

Chapter 10 Answer Key

Open-Ended Assessment
Sample Answers
Page 189

1. length and width 6 inches

2. $4(4 + 5x)$ or $(16 + 20x)$ square meters

3. $\ell^2 + \ell - 30$ or $(\ell + 6)(\ell - 5)$

4. $2x$, $3x + 1$, $2x + 1$

5. $8(x - 3)$ or $4(2x - 6)$

Chapter 10 Answer Key

Mid-Chapter Test
Page 190

1. 9 in., 10 in.

2. $2^2 \cdot 3 \cdot 5$

3. $2 \cdot 3 \cdot b \cdot b \cdot b$

4. $2 \cdot 2 \cdot 2 \cdot x \cdot x$

5. $-1 \cdot 2 \cdot 2 \cdot m \cdot m \cdot n$

6. $7ax$

7. $3p$

8. $5ab + bc$

9. $6d^2 - 2bc^2d$

10. $10f^2g + 7h$

11. $8 - 10z^2$

12. $2(3x - 4)$

13. $4a(a + 2)$

14. prime

15. $(x + 1)(x + 6)$

16. $(a + 2)(a + 3)$

17. $(g + 5)(g - 3)$

18. $(z - 2)(z + 5)$

19. $(y + 4)(y - 5)$

20. $2k(k + 4)(k - 2)$

Quiz A
Page 191

1. 1, 2, 4, 7, 14, 28; composite

2. 1, 31; prime

3. 2

4. $6x$

5. d

6. $2 + 5y$

7. $5a - 3y^2$

8. $6x(1 + 4x)$

9. prime

10. $8c(c + 5cd + 7d^3)$

Quiz B
Page 191

1. $(x + 1)(x + 7)$

2. $(a + 2)(a - 4)$

3. $2(m + 1)(m + 8)$

4. $(5b + 1)(b + 2)$

5. $(3y - 2)(y - 3)$

6. $(c - 1)(5c + 1)$

7. $(x + 11)^2$

8. $(2y - 1)^2$

9. $(a - 9)(a + 9)$

10. $(6b - 13)(6b + 13)$

Chapter 10 Answer Key

Cumulative Review	Standardized Test Practice
Page 192	Page 193 Page 194

Cumulative Review — Page 192

1. $24 = 2xz$
2. $-13y$
3. -2
4. 32.8
5. 16.2
6. 800
7. 54
8. 24
9. parallel
10. perpendicular
11. 7^2
12. $-3x^3y^2$
13. $4x - 8$
14. $7y^2 - 7y^3$
15. 1
16. 4

Standardized Test Practice — Page 193

1. A
2. B
3. A
4. D
5. B
6. C
7. C
8. D
9. A
10. A
11. B
12. D

Page 194

13. D
14. A
15. A
16. B
17. B
18. B
19. A
20. D
21. D
22. C
23. A
24. A
25. B

Write the letter for the correct answer in the blank at the right of each problem.

1. Which quadratic function has a graph that opens downward?
   A. $y = 3x^2 + x + 1$ **B.** $y = 3x^2 - x + 1$
   C. $y = 3x^2 + x - 1$ **D.** $y = -3x^2 + x + 1$

   1. _____

2. Which is the graph of $y = x^2 + 2$?
   A.   **B.**   **C.**   **D.**

   2. _____

3. Name the coordinates of the vertex of the graph of $y = 2x^2 + 4x - 1$.
   A. $(-1, -3)$ **B.** $(1, 5)$ **C.** $(-2, -1)$ **D.** $(0, -1)$

   3. _____

4. Which statement best describes how the graph of $y = x^2 + 4$ changes from the parent graph of $y = x^2$?
   A. left 4 units   **B.** right 4 units   **C.** up 4 units   **D.** down 4 units

   4. _____

5. Name the coordinates of the vertex of the graph of $y = (x + 1)^2 + 2$.
   A. $(-1, 2)$ **B.** $(1, 2)$ **C.** $(-1, -2)$ **D.** $(1, -2)$

   5. _____

6. Which is the graph of $y = (x + 3)^2$?
   A.   **B.**   **C.**   **D.**

   6. _____

7. Which graph has roots 2 and -3?
   A.   **B.** 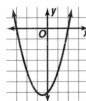   **C.** 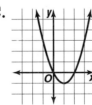   **D.**

   7. _____

8. Find the roots of $x^2 - 4x + 3 = 0$ by graphing the related function.
   A. $-4, 3$ **B.** $-1, -3$ **C.** $1, 3$ **D.** $0, 3$

   8. _____

9. Estimate the roots of $x^2 - 2x - 2 = 0$.
   A. Between -2 and -1 and between 2 and 3
   B. Between -1 and 0 and between 2 and 3
   C. Between -2 and -1 and between -2 and -3
   D. Between -4 and -3 and between 0 and 1

   9. _____

For Questions 10–12, solve each equation.

10. $4m(m - 2) = 0$

   A. $4, -2$ **B.** $0, 2$ **C.** 2 only   **D.** 0 only   **10.** _____

11. $(p - 3)(p + 1) = 0$

   A. $-3, 1$ **B.** $3, -1$ **C.** $-3, -1$ **D.** $0, 3$ **11.** _____

12. $x^2 + 5x + 4 = 0$

   A. $4, 5$ **B.** $1, 4$ **C.** $-1, -4$ **D.** $1, -4$ **12.** _____

13. Find the value of c that makes the trinomial $x^2 + 12x + c$ a perfect square.

   A. -36 **B.** 9 **C.** 24 **D.** 36 **13.** _____

14. Find the value of c that makes the trinomial $y^2 + 9y + c$ a perfect square.

   A. $\frac{9}{2}$ **B.** $\frac{81}{4}$ **C.** 36 **D.** 81 **14.** _____

15. Solve $x^2 - 8x = 0$ by completing the square.

   A. 0 only   **B.** -8 only   **C.** $0, -8$ **D.** $0, 8$ **15.** _____

For Questions 16–18, use the Quadratic Formula to solve each equation.

16. $x^2 - 6x - 7 = 0$

   A. $-1, 6$ **B.** $-1, 7$ **C.** $1, -7$ **D.** $1, 7$ **16.** _____

17. $x^2 + 4x + 3 = 0$

   A. $1, 3$ **B.** $1, 4$ **C.** $-1, -3$ **D.** $-1, 4$ **17.** _____

18. $3x^2 + 3x - 6 = 0$

   A. $-2, -1$ **B.** $-2, 1$ **C.** $1, 2$ **D.** $3, -2$ **18.** _____

19. Which is the graph of $y = 2^x$?

   A. 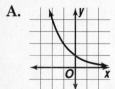   **B.**   **C.** 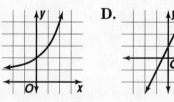   **D.**

   19. _____

20. Find the y-intercept of the graph of $y = 3^x + 1$.

   A. 0 **B.** 1 **C.** 2 **D.** 3 **20.** _____

Bonus Find the y-intercept of the graph of $y = 2^{x-1}$.

   A. -1 **B.** 0 **C.** $\frac{1}{2}$ **D.** 2 **Bonus** _____

11

Chapter 11 Test, Form 1B

Write the letter for the correct answer in the blank at the right of each problem.

1. Which quadratic function has a graph that opens upward?
A. $y = -3x^2 + x + 1$ **B.** $y = -3x^2 - x + 1$
C. $y = 3x^2 + x - 1$ **D.** $y = -3x^2 + x + 1$

1. _____

2. Which is the graph of $y = x^2 + 1$?

A. 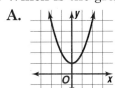   **B.** 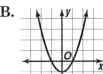   **C.** 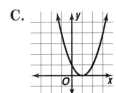   **D.**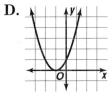

2. _____

3. Name the coordinates of the vertex of the graph of $y = 3x^2 - 6x + 2$.
A. $(-1, -1)$ **B.** $(-1, 1)$ **C.** $(1, -1)$ **D.** $(0, 2)$

3. _____

4. Which statement best describes how the graph of $y = (x - 2)^2$ changes from the parent graph of $y = x^2$?
A. left 2 units   **B.** right 2 units   **C.** up 2 units   **D.** down 2 units

4. _____

5. Name the coordinates of the vertex of the graph of $y = (x - 1)^2 + 2$.
A. $(-1, 2)$ **B.** $(1, 2)$ **C.** $(-1, -2)$ **D.** $(1, -2)$

5. _____

6. Which is the graph of $y = (x - 3)^2$?

A. 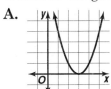   **B.** 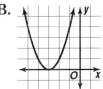   **C.** 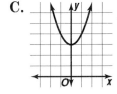   **D.**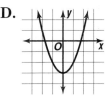

6. _____

7. Which graph has roots 1 and -2?

A. 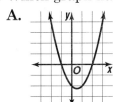   **B.** 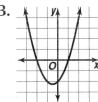   **C.** 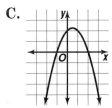   **D.**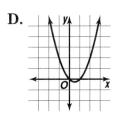

7. _____

8. Find the roots of $x^2 + 6x + 5 = 0$ by graphing the related function.
A. $-6, 5$ **B.** $-1, -5$ **C.** $1, 5$ **D.** $0, 5$

8. _____

9. Estimate the roots of $x^2 + 2x - 2 = 0$.
A. Between -3 and -2 and between 1 and 2
B. Between -1 and 0 and between 2 and 3
C. Between -3 and -2 and between 0 and 1
D. Between 1 and 2 and between 2 and 3

9. _____

For Questions 10–12, solve each equation.

10. $3m(m + 4) = 0$

    A. 3, 4   **B.** 0, −4   **C.** −4 only   **D.** 0 only   **10.** _____

11. $(k − 4)(k + 2) = 0$

    A. −4, 2   **B.** 4, −2   **C.** −4, −2   **D.** 0, 4   **11.** _____

12. $x^2 + 3x + 2 = 0$

    A. 2, 3   **B.** 1, 2   **C.** −1, −2   **D.** 1, −2   **12.** _____

13. Find the value of c that makes the trinomial $x^2 + 8x + c$ a perfect square.

    A. −16   **B.** 4   **C.** 16   **D.** 64   **13.** _____

14. Find the value of c that makes the trinomial $y^2 + 3y + c$ a perfect square.

    A. $\frac{3}{2}$ **B.** $\frac{9}{4}$ **C.** 6   **D.** 9

                                                                    14. _____

15. Solve $x^2 + 6x = 0$ by completing the square.

    A. 0 only   **B.** −6 only   **C.** 0, −6   **D.** 0, 6   **15.** _____

For Questions 16–18, use the Quadratic Formula to solve each equation.

16. $x^2 − 6x + 5 = 0$

    A. −1, −5   **B.** −1, 6   **C.** 1, −5   **D.** 1, 5   **16.** _____

17. $x^2 + 8x + 7 = 0$

    A. 1, 8   **B.** 1, 7   **C.** −1, −7   **D.** −1, 7   **17.** _____

18. $2x^2 − 14x + 24 = 0$

    A. −3, −4   **B.** 3, 4   **C.** 6, 4   **D.** 2, 12   **18.** _____

19. Which is the graph of $y = 3^x$?

    A.   **B.**   **C.**   **D.**

                                                                           19. _____

20. Find the y-intercept of the graph of $y = 2^x − 1$.

    A. −1   **B.** 0   **C.** 1   **D.** 2   **20.** _____

Bonus Find the y-intercept of the graph of $y = 3^{x + 1}$.

    A. 0   **B.** $\frac{1}{3}$ **C.** 1   **D.** 3

                                                                                 Bonus _____

11

Chapter 11 Test, Form 2A

For Questions 1–2, graph each function.

1. $y = x^2 + 2$

1.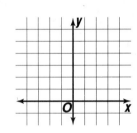

2. $y = -x^2 + 3x$

2.

3. For $y = x^2 + 4x + 3$, write the equation of the axis of symmetry and name the vertex.

3. _____

4. Describe how the graph of $y = x^2 + 3$ changes from the parent graph of $y = x^2$. Name the vertex of each graph.

4. _____

5. Describe how the graph of $y = -3x^2$ changes from the parent graph of $y = x^2$. Name the vertex of each graph.

5. _____

6. Graph $y = x^2$, $y = (x - 1)^2$, and $y = (x - 2)^2$ on the same screen. Compare and contrast the graphs.

6. _____

Solve each equation by graphing the related function. If exact roots cannot be found, state the consecutive integers between which the roots are located.

7. $x^2 + 3x + 2 = 0$

7. _____

8. $x^2 + 3x - 5 = 0$

8. _____

9. $-x^2 + 5x - 4 = 0$

9. _____

10. $x^2 + 5x - 6 = 0$

10. _____

Solve each equation by factoring. Check your solution.

11. $2n(n + 5) = 0$

11. _____

12. $-6y(y - 2) = 0$

12. _____

13. $(p - 8)(p + 1) = 0$

13. _____

14. $x^2 + 4x - 5 = 0$

14. _____

Find the value of c that makes each trinomial a perfect square.

15. $x^2 + 4x + c$ **15.** _____

16. $z^2 - 10z + c$ **16.** _____

Solve each equation by completing the square.

17. $x^2 + 6x + 5 = 0$ **17.** _____

18. $p^2 - 12p + 11 = 0$ **18.** _____

Use the Quadratic Formula to solve each equation.

19. $z^2 - 10z + 9 = 0$ **19.** _____

20. $m^2 + 7m + 6 = 0$ **20.** _____

21. $2x^2 + 5x - 12 = 0$ **21.** _____

22. $n^2 + n + 1 = 0$ **22.** _____

For Questions 23–24, graph each function.

23. $y = 2^x$ **23.**

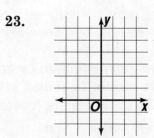

24. $y = 3^x - 1$ **24.**

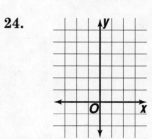

25. Find the amount of money in a bank given an initial deposit of \$2000 at an annual rate of 5% for a period of 3 years.   **25.** _____

Bonus Jerome bought a car for \$15,000. If it depreciates at a rate of 10% per year, how long will it take before the car is worth \$10,000?

Bonus _____

11

Chapter 11 Test, Form 2B

For Questions 1–2, graph each function.

1. $y = 4x^2$

1.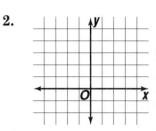

2. $y = x^2 - 2$

2.

3. For $y = -2x^2$, write the equation of the axis of symmetry and name the vertex.

3. _____

4. Describe how the graph of $y = x^2 - 1$ changes from the parent graph of $y = x^2$. Name the vertex of each graph.

4. _____

5. Describe how the graph of $y = -6x^2$ changes from the parent graph of $y = x^2$. Name the vertex of each graph.

5. _____

6. Graph $y = x^2$, $y = (x + 2)^2$, and $y = (x + 4)^2$ on the same screen. Compare and contrast the graphs.

6. _____

Solve each equation by graphing the related function. If exact roots cannot be found, state the consecutive integers between which the roots are located.

7. $x^2 - 4x + 3 = 0$

7. _____

8. $x^2 + 6x - 2 = 0$

8. _____

9. $-x^2 + 6x - 5 = 0$

9. _____

10. $x^2 + 7x - 8 = 0$

10. _____

Solve each equation by factoring. Check your solution.

11. $4p(p - 1) = 0$

11. _____

12. $-2y(y + 4) = 0$

12. _____

13. $(m - 6)(m + 5) = 0$

13. _____

14. $x^2 + 3x + 2 = 0$

14. _____

Find the value of c that makes each trinomial a perfect square.

15. $x^2 + 16x + c$

15. _____

16. $z^2 - 8z + c$

16. _____

Solve each equation by completing the square.

17. $x^2 + 4x - 5 = 0$

17. _____

18. $p^2 - 8p = 0$

18. _____

Use the Quadratic Formula to solve each equation.

19. $x^2 + 8x + 7 = 0$

19. _____

20. $m^2 + 12m + 11 = 0$

20. _____

21. $-x^2 + 7x - 10 = 0$

21. _____

22. $n^2 - n + 1 = 0$

22. _____

For Questions 23–24, graph each function.

23. $y = 2^x$

23.

24. $y = 2^x - 1$

24.

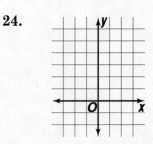

25. Find the amount of money in a bank given an initial deposit of $4000 at an annual rate of 4% for a period of 5 years.

25. _____

Bonus Bonnie bought a car for $18,000. If it depreciates at a rate of 10% per year, how long will it take before the car is worth $15,000?

Bonus _____

Instructions: Demonstrate your knowledge by giving a clear, concise solution for each problem. Be sure to include all relevant graphs and to justify your answers. You may show your solutions in more than one way or investigate beyond the requirements of the problem.

1. A team of students designed an experiment involving quadratic functions. They knew that if they tossed a ball upward, then its height could be modeled by the quadratic function $h(t) = -16t^2 + 24t + 4$, where $h(t)$ represents the height in feet at any time t in seconds after the ball is tossed.

   a. Graph this quadratic function. Name its shape.

   b. Find the equation of the axis of symmetry and the vertex.

   c. At the beginning of the experiment, the time is 0 seconds. From what height is the ball thrown?

   d. How many seconds does it take for the ball to reach its highest point?

   e. How high is the ball at its highest point? Can it be caught at that height by one of the team members? Explain.

   f. When the ball hits the ground, the height is 0. How many seconds does it take for the ball to hit the ground?

2. The balance of a savings account can be modeled by the exponential function $A(t) = P(1 + r)^t$, where $A(t)$ is the balance after time t in years, P is the initial amount deposited (the *principal*), and r is the annual interest rate expressed as a decimal.

   a. Find the amount of money in a bank account with an initial deposit of $5000 at an annual rate of 4% for 3 years.

   b. Find the amount of money in a bank account with an initial deposit of $4000 at an annual rate of 5% for 3.5 years.

   c. Which results in a greater amount: depositing $2000 at an annual rate of 3% for 4 years, or depositing $2000 at an annual rate of 3.5% for 3 years? Explain.

   d. If $y = 5000(1 + 0.04)^x$ represents the balance of a savings account, what variable represents time? What is the principal? What is the interest rate?

   e. Graph $y = 5000(1 + 0.04)^x$ and $y = 10000$ in the same screen with a graphing calculator. Be careful to choose a window that shows both functions. List a table of values for the first function. Find the intersection of the functions to find how long it takes for the balance to reach $10,000.

11

Chapter 11 Mid-Chapter Test
(Lessons 11–1 through 11–4)

Graph each quadratic equation by making a table of values.

1. $y = 2x^2 + 1$

1.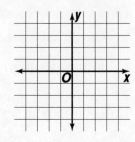

2. $y = -x^2 - 1$

2.

Graph each group of equations on the same screen. Compare and contrast the graphs.

3. $y = -x^2$
$y = -3x^2$
$y = -5x^2$

3. _____

4. $y = x^2$
$y = (x - 1)^2$
$y = (x - 3)^2$

4. _____

Describe how each graph changes from the parent graph of $y = x^2$. Then name the vertex of each graph.

5. $y = (x + 4)^2$

5. _____

6. $y = x^2 - 2$

6. _____

Solve each quadratic equation by graphing the related function. If exact roots cannot be found, state the consecutive integers between which the roots are located.

7. $x^2 + 6x + 9 = 0$

7. _____

8. $p^2 - 4p + 3 = 0$

8. _____

9. $m^2 + 5m + 2 = 0$

9. _____

10. $y^2 + y - 2 = 0$

10. _____

Solve each equation. Check your solution.

11. $m^2 - 9m + 8 = 0$

11. _____

12. $(s - 3)(s + 2) = 0$

12. _____

13. $-3s(s - 4) = 0$

13. _____

14. $m^2 - m - 6 = 0$

14. _____

NAME _____ DATE _____ PERIOD _____

Chapter 11 Quiz A
(Lessons 11–1 through 11–3)

1. Write the equation of the axis of symmetry and the coordinates of the vertex of the quadratic function $y = x^2 - 2x + 3$. Then graph the function.

1. _____

Describe how each graph changes from its parent graph of $y = x^2$. Then name the vertex of each graph.

2. $y = -3x^2$

2. _____

3. $y = (x + 2)^2$

3. _____

Solve each equation by graphing the related function. If exact roots cannot be found, state the consecutive integers between which the roots are located.

4. $x^2 + 6x - 7 = 0$

4. _____

5. $x^2 + 4x - 1 = 0$

5. _____

NAME _____ DATE _____ PERIOD _____

Chapter 11 Quiz B
(Lessons 11–4 through 11–7)

Solve each quadratic equation by factoring. Check your solution.

1. $-2n(n + 5) = 0$

1. _____

2. $x^2 + 10x + 16 = 0$

2. _____

Solve each quadratic equation by completing the square.

3. $x^2 - 4x - 5 = 0$

3. _____

4. $x^2 + 8x + 5 = 0$

4. _____

For Questions 5–6, use the Quadratic Formula to solve each equation.

5. $x^2 + 2x - 1 = 0$

5. _____

6. $x^2 + 7x - 8 = 0$

6. _____

7. Graph $y = 2^x - 2$. Then state the y-intercept.

7. _____

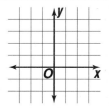

NAME _____ DATE _____ PERIOD _____

Chapter 11 Cumulative Review

1. Name the property of equality used to state that $36 + 0 = 36$.
   (Lesson 1–2)

   1. _____

2. Evaluate $8 + (-3) + (-9)$. *(Lesson 2–3)*

   2. _____

3. Simplify $(-3m)(-4n)$. *(Lesson 2–5)*

   3. _____

4. Solve $\frac{2}{3} = z - \left(-\frac{5}{6}\right)$. *(Lesson 3–6)*

   4. _____

5. Evaluate the expression $\frac{-j}{4}$ if $j = \frac{3}{4}$. *(Lesson 4–3)*

   5. _____

6. Solve $-8 - 0.6n = -9.5$. *(Lesson 4–5)*

   6. _____

7. Solve $\frac{6}{y} = \frac{18}{24}$. *(Lesson 5–1)*

   7. _____

8. Suppose you answered 34 questions correctly on a 40-question test. What percent did you answer correctly? *(Lesson 5–3)*

   8. _____

9. For the relation $\{(4, -3), (4, 2), (-2, 8), (-3, 6)\}$, find the domain. *(Lesson 6–1)*

   9. _____

10. Write the slope-intercept form of an equation for the line passing through the point at $(2, -4)$ and having a slope of $-\frac{1}{2}$. *(Lesson 7–3)*

    10. _____

11. For what value of k are the graphs of the lines $y = kx + 5$ and $y = \frac{3}{2}x - 2$ parallel? *(Lesson 7–7)*

    11. _____

12. Evaluate $6x + y^3$ if $x = -2$ and $y = -3$. *(Lesson 8–1)*

    12. _____

13. Simplify $(m^3n^2)(m^5n^4)$. *(Lesson 8–2)*

    13. _____

14. Simplify $(2x^2 + 4x - 2) + (-2 - x^2)$. *(Lesson 9–2)*

    14. _____

15. Find $(x - 2)(x + 4)$. *(Lesson 9–4)*

    15. _____

16. Find $(12x^3 + 8x^2) \div 4x$. *(Lesson 10–2)*

    16. _____

17. Solve $-b^2 - b + 9 = 0$. *(Lesson 11–6)*

    17. _____

Chapter 11 Standardized Test Practice
(Chapters 1–11)

Write the letter for the correct answer in the blank at the right of each problem.

1. Which equation represents the sentence *four more than twice a number is 8*?

   A. $n + 4 = 8$ **B.** $4n + 2 = 8$ **C.** $2n + 4 = 8$ **D.** $2n - 4 = 8$

   1. _____

2. Evaluate $|a| - b - c$ if $a = -6$, $b = -2$, and $c = 8$.

   A. -16 **B.** -4 **C.** 0 **D.** 16

   2. _____

3. Find the median of the data 18, 28, 12, 14, and 28.

   A. 12   **B.** 18   **C.** 20   **D.** 28

   3. _____

4. For what value of x is $-38 = x - (-8)$ true?

   A. -46 **B.** -30 **C.** 30 **D.** 46

   4. _____

5. For what value of x is $-\dfrac{x}{4} = -12$ true?

   A. -48 **B.** -3 **C.** 3 **D.** 48

   5. _____

6. For what value of x is $16 = 3x + 2 + 2x - 8$ true?

   A. -2 **B.** 1.2 **C.** 2 **D.** 4.4

   6. _____

7. Find the value of x in $\dfrac{x - 8}{x + 2} = \dfrac{2}{12}$.

   A. -10 **B.** 1 **C.** 10 **D.** 12

   7. _____

8. A card is drawn from a deck of ten cards numbered 1 through 10. The card is replaced, the deck is shuffled, and another card is drawn. Find the probability that an odd number is drawn first and an even number is drawn second.

   A. $\dfrac{1}{10}$ **B.** $\dfrac{1}{4}$ **C.** $\dfrac{1}{2}$ **D.** 1

   8. _____

9. Which is the correct graph of $2x + 3y = 12$?

   A. 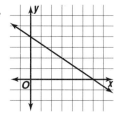   **B.**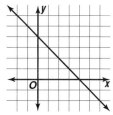

   C. 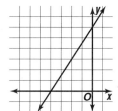   **D.**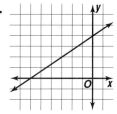

   9. _____

10. The volume of a gas varies directly with its temperature. If the volume of a gas is 100 milliliters when the temperature is 10°, find the volume when the temperature is 25°.

    A. 40 mL   **B.** 150 mL   **C.** 250 mL   **D.** 1500 mL

    10. _____

11

Chapter 11 Standardized Test Practice
(Chapters 1–11) *(continued)*

11. Determine the equation of the line shown at the right.

    A. $y = -\frac{1}{2}x + 3$ **B.** $y = -2x + 3$

    C. $y = \frac{1}{2}x + 3$ **D.** $y = 2x + 3$

    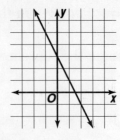

    11. _____

12. Find the slope-intercept form of an equation for the line that is perpendicular to the line $y = -\frac{3}{2}x - 2$ and that passes through the point at $(-3, 4)$.

    A. $y = -\frac{3}{2}x + 6$ **B.** $y = \frac{2}{3}x + 6$

    C. $y = -\frac{2}{3}x + 6$ **D.** $y = -\frac{3}{2}x + 6$

    12. _____

13. Simplify $\frac{15x^5y^3}{20x^{-2}y^5}$.

    A. $\frac{3x^7y^8}{4}$ **B.** $\frac{3x^7y^2}{4}$ **C.** $\frac{3x^7}{4y^2}$ **D.** $\frac{3x^3}{4y^2}$

    13. _____

14. The following numbers represent the lengths of the sides of a triangle. Which *cannot* represent a right triangle?

    A. 6, 8, 10 **B.** 7, 24, 25 **C.** 10, 24, 26 **D.** 15, 25, 35

    14. _____

15. For what value of x is $-3(2x - 3) + 8 = -2(x - 1) - 1$ true?

    A. 0 **B.** $\frac{9}{4}$ **C.** $\frac{5}{2}$ **D.** 4

    15. _____

16. Which expression represents $(3x - 4)(x + 2)$?

    A. $3x^2 + 2x - 8$ **B.** $3x^2 - 8x - 8$
    C. $3x^2 - 2x - 8$ **D.** $3x^2 + 2x - 2$

    16. _____

17. Factor $x^2 + x - 12$.

    A. $(x - 2)(x + 6)$ **B.** $(x - 3)(x + 4)$
    C. $(x - 4)(x + 3)$ **D.** $(x - 4)(x - 3)$

    17. _____

18. Which of the following is *not* a perfect square trinomial?

    A. $x^2 + 2x + 1$ **B.** $x^2 - 8x - 16$
    C. $x^2 + 6x + 9$ **D.** $x^2 - 10x + 25$

    18. _____

19. Which of the following is the vertex of the graph of $y = -x^2 - 2x$?

    A. $(0, 0)$ **B.** $(1, -1)$ **C.** $(-2, 0)$ **D.** $(-1, 1)$

    19. _____

20. Which of the following is a root of the equation $(y + 2)^2 = 23$?

    A. 5 **B.** $-2 - \sqrt{23}$ **C.** $2 - \sqrt{23}$ **D.** 21

    20. _____

Chapter 11 Answer Key

Form 1A

Page 201

1. __D__

2. __A__

3. __A__

4. __C__

5. __A__

6. __B__

7. __B__

8. __C__

9. __B__

Page 202

10. __B__

11. __B__

12. __C__

13. __D__

14. __B__

15. __D__

16. __B__

17. __C__

18. __B__

19. __B__

20. __C__

Bonus __C__

Form 1B

Page 203

1. __C__

2. __A__

3. __C__

4. __B__

5. __B__

6. __A__

7. __B__

8. __B__

9. __C__

Page 204

10. __B__

11. __B__

12. __C__

13. __C__

14. __B__

15. __C__

16. __D__

17. __C__

18. __B__

19. __B__

20. __B__

Bonus __D__

Algebra: Concepts and Applications

Chapter 11 Answer Key

Form 2A

Page 205

1.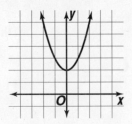

2.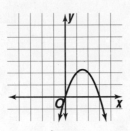

3. $x = -2$; $(-2, -1)$

4. up 3 units; (0, 3); (0, 0)

5. narrows; opens down; (0, 0), (0, 0)

6. all 3 open up; shift one unit right for each graph

7. $-1, -2$

8. between -5 and -4; between 1 and 2

9. 1, 4

10. 1, -6

11. 0, -5

12. 0, 2

13. $-1, 8$

14. 1, -5

Page 206

15. 4

16. 25

17. $-1, -5$

18. 1, 11

19. 1, 9

20. $-1, -6$

21. $\frac{3}{2}, -4$

22. no real solutions

23.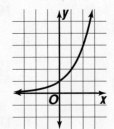

24.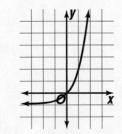

25. $2315.25

Bonus ___ 3.85 yr

1.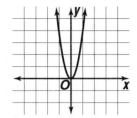

2.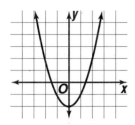

3. $x = 0; (0, 0)$

4. down 1 unit; $(0, -1); (0, 0)$

5. narrows; opens down; $(0, 0); (0, 0)$

6. all graphs open upward; graphs shift left

7. 1, 3

8. between -7 and -6; between 0 and 1

9. 1, 5

10. 1, -8

11. 0, 1

12. 0, -4

13. $-5, 6$

14. $-1, -2$

15. 64

16. 16

17. 1, -5

18. 0, 8

19. $-1, -7$

20. $-11, -1$

21. 2, 5

22. no real solutions

23.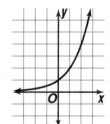

24.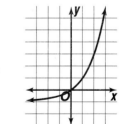

25. $4866.61

Bonus 1.73 yr

Algebra: Concepts and Applications

Chapter 11 Answer Key

Open-Ended Assessment
Sample Answers
Page 209

1. a. 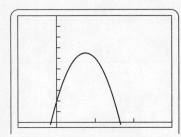 ; parabola

b. $x = 0.75$; (0.75, 13)

c. 4 ft

d. 0.75 s

e. 13 ft; no; a person cannot jump that high.

f. 1.65 s

2. a. $5624.32

b. $4744.85

c. At a rate of 3% for 4 years, the amount is $2251.02; at a rate of 3.5% for 3 years, the amount is $2217.44. The account that earned 3% for 4 years has the greater value.

d. x = time; principal = $5000; interest rate = 4%

e.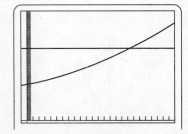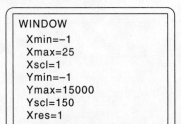

X	Y1	
0	5000	
1	5200	
2	5408	
3	5624.3	
4	5849.3	
5	6083.3	
6	6326.6	
X=6		

The intersection is approximately (17.673,10000); it takes about 17.7 years for the balance to double and reach $10,000.

Chapter 11 Answer Key

Mid-Chapter Test
Page 210

1.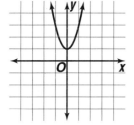

2.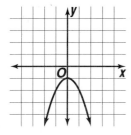

3. all graphs open downwards; the graphs get narrower

4. all graphs open upwards; the graphs shift right

5. shift left 4 units; (−4, 0)

6. shift down 2 units, (0, −2)

7. −3

8. 1, 3

9. between −5 and −4, between −1 and 0

10. −2, 1

11. 1, 8

12. −2, 3

13. 0, 4

14. −2, 3

Quiz A
Page 211

1. $x = 1; (1, 2)$

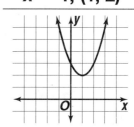

2. narrows, opens down; (0, 0)

3. shifts left 2 units; (−2, 0)

4. −7, 1

5. between −5 and −4, between 0 and 1

Quiz B
Page 211

1. 0, −5

2. −2, −8

3. −1, 5

4. $-4 \pm \sqrt{11}$

5. $-1 \pm \sqrt{2}$

6. −8, 1

7. −1

Algebra: Concepts and Applications

Chapter 11 Answer Key

Cumulative Review
Page 212

1. Additive Identity Property

2. -4

3. $12mn$

4. $-\dfrac{1}{6}$

5. $-\dfrac{3}{16}$

6. 2.5

7. 8

8. 85%

9. $\{-3, -2, 4\}$

10. $y = -\dfrac{1}{2}x - 3$

11. $\dfrac{3}{2}$

12. -39

13. m^8n^6

14. $x^2 + 4x - 4$

15. $x^2 + 2x - 8$

16. $3x^2 + 2x$

17. $\dfrac{1 \pm \sqrt{37}}{-2}$

Standardized Test Practice
Page 213

1. C

2. C

3. B

4. A

5. D

6. D

7. C

8. B

9. A

10. C

Page 214

11. B

12. B

13. C

14. D

15. D

16. A

17. B

18. B

19. D

20. B

12

Chapter 12 Test, Form 1A

Write the letter for the correct answer in the blank at the right of each problem.

1. Which of the following inequalities describes a number that is less than or equal to 12?

   A. $x > 12$ **B.** $x \geq 12$ **C.** $x < 12$ **D.** $x \leq 12$

   1. _____

2. Which is the graph of $x < 5$?

   A.   3 4 5 6 7   **B.**   3 4 5 6 7   **C.**   3 4 5 6 7   **D.**   3 4 5 6 7

   2. _____

3. Which inequality matches the graph at the right?

   0 1 2 3 4 5 6 7 8 9

   A. $x \leq 4$ **B.** $x \geq 4$ **C.** $x < 4$ **D.** $x > 4$

   3. _____

4. Which is the solution of $n + 8 > -5$?

   A. $\{n \mid n > -13\}$ **B.** $\{n \mid n < -13\}$ **C.** $\{n \mid n < 3\}$ **D.** $\{n \mid n > 3\}$

   4. _____

5. Which is the solution of $x - 5 \leq -2$?

   A. $\{x \mid x \leq -7\}$ **B.** $\{x \mid x \geq -7\}$ **C.** $\{x \mid x \leq 3\}$ **D.** $\{x \mid x \geq 3\}$

   5. _____

6. Which is the graph of the solution of $2 < 3 + m$?

   A.   -1 0 1 2 3   **B.**   -1 0 1 2 3   **C.**   -3 -2 -1 0 1   **D.**   -3 -2 -1 0 1

   6. _____

For Questions 7–13, solve each inequality.

7. $-5x \leq 20$

   A. $\{x \mid x \leq -4\}$ **B.** $\{x \mid x \geq -4\}$ **C.** $\{x \mid x \leq 25\}$ **D.** $\{x \mid x \geq -100\}$

   7. _____

8. $\frac{x}{3} > 6$

   A. $\{x \mid x < -18\}$ **B.** $\{x \mid x > 18\}$ **C.** $\{x \mid x < -2\}$ **D.** $\{x \mid x > -18\}$

   8. _____

9. $-2x \geq 8$

   A. $\{x \mid x \leq -4\}$ **B.** $\{x \mid x \geq -4\}$ **C.** $\{x \mid x \leq -16\}$ **D.** $\{x \mid x \leq 16\}$

   9. _____

10. $-12 > -4w$

   A. $\{w \mid w < 3\}$ **B.** $\{w \mid w > 3\}$ **C.** $\{w \mid w < -48\}$ **D.** $\{w \mid w > 48\}$

   10. _____

11. $3p - 6 > 12$

   A. $\{p \mid p < 2\}$ **B.** $\{p \mid p > 2\}$ **C.** $\{p \mid p < 6\}$ **D.** $\{p \mid p > 6\}$

   11. _____

12. $8 \leq 12 - 4x$

   A. $\{x \mid x \leq 1\}$ **B.** $\{x \mid x \geq -5\}$ **C.** $\{x \mid x \leq 5\}$ **D.** $\{x \mid x \leq 11\}$

   12. _____

13. $3 - 2x > 7$

   A. $\{x \mid x < 2\}$ **B.** $\{x \mid x > -2\}$ **C.** $\{x \mid x < 5\}$ **D.** $\{x \mid x < -2\}$

   13. _____

14. Which is the solution of $-10 \leq 12 - 2x$?

   A. $\{x \mid x \leq -1\}$ **B.** $\{x \mid x \geq -1\}$ **C.** $\{x \mid x \geq -11\}$ **D.** $\{x \mid x \leq 11\}$

   14. _____

15. Write the compound inequality $y \leq 3$ and $y \geq -2$ without using the word *and*.

   A. $-2 \geq y \geq 3$ **B.** $-2 \leq y \leq 3$ **C.** $y \leq -2$ **D.** $y \geq -6$

   15. _____

    221   *Algebra: Concepts and Applications*

12

Chapter 12 Test, Form 1A *(continued)*

16. Which is the graph of $x < -4$ or $x > 1$?

A. ![number line -3 to 6] B. ![number line -6 to 3]

C. ![number line -6 to 3] D. ![number line -6 to 3]

16. _____

17. Which graph matches the compound inequality $-3 \le x < 1$?

A. ![number line -6 to 3] B. ![number line -6 to 3]

C. ![number line -6 to 3] D. ![number line -6 to 3]

17. _____

Solve each compound inequality.

18. $-3 \le x - 1 < 4$

A. $\{x \mid -4 \le x < 3\}$ B. $\{x \mid -2 \le x < 5\}$

C. $\{x \mid -4 \le x < 5\}$ D. $\{x \mid -2 \le x < 3\}$

18. _____

19. $x - 2 > 4$ or $x + 3 < 6$

A. $\{x \mid 3 < x < 6\}$ B. $\{x \mid x > 6$ or $x < 3\}$

C. $\{x \mid x < -6$ or $x > 3\}$ D. $\{x \mid x > -6$ or $x < -3\}$

19. _____

For Questions 20–22, solve each inequality.

20. $|5x| < 20$

A. $\{x \mid x > -4\}$ B. $\{x \mid x < -4\}$

C. $\{x \mid -4 < x < 4\}$ D. $\{x \mid x > 4\}$

20. _____

21. $|x + 2| < 6$

A. $\{x \mid x < 4\}$ B. $\{x \mid -4 < x < 4\}$

C. $\{x \mid -8 < x < 4\}$ D. $\{x \mid -8 > x > 4\}$

21. _____

22. $|x - 3| \ge 6$

A. $\{x \mid x \le 9\}$ B. $\{x \mid x \ge -9$ or $x \le 3\}$

C. $\{x \mid x \ge 9$ or $x \le -3\}$ D. $\{x \mid -3 \le x \le 9\}$

22. _____

23. Which inequality is shown in the graph?

A. $x \ge 2$ B. $x \le 2$

C. $y \ge 2$ D. $y \le 2$

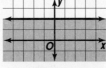

23. _____

24. Which inequality is shown in the graph?

A. $y > x + 3$ B. $y > x - 3$

C. $y > -x - 3$ D. $y < -x - 3$

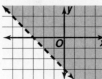

24. _____

25. Which inequality is shown in the graph?

A. $y \le x + 2$ B. $y \le \frac{1}{2}x + 1$

C. $y \ge 2x + 1$ D. $y \le 2x + 1$

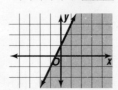

25. _____

Bonus Graph $y \le x + 2$ and $y > \frac{1}{2}x + 2$ on the same coordinate plane.

Which point is contained in both graphs?

A. $(2, 4)$ B. $(0, 3)$ C. $(-2, 0)$ D. $(-4, 4)$ **Bonus** _____

          Algebra: Concepts and Applications

12

Chapter 12 Test, Form 1B

Write the letter for the correct answer in the blank at the right of each problem.

1. Which of the following inequalities describes a number that is more than 8?

    A. $x > 8$ **B.** $x \geq 8$ **C.** $x < 8$ **D.** $x \leq 8$

    1. _____

2. Which is the graph of $x > -2$?

    A. **B.** **C.** **D.**

    2. _____

3. Which inequality matches the graph at the right?

    A. $x \leq -3$ **B.** $x \geq -3$ **C.** $x < -3$ **D.** $x > -3$

    3. _____

4. Which is the solution of $n - 6 > -2$?

    A. $\{n \mid n > 4\}$ **B.** $\{n \mid n < 4\}$ **C.** $\{n \mid n < -8\}$ **D.** $\{n \mid n > -8\}$

    4. _____

5. Which is the solution of $x + 3 \leq -5$?

    A. $\{x \mid x \leq -8\}$ **B.** $\{x \mid x \geq -8\}$ **C.** $\{x \mid x \leq -2\}$ **D.** $\{x \mid x \geq -2\}$

    5. _____

6. Which is the graph of the solution of $-1 < -2 + x$?

    A. **B.** **C.** **D.**

    6. _____

For Questions 7–13, solve each inequality.

7. $-3x \leq 12$

    A. $\{x \mid x \leq -4\}$ **B.** $\{x \mid x \geq -4\}$ **C.** $\{x \mid x \leq 15\}$ **D.** $\{x \mid x \geq -36\}$

    7. _____

8. $\frac{x}{4} < -8$

    A. $\{x \mid x < -32\}$ **B.** $\{x \mid x > -32\}$ **C.** $\{x \mid x < -2\}$ **D.** $\{x \mid x > -2\}$

    8. _____

9. $-4x \geq 16$

    A. $\{x \mid x \leq -64\}$ **B.** $\{x \mid x \geq -4\}$ **C.** $\{x \mid x \leq -4\}$ **D.** $\{x \mid x \leq 64\}$

    9. _____

10. $-9 < -3w$

    A. $\{w \mid w < 3\}$ **B.** $\{w \mid w > 3\}$ **C.** $\{w \mid w < -27\}$ **D.** $\{w \mid w > 27\}$

    10. _____

11. $2p - 4 > 16$

    A. $\{p \mid p < 6\}$ **B.** $\{p \mid p > 6\}$ **C.** $\{p \mid p < 10\}$ **D.** $\{p \mid p > 10\}$

    11. _____

12. $12 \leq 16 - 4x$

    A. $\{x \mid x \leq -1\}$ **B.** $\{x \mid x \geq -7\}$ **C.** $\{x \mid x \leq 7\}$ **D.** $\{x \mid x \leq 1\}$

    12. _____

13. $6 - 3x > 3$

    A. $\{x \mid x < 1\}$ **B.** $\{x \mid x > -1\}$ **C.** $\{x \mid x < 3\}$ **D.** $\{x \mid x < -3\}$

    13. _____

14. Which is the solution of $-6 \leq 12 - 3x$?

    A. $\{x \mid x \leq 2\}$ **B.** $\{x \mid x \geq 6\}$ **C.** $\{x \mid x \geq -6\}$ **D.** $\{x \mid x \leq 6\}$

    14. _____

15. Write the compound inequality $y \leq 2$ and $y \geq -3$ without using the word *and*.

    A. $-3 \geq y \geq 2$ **B.** $-3 \leq y \leq 2$ **C.** $y \leq 2$ **D.** $y \geq -6$

    15. _____

       Algebra: Concepts and Applications

16. Which is the graph of $x < -2$ or $x \geq 3$?

A.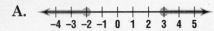

B.

C.

D.

16. _____

17. Which graph matches the compound inequality $-2 \leq x < 4$?

A.

B.

C.

D.

17. _____

Solve each compound inequality.

18. $-2 \leq x + 2 < 5$

   A. $\{x \mid -4 \leq x < 3\}$ B. $\{x \mid 0 \leq x < 7\}$

   C. $\{x \mid -4 \leq x < 7\}$ D. $\{x \mid 0 \leq x < 3\}$

18. _____

19. $x - 4 > 6$ or $x + 2 < 4$

   A. $\{x \mid 2 < x < 10\}$ B. $\{x \mid x > 10$ or $x < 2\}$

   C. $\{x \mid x < -10$ or $x > 2\}$ D. $\{x \mid x > -10$ or $x < -2\}$

19. _____

For Questions 20–22, solve each Inequality.

20. $|6x| < 24$

   A. $\{x \mid x > -4\}$ B. $\{x \mid x < -4\}$

   C. $\{x \mid -4 < x < 4\}$ D. $\{x \mid x > 4\}$

20. _____

21. $|x + 4| < 8$

   A. $\{x \mid x < 4\}$ B. $\{x \mid -4 < x < 4\}$

   C. $\{x \mid -12 < x < 4\}$ D. $\{x \mid -12 > x > 4\}$

21. _____

22. $|x - 2| \geq 7$

   A. $\{x \mid x \leq 9\}$ B. $\{x \mid x \geq -5$ or $x \leq 9\}$

   C. $\{x \mid x \geq 9$ or $x \leq -5\}$ D. $\{x \mid -5 \leq x \leq 9\}$

22. _____

23. Which inequality is shown in the graph?

   A. $x \geq 4$ B. $x \leq 4$

   C. $y \geq 4$ D. $y \leq 4$

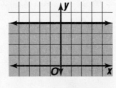

23. _____

24. Which inequality is shown in the graph?

   A. $y \leq -2x + 3$ B. $y \geq 2x - 3$

   C. $y \leq -2x - 3$ D. $y \geq -2x + 3$

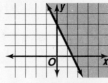

24. _____

25. Which inequality is shown in the graph?

   A. $y < -x - 1$ B. $y > -x - 1$

   C. $y \geq -x - 1$ D. $y < x - 1$

25. _____

Bonus Graph $y > x - 2$ and $y \leq -\frac{1}{2}x + 3$ on the same coordinate plane.

Which point is contained in both graphs?

   A. $(7, -2)$ **B.** $(0, 4)$ **C.** $(-2, 0)$ **D.** $(6, 4)$ **Bonus** _____

Chapter 12 Test, Form 2A

Write an inequality to describe each number. Use x as the variable.

1. a number that is at least -2

1. _____

2. a number that has a maximum value of 8

2. _____

For Questions 3–5, graph each inequality on a number line.

3. $x \leq 5$

3.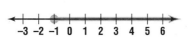

4. $y > -3$

4. ![number line -4 to 5]

5. $d < 1.5$

5. ![number line -4 to 5]

6. Write an inequality for the graph at the right.

![number line -3 to 6]

6. _____

Solve each inequality.

7. $x + 4 \leq 2$

7. _____

8. $y - 8 > -4$

8. _____

9. $r - 3 < -5$

9. _____

10. $12 \leq y + 5$

10. _____

11. $-4.2 \geq p - 1.8$

11. _____

12. $\frac{5}{4} \geq y + \frac{1}{4}$

12. _____

13. $-8h < 32$

13. _____

14. $\frac{g}{6} > -3$

14. _____

15. $8y \geq 64$

15. _____

16. $-3t \leq 33$

16. _____

17. $16 < \frac{y}{-4}$

17. _____

18. $-\frac{1}{5}v \geq 5$

18. _____

19. $4h - 3 < 21$

19. _____

20. $3b + 14 \geq 11$

20. _____

Solve each inequality.

21. $12 \le 8y + 4$

22. $6 - 2x > 22$

23. $\frac{y}{3} - 4 \ge 12$

24. $8 + 0.2h > 2$

21. _____

22. _____

23. _____

24. _____

Graph the solution of each compound inequality.

25. $x > 1$ and $x < 4$

26. $y > 3$ or $y < -2$

27. $m \le 2$ and $m > -4$

25. ![number line from -4 to 5]

26. ![number line from -4 to 5]

27. ![number line from -5 to 4]

Solve each inequality. Graph the solution.

28. $|3x| < 12$

28. _____

![number line from -4 to 5]

29. $|p + 1| \le 4$

29. _____

![number line from -5 to 4]

30. $|z - 2| \ge 1$

30. _____

![number line from -4 to 5]

For Questions 31–33, graph each inequality.

31. $y \le 3x - 1$

31.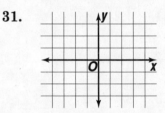

32. $y > -2x + 2$

32.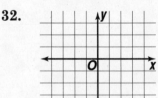

33. $y < -x + 3$

33.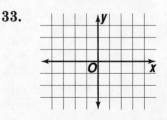

Bonus Solve the inequality $1 < |n - 1| < 3$. (*Hint:* There are two cases, one where $n - 1$ is positive and one where $n - 1$ is negative.)

Bonus _____

12

Chapter 12 Test, Form 2B

Write an inequality to describe each number. Use x as the variable.

1. a number greater than 3

1. _____

2. a number less than -5

2. _____

For Questions 3–5, graph each inequality on a number line.

3. $x \geq -2$

3. ← +++++++++ →
   -4 -3 -2 -1 0 1 2 3 4 5

4. $y < 1$

4. ← +++++++++ →
   -4 -3 -2 -1 0 1 2 3 4 5

5. $d > -2.5$

5. ← +++++++++ →
   -4 -3 -2 -1 0 1 2 3 4 5

6. Write an inequality for the graph at the right.

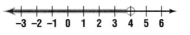
-3 -2 -1 0 1 2 3 4 5 6

6. _____

Solve each inequality.

7. $x - 3 \leq 5$

7. _____

8. $y + 4 > -2$

8. _____

9. $p + 2 < -6$

9. _____

10. $10 \leq y - 4$

10. _____

11. $-3.1 \geq p + 1.4$

11. _____

12. $-\frac{2}{3} < y - \frac{1}{3}$

12. _____

13. $-6h > 36$

13. _____

14. $\frac{d}{-2} < -4$

14. _____

15. $-2y \leq 26$

15. _____

16. $-8t \geq 32$

16. _____

17. $18 > \frac{x}{-3}$

17. _____

18. $-\frac{1}{4}v > 12$

18. _____

19. $3h + 6 < 33$

19. _____

20. $2b - 12 \geq 13$

20. _____

Solve each inequality.

21. $18 \leq 6y - 12$

22. $8 - 3x > 35$

23. $\frac{b}{12} - 2 \geq 4$

24. $10 + 1.2h > 0.4$

21. _____

22. _____

23. _____

24. _____

Graph the solution of each compound inequality.

25. $x < 2$ and $x > -4$

26. $y > 5$ or $y < -1$

27. $m \leq 3$ and $m > -1$

25.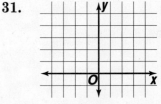

26.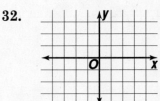

27.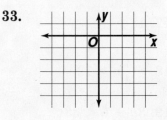

Solve each inequality. Graph the solution.

28. $|2x| < 8$

28. _____

29. $|p + 2| \leq 6$

29. _____

30. $|z + 3| \geq 2$

30. _____

For Questions 31–33, graph each inequality.

31. $y \leq 2x + 3$

31.

32. $y > -3x - 1$

32.

33. $y < -x - 4$

33.

Bonus Solve the inequality $1 < |n| < 3$. (*Hint:* There are two cases, one where n is positive and one where n is negative.)

Bonus _____

12

Chapter 12 Open-Ended Assessment

Instructions: Demonstrate your knowledge by giving a clear, concise solution for each problem. Be sure to include all relevant graphs and to justify your answers. You may show your solutions in more than one way or investigate beyond the requirements of the problem.

1. Suppose all persons who use a local airport live in any direction within 30 miles, inclusive, of the airport.

   a. Let d represent the distance that a person lives from the airport. Write and graph an absolute value inequality for d for all persons who use the airport.

   b. What is the maximum distance traveled to use the airport?

   c. The residents of Town A use the local airport. What is the airport's distance from Town A? Express the answer as an inequality.

   d. Suppose the residents of Town B do not use the local airport because they live outside the range given in part b. Write an absolute value inequality to describe Town B's distance from the airport.

2. Two friends pool their money to buy CDs and music tapes. Together they have $150. Each CD costs $15 and each tape costs $10. They want to know how many of each type they can buy. Let x represent the number of CDs that can be purchased. Let y represent the number of tapes that can be purchased.

   a. Write an inequality involving x that represents the number of CDs alone that can be purchased. *Note:* They cannot buy a negative number of CDs.

   b. Write an inequality involving y that represents the number of tapes alone that can be purchased.

   c. Write an inequality that represents the number of each that can be purchased.

   d. Graph parts a–c on the same coordinate plane. Shade the solution representing all conditions in the problem. Use "dots" for integer values for points in your graph.

   e. List at least three integer points that are solutions. How many of each type can be purchased?

   f. If they want to buy exactly 4 CDs, how many tapes can be purchased? Represent the solution as an inequality.

12

Chapter 12 Mid-Chapter Test
(Lessons 12–1 through 12–4)

1. The average summer temperature t in one region is less than 72 degrees Fahrenheit. Express t as an inequality.

1. _____

2. An *acute angle* has a measure less than 90 degrees. If the measure of a particular acute angle is $2x$, write an inequality to express the value of x.

2. _____

3. Write an inequality to describe the maximum number of tickets that can be sold for a hockey game if the hockey arena has 2000 seats.

3. _____

4. Write an inequality for the graph at the right.

$$\xleftarrow{\hspace{0.5em}}\begin{array}{ccccccccccc} & & & & & & & & & & \\ -3 & -2 & -1 & 0 & 1 & 2 & 3 & 4 & 5 & 6 \end{array}\xrightarrow{\hspace{0.5em}}$$

4. _____

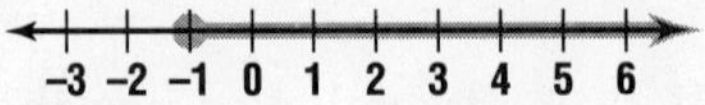

5. Graph all numbers greater than or equal to 4.

5. $\xleftarrow{\hspace{0.5em}}\begin{array}{ccccccccccc} -4 & -3 & -2 & -1 & 0 & 1 & 2 & 3 & 4 & 5 \end{array}\xrightarrow{\hspace{0.5em}}$

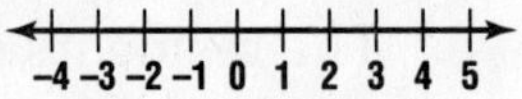

Solve each inequality. Graph the solution.

6. $n + 4 \leq 2$

6. _____
$\xleftarrow{\hspace{0.5em}}\begin{array}{cccccccccc} -4 & -3 & -2 & -1 & 0 & 1 & 2 & 3 & 4 & 5 \end{array}\xrightarrow{\hspace{0.5em}}$

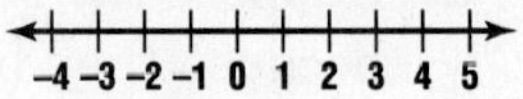

7. $g - 8 > -4$

7. _____
$\xleftarrow{\hspace{0.5em}}\begin{array}{cccccccccc} -4 & -3 & -2 & -1 & 0 & 1 & 2 & 3 & 4 & 5 \end{array}\xrightarrow{\hspace{0.5em}}$

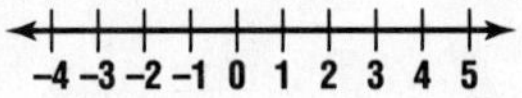

8. $6z + 3 > 7z$

8. _____
$\xleftarrow{\hspace{0.5em}}\begin{array}{cccccccccc} -4 & -3 & -2 & -1 & 0 & 1 & 2 & 3 & 4 & 5 \end{array}\xrightarrow{\hspace{0.5em}}$

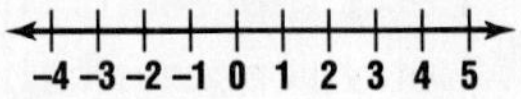

9. $5y \geq -25$

9. _____
$\xleftarrow{\hspace{0.5em}}\begin{array}{ccccccccccc} -6 & -5 & -4 & -3 & -2 & -1 & 0 & 1 & 2 & 3 \end{array}\xrightarrow{\hspace{0.5em}}$

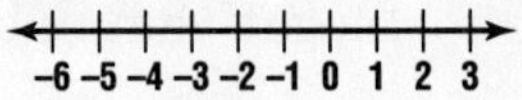

10. $-\dfrac{v}{2} > 4$

10. _____
$\xleftarrow{\hspace{0.5em}}\begin{array}{ccccccccccc} -10 & -9 & -8 & -7 & -6 & -5 & -4 & -3 & -2 & -1 \end{array}\xrightarrow{\hspace{0.5em}}$

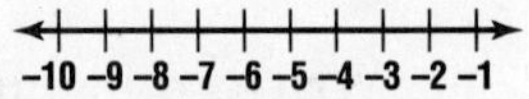

11. $\dfrac{y}{3} > -6$

11. _____
$\xleftarrow{\hspace{0.5em}}\begin{array}{ccccc} -20 & -18 & -16 & -14 & -12 \end{array}\xrightarrow{\hspace{0.5em}}$

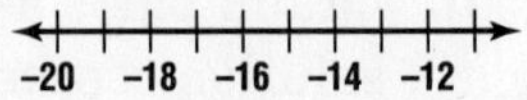

Solve each inequality.

12. $4n - 8 \leq 12$

12. _____

13. $-3 - 4z > 6z$

13. _____

14. $\dfrac{1}{2}x - 3 \leq 5$

14. _____

15. $\dfrac{n}{4} + 6 < -2$

15. _____

Algebra: Concepts and Applications

NAME _____ DATE _____ PERIOD _____

Chapter 12 Quiz A
(Lessons 12–1 through 12–3)

Graph each inequality on a number line.

1. $x < -3$

1. ![number line from -6 to 3]
    -6 -5 -4 -3 -2 -1 0 1 2 3

2. $2 \leq z$

2. ![number line from -3 to 6]
    -3 -2 -1 0 1 2 3 4 5 6

Solve each inequality. Check the solution.

3. $n - 3 \geq 8$

3. _____

4. $6 + g < 2$

4. _____

5. $7y \leq 28$

5. _____

6. $-\dfrac{v}{6} \leq 2$

6. _____

NAME _____ DATE _____ PERIOD _____

Chapter 12 Quiz B
(Lessons 12–4 through 12–7)

1. Solve $-8 + 4z > 6z$. Check your solution.

1. _____

For Question 2–3, solve each compound inequality. Graph the solution.

2. $1 < 3 + z < 6$

2. _____

    -5 -4 -3 -2 -1 0 1 2 3 4

3. $p + 3 > 4$ or $p - 2 < -2$

3. _____

    -4 -3 -2 -1 0 1 2 3 4 5

4. Solve $|2 + z| > 8$. Graph the solution.

4. _____

    -10 -8 -6 -4 -2 0 2 4 6

5. Graph $-2y < -8$.

5. ![number line from -4 to 5]
    -4 -3 -2 -1 0 1 2 3 4 5

6. Graph $x - y \geq -3$.

6.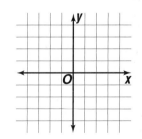

Chapter 12 Cumulative Review

1. Simplify $12x - 3 - 8x + 4$. *(Lesson 1–4)*

2. Give the coordinates of the points graphed at the right. *(Lesson 2–1)*
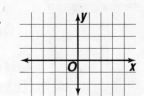
$$-5 \quad -4 \quad -3 \quad -2 \quad -1 \quad 0 \quad 1 \quad 2 \quad 3 \quad 4$$

3. Simplify $-34 \div (-17)$. *(Lesson 2–6)*

4. Solve $k + (-6) = -13$. *(Lesson 3–6)*

5. Simplify $-9.5 \div 5$. *(Lesson 4–3)*

6. Solve $\frac{2}{3}x = 6$. *(Lesson 4–4)*

7. Solve $\frac{y}{6} = \frac{y+3}{24}$. *(Lesson 5–1)*

8. A single die labeled 1 through 6 is rolled. Find the odds of rolling a number greater than 4. *(Lesson 5–6)*

9. Graph $y = -2x + 2$. *(Lesson 6–3)*

10. Suppose y varies inversely as x and $y = 12$ when $x = -4$. Find y when $x = 2$. *(Lesson 6–6)*

11. For what value of k are the graphs of $y = kx + 5$ and $y = \frac{1}{2}x + 1$ perpendicular? *(Lesson 7–7)*

12. A triangle has sides of 7, 8, and 12 inches. Determine whether the triangle is a right triangle. *(Lesson 8–7)*

13. Simplify $(x + 3)(x - 5)$. *(Lesson 9–4)*

14. Factor $8x^3 - 4x^2y$. *(Lesson 10–2)*

15. Factor $2x^2 + 7x + 5$. *(Lesson 10–4)*

16. Use the Quadratic Formula to solve $x^2 - x - 6 = 0$. *(Lesson 11–6)*

17. Graph $y = 2^x + 1$. *(Lesson 11–7)*

18. The minimum telephone service costs the Smiths $24.95 per month. Express the monthly cost as an inequality using the variable x. *(Lesson 12–1)*

19. Solve $|x + 8| < 2$. *(Lesson 12–6)*

20. Graph $y \le -x - 2$. *(Lesson 12–7)*

1. _____

2. _____

3. _____

4. _____

5. _____

6. _____

7. _____

8. _____

9.

10. _____

11. _____

12. _____

13. _____

14. _____

15. _____

16. _____

17.

18. _____

19. _____

20.

Algebra: Concepts and Applications

12

Chapter 12 Standardized Test Practice
(Chapters 1–12)

Write the letter for the correct answer in the blank at the right of each problem.

1. Tell which sentence represents the equation $n + 8 = 12$.
   A. Eight more than a number is twelve.
   B. Twelve more than a number is eight.
   C. Eight is twelve less than a number.
   D. The difference of a number and eight is twelve.   1. _____

2. Suppose you wanted to buy a music CD and DVD movie. The movie costs $10 more than the CD. The CD costs $15. Which of the following statements is true?
   A. The movie costs $25.   B. The movie costs $10.
   C. Together, they cost $25.   D. None are true.   2. _____

3. Evaluate $|-5| - |3|$.
   A. -8 B. -2 C. 2   D. 8   3. _____

4. In a football game, the team first lost 18 yards, then gained 16 yards. Which integer represents the net gain in yards?
   A. -34 B. -2 C. 2   D. 34   4. _____

5. For what value in the replacement set $\{-1, 0, 1, 2\}$ is the equation $x + 4 = 3x$ true?
   A. -1 B. 0   C. 1   D. 2   5. _____

6. For what value of x is the equation $-24 = x - (-6)$ true?
   A. -30 B. -18 C. 18   D. 30   6. _____

7. A sandwich can be made of turkey, tuna, or ham and be put on white or wheat bread. Find the number of possible sandwiches.
   A. 2   B. 3   C. 5   D. 6   7. _____

8. For what value of x is $-23 = 3x + 4$ true?
   A. -27 B. -19 C. -9 D. 9   8. _____

9. A coat was on sale for $75. It originally cost $90. Which of the following represents the percent of change?
   A. 15%   B. 16.7%   C. 20%   D. 120%   9. _____

10. Ten cards in a deck are numbered from 1 to 10. A card is drawn and then replaced. Another card is drawn. Find the probability of drawing a 4 and then a 3.
    A. $\frac{1}{100}$ B. $\frac{1}{10}$ C. $\frac{1}{5}$ D. $\frac{1}{2}$ 10. _____

11. Which ordered pair is *not* a solution to $2x - 3y = 6$?
    A. $(4, 0)$ B. $(0, -2)$ C. $(3, 0)$ D. $(-3, -4)$ 11. _____

12. The number of gallons of gas needed to drive on a trip varies directly as the number of miles traveled. If 20 gallons of gas are used to drive 250 miles, how many gallons are used to drive 400 miles?
    A. 30 gal   B. 32 gal   C. 40 gal   D. 64 gal   12. _____

13. Determine the equation of the line shown at the right.

    A. $y = -\frac{1}{2}x + 3$ **B.** $y = \frac{1}{2}x + 3$

    C. $y = -2x + 3$ **D.** $y = 2x + 3$

    13. _____

14. Find the slope-intercept form of an equation for the line passing through the point at (2, 3) and parallel to the graph of $y = -\frac{3}{2}x - 2$.

    A. $y = -\frac{3}{2}x + 6$ **B.** $y = \frac{2}{3}x + 6$

    C. $y = -\frac{2}{3}x + 6$ **D.** $y = -\frac{3}{2}x + 6$

    14. _____

15. Simplify $\frac{12x^9y^5}{16x^2y^7}$.

    A. $\frac{3x^7y^8}{4}$ **B.** $\frac{3x^7y^2}{4}$ **C.** $\frac{3x^7}{4y^2}$ **D.** $\frac{3x^3}{4y^2}$

    15. _____

16. Simplify $\frac{6 \times 10^8}{3 \times 10^2}$.

    A. 18×10^6 **B.** 2×10^6 **C.** 2×10^{10} **D.** 2×10^{16} 16. _____

17. A 10-foot ladder is placed against a vertical wall of a building with the bottom of the ladder 6 feet from the building. How high up the building is the ladder placed?

    A. 5 ft   **B.** 6 ft   **C.** 8 ft   **D.** 10 ft   17. _____

18. Which expression is equivalent to $(5x - 3) - 2(x - 1)$?

    A. $-10x^2 + x + 6$ **B.** $3x - 1$

    C. $7x - 1$ **D.** $7x - 5$ 18. _____

19. Which expression is equivalent to $(3p - 4)^2$?

    A. $9p^2 - 24p + 16$ **B.** $9p^2 - 12p + 16$

    C. $9p^2 - 7p + 16$ **D.** $9p^2 - 16$ 19. _____

20. Which expression represents $(6x^3 - 2x) \div 2x$?

    A. $3x^2$ **B.** $3x^2 - 2$ **C.** $3x^2 - 1$ **D.** $4x^2 - 1$ 20. _____

21. Which expression is equivalent to $x^2 + 4x - 12$?

    A. $(x - 2)(x + 6)$ **B.** $(x - 3)(x + 4)$ **C.** $(x - 4)(x + 3)$ **D.** $(x - 2)(x - 6)$ 21. _____

22. Find the equation of the axis of symmetry for the graph of $y = -2x^2 - 2x + 1$.

    A. $x = -2$ **B.** $x = -\frac{1}{2}$ **C.** $x = 1$ **D.** $y = 1$

    22. _____

23. Which of the following is the vertex of the graph of $y = x^2 + 2x + 1$?

    A. (0, 0)   **B.** (−1, 0)   **C.** (−2, 0)   **D.** (−1, −1)   23. _____

24. Which of the following is the solution of $1 + x < -2$ or $1 + x > 3$?

    A. $\{x \,|\, -3 < x < 2\}$ **B.** $\{x \,|\, x > -3 \text{ or } x < 2\}$

    C. $\{x \,|\, x < -3 \text{ or } x < 2\}$ **D.** $\{x \,|\, x < -3 \text{ or } x > 2\}$ 24. _____

25. Which of the following is the solution of $|y + 2| \leq 8$?

    A. $\{y \,|\, y \leq 6\}$ **B.** $\{y \,|\, y \leq 10\}$

    C. $\{y \,|\, -10 \leq y \leq 6\}$ **D.** $\{y \,|\, y \geq -10\}$ 25. _____

Chapter 12 Answer Key

Form 1A

Page 221

1. __D__
2. __A__
3. __B__
4. __A__
5. __C__
6. __D__
7. __B__
8. __B__
9. __A__
10. __B__
11. __D__
12. __A__
13. __D__
14. __D__
15. __B__

Page 222

16. __D__
17. __C__
18. __B__
19. __B__
20. __C__
21. __C__
22. __C__
23. __D__
24. __C__
25. __D__

Bonus __A__

Form 1B

Page 223

1. __A__
2. __B__
3. __A__
4. __A__
5. __A__
6. __A__
7. __B__
8. __A__
9. __C__
10. __A__
11. __D__
12. __D__
13. __A__
14. __D__
15. __B__

Page 224

16. __B__
17. __C__
18. __A__
19. __B__
20. __C__
21. __C__
22. __C__
23. __D__
24. __D__
25. __B__

Bonus __C__

Chapter 12 Answer Key
Form 2A

Page 225

1. $x \geq -2$

2. $x \leq 8$

3. (number line: points from 5 to the left, shaded left, closed circle at 5) −3 −2 −1 0 1 2 3 4 5 6

4. (number line: open circle at −4, shaded right) −4 −3 −2 −1 0 1 2 3 4 5

5. (number line: open circle at 2, shaded left) −4 −3 −2 −1 0 1 2 3 4 5

6. $\{x|x \geq -1\}$

7. $\{x|x \leq -2\}$

8. $\{y|y > 4\}$

9. $\{r|r < -2\}$

10. $\{y|y \geq 7\}$

11. $\{p|p \leq -2.4\}$

12. $\{y|y \leq 1\}$

13. $\{h|h > -4\}$

14. $\{g|g > -18\}$

15. $\{y|y \geq 8\}$

16. $\{t|t \geq -11\}$

17. $\{y|y < -64\}$

18. $\{v|v \leq -25\}$

19. $\{h|h < 6\}$

20. $\{b|b \geq -1\}$

Page 226

21. $\{y|y \geq 1\}$

22. $\{x|x < -8\}$

23. $\{y|y \geq 48\}$

24. $\{h|h > -30\}$

25. (number line: open circles at 1 and 4, shaded between/outside) −4 −3 −2 −1 0 1 2 3 4 5

26. (number line: open circle at 1, shaded left) −4 −3 −2 −1 0 1 2 3 4 5

27. (number line: open circle at −4, closed circle at 2) −5 −4 −3 −2 −1 0 1 2 3 4

28. $\{x|-4 < x < 4\}$
(number line: open circles at −4 and 4, shaded between) −4 −3 −2 −1 0 1 2 3 4 5

29. $\{p|-5 \leq p \leq 3\}$
(number line: closed circles at −5 and 3, shaded between) −5 −4 −3 −2 −1 0 1 2 3 4

30. $\{z|z \geq 3 \text{ or } z \leq 1\}$
(number line: closed circles at 1 and 3) −4 −3 −2 −1 0 1 2 3 4 5

31.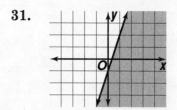

32.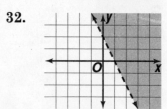

33.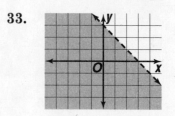

Bonus $\{n|-2 < n < 0 \text{ or } 2 < n < 4\}$

Chapter 12 Answer Key

Form 2B

Page 227

1. ___ $x > 3$ ___

2. ___ $x < -5$ ___

3. (number line from -4 to 5)

4. (number line from -4 to 5)

5. (number line from -4 to 5)

6. ___ $\{x|x < 4\}$ ___

7. ___ $\{x|x \leq 8\}$ ___

8. ___ $\{y|y > -6\}$ ___

9. ___ $\{p|p < -8\}$ ___

10. ___ $\{y|y \geq 14\}$ ___

11. ___ $\{p|p \leq -4.5\}$ ___

12. ___ $\left\{y|y > -\frac{1}{3}\right\}$ ___

13. ___ $\{h|h < -6\}$ ___

14. ___ $\{d|d > 8\}$ ___

15. ___ $\{y|y \geq -13\}$ ___

16. ___ $\{t|t \leq -4\}$ ___

17. ___ $\{x|x > -54\}$ ___

18. ___ $\{v|v < -48\}$ ___

19. ___ $\{h|h < 9\}$ ___

20. ___ $\{b|b \geq 12.5\}$ ___

Page 228

21. ___ $\{y|y \geq 5\}$ ___

22. ___ $\{x|x < -9\}$ ___

23. ___ $\{b|b \geq 72\}$ ___

24. ___ $\{h|h > -8\}$ ___

25. (number line from -5 to 4)

26. (number line from -2 to 7)

27. (number line from -5 to 4)

28. $\{x|-4 < x < 4\}$
(number line from -4 to 5)

29. $\{p|-8 \leq p \leq 4\}$
(number line from -10 to 8)

30. $\{z|z \geq -1 \text{ or } z \leq -5\}$
(number line from -7 to 2)

31.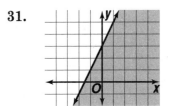

32.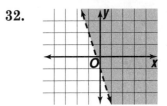

33.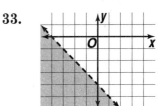

Bonus ___ $\{n|-3 < n < -1 \text{ or } 1 < n < 3\}$ ___

Chapter 12 Answer Key

Open-Ended Assessment
Sample Answers
Page 229

1. a. $\{d \mid 0 \le d \le 30\}$

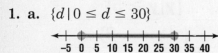

b. 30 mi

c. $\{d \mid 0 \le d \le 30\}$

d. $\{d \mid d > 30\}$

2. a. $\{x \mid 0 \le x \le 10\}$

b. $\{y \mid 0 \le y \le 15\}$

c. $15x + 10y \le 150$

d.

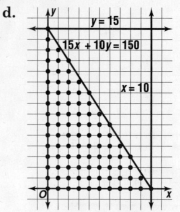

e. (0, 15), (5, 5), (10, 0); 0 CDs and 15 tapes, 5 CDs and 5 tapes, 10 CDs and 0 tapes

f. $\{y \mid y \le 9\}$

Chapter 12 Answer Key

Mid-Chapter Test
Page 230

1. $\{t \mid t < 72\}$

2. $x < 45$

3. $\{x \mid x \leq 2000\}$

4. $\{x \mid x \geq -1\}$

5. (number line from −4 to 5, open circle at 4, shaded right)

6. $\{n \mid n \leq -2\}$
(number line from −4 to 5, closed circle at −2, shaded left)

7. $\{g \mid g > 4\}$
(number line from −4 to 5, open circle at 4, shaded right)

8. $\{z \mid z < 3\}$
(number line from −4 to 5, open circle at 3, shaded left)

9. $\{y \mid y \geq -5\}$
(number line from −6 to 3, closed circle at −5, shaded right)

10. $\{v \mid v < -8\}$
(number line from −10 to −1, open circle at −8, shaded left)

11. $\{y \mid y > -18\}$
(number line from −20 to −12, open circle at −18, shaded right)

12. $\{n \mid n \leq 5\}$

13. $\{z \mid z < -0.3\}$

14. $\{x \mid x \leq 16\}$

15. $\{n \mid n < -32\}$

Quiz A
Page 231

1. (number line from −6 to 3, open circle at −3, shaded right)

2. (number line from −3 to 6, closed circle at 2, shaded right)

3. $\{n \mid n \geq 11\}$

4. $\{g \mid g < -4\}$

5. $\{y \mid y \leq 4\}$

6. $\{v \mid v \geq -12\}$

Quiz B
Page 231

1. $\{z \mid z < -4\}$

2. $\{z \mid -2 < z < 3\}$
(number line from −5 to 4, closed circle at −2, open circle at 3, shaded between)

3. $\{p \mid p > 1$ or $p < 0\}$
(number line from −4 to 5, open circles at 0 and 1, shaded outer)

4. $\{z \mid z > 6$ or $z < -10\}$
(number line from −10 to 6, open circles at −10 and 6, shaded outer)

5. (number line from −4 to 5, open circle at 4, shaded left)

6.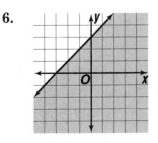

Chapter 12 Answer Key

Cumulative Review
Page 232

1. $4x + 1$

2. $-4, 0, 1, 3$

3. 2

4. -7

5. -1.9

6. 9

7. 1

8. $1:2$

9.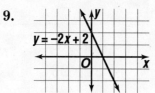

10. -24

11. -2

12. no

13. $x^2 - 2x - 15$

14. $4x^2(2x - y)$

15. $(2x + 5)(x + 1)$

16. $-2, 3$

17.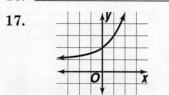

18. $x \geq 24.95$

19. $-10 < x < -6$

20.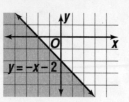

Standardized Test Practice
Page 233

1. A

2. A

3. C

4. B

5. D

6. A

7. D

8. C

9. B

10. A

11. A

12. B

Page 234

13. D

14. D

15. C

16. B

17. C

18. B

19. A

20. C

21. A

22. B

23. B

24. D

25. C

13

Chapter 13 Test, Form 1A

Write the letter for the correct answer in the blank at the right of each problem.

For Questions 1–2, solve each system of equations by graphing.

1. $y = x - 2$
   $y = 2x - 7$
   A. (3, 1)   **B.** (5, 3)   **C.** (4, 2)   **D.** (−1, 3)

   1. _____

2. $2x - 3y = 7$
   $x + y = 1$
   A. (4, −1)   **B.** (5, 1)   **C.** (3, −2)   **D.** (2, −1)

   2. _____

3. Which system is consistent and dependent?

   A.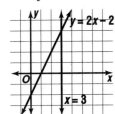

   B.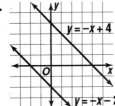

   C.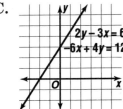

   D.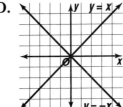

   3. _____

4. How many solutions does the system $2x + y = 3$ and $2y = 4x - 3$ have?
   A. 0   **B.** 1   **C.** 2   **D.** infinitely many

   4. _____

5. The equation $2x - y = 5$ forms an inconsistent system together with which equation?
   A. $x + 2y = 5$ **B.** $x + y = 5$ **C.** $y = -2x + 5$ **D.** $2y = 4x - 5$

   5. _____

For Questions 6–7, use substitution to solve each system of equations.

6. $x = 2y + 1$
   $2x - y = -7$
   A. (5, 11)   **B.** (−5, −3)   **C.** (2, −5)   **D.** (7, 3)

   6. _____

7. $3y - x = 4$
   $2x + 2y = 24$
   A. (5, 3)   **B.** (6, 6)   **C.** (8, 4)   **D.** (10, 2)

   7. _____

8. Use elimination to solve the system of equations $x - 2y = 3$ and $4x + 2y = 12$.
   A. (3, 0)   **B.** (0, 6)   **C.** (−1, −2)   **D.** (2, 2)

   8. _____

9. Find the solution of the system $\frac{x}{3} + 4y = 10$ and $2x + 3y = 18$.

   A. $\left(4, \frac{7}{3}\right)$ **B.** (6, 2)   **C.** (12, −2)   **D.** $\left(10, -\frac{2}{3}\right)$

   9. _____

For Questions 10–11, use elimination to solve each system of equations.

10. $-3x + 5y = 9$
$9x - 10y = -12$
A. $(-3, 0)$ **B.** $(-8, -6)$ **C.** $(-2, -3)$ **D.** $(2, 3)$ 10. _____

11. $2x - 3y = 28$
$6x + 10y = 8$
A. $(5, -6)$ **B.** $(20, 16)$ **C.** $(8, -4)$ **D.** $(44, 20)$ 11. _____

12. Find the solution of the system $y = -x^2 + 8$ and $y = -4x + 3$.
A. $(-3, -1), (1, -1)$ **B.** $(-5, 23), (1, -1)$
C. $(5, -17), (-1, 7)$ **D.** no solution 12. _____

13. Solve the system of equations by substitution.
$y = x + 2$
$y = 3x^2 - 28$
A. $(-3, -1), \left(\frac{10}{3}, \frac{16}{3}\right)$ **B.** $(-5, 3), (0, 28)$
C. $(3, 5), (2, -16)$ **D.** no solution 13. _____

14. What is the solution of the system $y = 3x - 1$ and $y = x^2 - 5$?
A. $(2, 5), (3, 4)$ **B.** $(4, 11), (-1, -4)$
C. $(3, 8), (-3, -10)$ **D.** no solution 14. _____

15. Which ordered pair is a solution of the system of inequalities?
$x + 2y \geq 8$
$-x - y < -2$
A. $(-4, 3)$ **B.** $(10, -1)$ **C.** $(5, -2)$ **D.** $(0, 3)$ 15. _____

16. Use graphing to solve the system of inequalities.
$2x + y > 5$
$y - x < 2$

A. **B.**

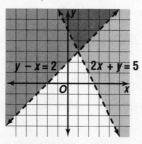

C. **D.**

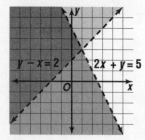 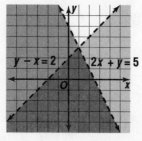

16. _____

Bonus Jared sells 450 pounds of scrap aluminum and copper to a recycling plant for $234. He gets $0.40 per pound for his aluminum cans and $0.60 per pound for copper tubing. How much copper did he sell?
A. 180 lb **B.** 210 lb **C.** 240 lb **D.** 270 lb **Bonus** _____

13

Chapter 13 Test, Form 1B

Write the letter for the correct answer in the blank at the right of each problem.

For Questions 1–2, solve each system of equations by graphing.

1. $x = 7$
   $y = x - 5$
   A. $(2, 7)$ **B.** $(12, 7)$ **C.** $(7, 2)$ **D.** $(7, 12)$ 1. _____

2. $y + 4x = 3$
   $2y - x = 6$
   A. $(0, 3)$ **B.** $(-2, 5)$ **C.** $(-2, 2)$ **D.** $(2, 3)$ 2. _____

3. How many solutions does the system $2x - 5y = 4$ and $15y = 6x - 12$ have?
   A. 0   **B.** 1   **C.** 2   **D.** infinitely many   3. _____

4. Which of the following systems is inconsistent?

   A.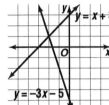

   B.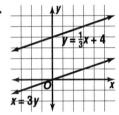

   C.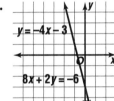

   D.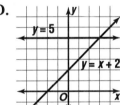

   4. _____

5. The equation $y = 3x + 2$ forms a consistent and independent system together with which equation?
   A. $y = 3x + 4$ **B.** $2y = 6x + 4$ **C.** $y = 2x + 2$ **D.** $y = 3x - 2$ 5. _____

For Questions 6–7, use substitution to solve each system of equations.

6. $y = -3x$
   $4x + y = 3$
   A. $(-1, 3)$ **B.** $(-3, 9)$ **C.** $(2, -6)$ **D.** $(3, -9)$ 6. _____

7. $x + y = -2$
   $2x + 5y = 2$
   A. $(-3, 1)$ **B.** $(0, -2)$ **C.** $(-4, 2)$ **D.** $(-2, -4)$ 7. _____

8. Use elimination to solve the system of equations $2x + y = 4$ and $4x - y = 8$.
   A. $(-2, 8)$ **B.** $(2, 0)$ **C.** $(0, 4)$ **D.** $(4, 8)$ 8. _____

9. Find the solution of the system $3x - 2y = 5$ and $6x - 2y = 6$.
   A. $\left(-\frac{1}{3}, 3\right)$ **B.** $\left(\frac{1}{3}, -4\right)$ **C.** $\left(-\frac{1}{3}, 2\right)$ **D.** $\left(\frac{1}{3}, -2\right)$ 9. _____

For Questions 10–11, use elimination to solve each system of equations.

10. $2x + 3y = 10$
    $4x - y = -8$
    A. $(5, 0)$ **B.** $(-1, 4)$ **C.** $(-2, 0)$ **D.** $(-4, -8)$ 10. _____

11. $2x + y = -8$
    $3x - 5y = 1$
    A. $(-3, -2)$ **B.** $(-5, 2)$ **C.** $(3, 2)$ **D.** $(2, -1)$ 11. _____

12. What is the solution of the system $x = 3$ and $y = -x^2 + 2$?
    A. $(3, 11)$ **B.** $(-1, 3)$ **C.** $(3, -7)$ **D.** $(-1, 8)$ 12. _____

13. Find the solution of the system $y = x^2 - 3$ and $y = x - 1$.
    A. $(3, 6), (3, 2)$ **B.** $(-1, -2), (2, 1)$
    C. $(1, -2), (2, 1)$ **D.** no solution   13. _____

14. Solve the system of equations by $y = x^2 + 4x + 3$
    substitution. $y = -1$
    A. $(-1, 3)$ **B.** $(2, -1)$ **C.** $(-2, -1)$ **D.** no solution   14. _____

15. Which ordered pair is a solution of the $x + y > 20$
    system of inequalities? $2x - y < 15$
    A. $(10, 4)$ **B.** $(9, 12)$ **C.** $(4, -12)$ **D.** $(25, -3)$ 15. _____

16. Use graphing to solve the system of $-3x + y \leq 3$
    inequalities. $3y > -9$

    A. 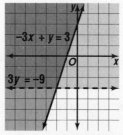   **B.**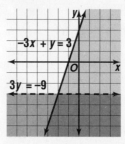

    C. 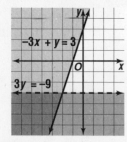   **D.**

    16. _____

Bonus Mrs. Doolittle has ten cats and dogs. To board all of her animals costs $104 per day. If the kennel charges $8 per day to board a cat and $14 for a dog, how many cats does she have?
    A. 4   **B.** 5   **C.** 6   **D.** 7   **Bonus** _____

Chapter 13 Test, Form 2A

Solve each system of equations by graphing.

1. $y = x + 3$
   $3x - y = 1$

1. _____

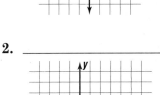

2. $2x - y = 7$
   $3x + y = 3$

2. _____

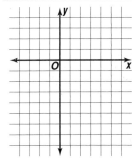

State whether each system is consistent and independent, consistent and dependent, **or** inconsistent.

3.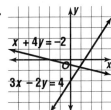

4.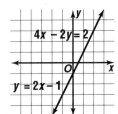

3. _____

4. _____

Determine whether each system of equations has one solution, no solution, **or** infinitely many solutions. If the system has one solution, name it.

5. $y = -2x + 1$
   $y = -\frac{1}{2}x - 2$

5. _____

6. $y = -\frac{x}{2} + 1$
   $x + 2y = 5$

6. _____

Use substitution to solve each system of equations.

7. $y = 4x + 7$
   $5x + 3y = -13$

7. _____

8. $x - 6y = -2$
   $7x + 3y = 1$

8. _____

Use elimination to solve each system of equations.

9. $-2x + 5y = 40$
   $2x - 3y = 24$

9. _____

10. $2x + 3y = 65$
    $7x + 3y = 25$

10. _____

For Questions 11–12, use elimination to solve each system of equations.

11. $\frac{x}{3} + 4y = 30$

    $2x - y = 5$

    11. _____

12. $6x - \frac{y}{4} = -9$

    $3x + 2y = -30$

    12. _____

13. Solve the following system of equations by graphing.

    $y = -x^2 + 2$

    $y = -x - 4$

    13. _____

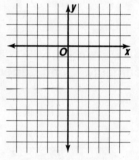

14. Solve the system of equations by substitution.

    $y = x^2 + 2x - 2$

    $y = 3x + 4$

    14. _____

15. Tell whether or not $(-1, -5)$ is a solution of the system of inequalities.

    $x + 2y < -12$

    $3x - y \geq -2$

    15. _____

16. Solve the following system of inequalities by graphing.

    $x + 2y \leq 8$

    $x - y < 3$

    16.

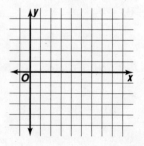

Bonus Mr. Adams buys a bag of apples and a bag of pears for a total of $14. There are eight pounds of fruit in all. The apples cost $1.50 per pound, and the pears cost $2.30 per pound. How many pounds of pears did he buy?

Bonus _____

13

Chapter 13 Test, Form 2B

Solve each system of equations by graphing.

1. $x + 2y = 5$
   $x - y = 2$

1. _____

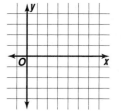

2. $4x - y = 6$
   $3x + y = 1$

2. _____

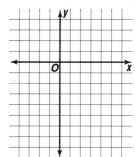

State whether each system is consistent and independent, consistent and dependent, or inconsistent.

3.

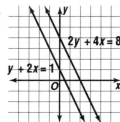

4.

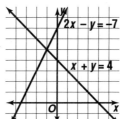

3. _____

4. _____

Determine whether each system of equations has one solution, no solution, or infinitely many solutions. If the system has one solution, name it.

5. $y = -x + 2$
   $3x + 3y = 6$

5. _____

6. $y = \frac{2}{3}x$
   $2x - y = -4$

6. _____

Use substitution to solve each system of equations.

7. $x = 3y - 2$
   $2x + 4y = 16$

7. _____

8. $2x + y = 7$
   $5x - 2y = 4$

8. _____

Use elimination to solve each system of equations.

9. $3x - y = 15$
   $5x + y = 9$

9. _____

10. $3x - 2y = 6$
    $x - 2y = -2$

10. _____

For Questions 11–12, use elimination to solve each system of equations.

11. $\frac{x}{2} + 2y = 9$
    $2x - y = 18$

11. _____

12. $4x - y = -3$
    $5x + 2y = -20$

12. _____

13. Solve the following system of equations by graphing.
    $y = x^2 - 4$
    $y = x - 2$

13. _____

14. Find the solution of the system $y = x^2 + 5$ and $y = 2x + 4$.

14. _____

15. Tell whether or not (2, 3) is a solution of $2x - 3y < 0$
    the system of inequalities. $x + y > 4$

15. _____

16. Solve the following system of inequalities by graphing.
    $y \geq 2$
    $3x + y < 10$

16.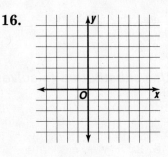

Bonus Sixty wedding guests are given a choice of prime rib or chicken for dinner. The bride and groom will be billed $30 for each guest who has prime rib, and $20 for each guest who has chicken. If the total dinner bill is $1470, how many guests had prime rib? **Bonus** _____

13

Chapter 13 Open-Ended Assessment

Instructions: Demonstrate your knowledge by giving a clear, concise solution to each problem. Be sure to include all relevant drawings and to justify your answers. You may show your solution in more than one way or investigate beyond the requirements of the problem.

1. You have $100 to spend on pizzas and foot-long sandwiches for a party. You decide that you will need at least three pizzas and eight foot-long sandwiches. The pizzas cost $12.50 each and the sandwiches cost $4 each.

   a. Write a system of inequalities to represent the situation. Use x for the number of pizzas you decide to buy and y for the number of sandwiches.

   b. Graph the system of inequalities in part a.

   c. What shape is the shaded region in your graph?

   d. What are the coordinates of the vertices of the shape?

   e. Write how you can use your answer in part d to tell the greatest number of pizzas that you can buy. What is the greatest number of pizzas you could buy? What is the greatest number of sandwiches?

   f. Write how you could use your graph to tell how many possible solutions there are.

2. Suppose that 46 people attend your party. Assume that everyone will choose to eat either pizza or part of a sandwich, and no one will each both pizza and a sandwich. The pizzas will serve four people on the average, and the sandwiches will serve two people. Your total bill for the pizzas and sandwiches is $128.

   a. Using the information in Question 1, write a system of equations to represent this situation. Use x for the number of pizza-eaters and y for the sandwich-eaters.

   b. What method would you use to solve the system? Why?

   c. Solve the system of equations.

3. The pizzas in Questions 1 and 2 are either cheese or pepperoni. People are three times more likely to choose cheese over pepperoni.

   a. Use the information from Question 2 to write a system of equations to find the number of cheese and pepperoni pizzas consumed. Use c for the number of cheese pizzas and p for the pepperoni pizzas.

   b. How would you solve this system? Why?

   c. Solve the system of equations.

13

Chapter 13 Mid-Chapter Test
(Lessons 13–1 through 13–4)

For Questions 1–2, solve each system of equations by graphing. Label the solution on each graph.

1. $x + 2y = -1$
   $y = 2$

1.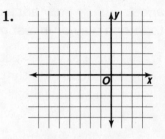

2. $y = 3x - 4$
   $y = 2x - 3$

2.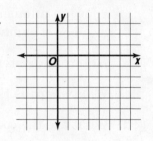

3. State whether the system of equations graphed at the right is *consistent and independent, consistent and dependent,* or *inconsistent.*

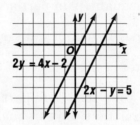
$2y = 4x - 2$
$2x - y = 5$

3. _____

Determine whether each system of equations has one solution, no solution, or infinitely many solutions. If the system has one solution, name it.

4. $2x + y = 0$
   $3x - y = -10$

4. _____

5. $y = \frac{x}{3} + 2$
   $x - 3y = -6$

5. _____

For Questions 6–7, use substitution to solve each system of equations.

6. $x - 2y = 10$
   $3x + 10y = 14$

6. _____

7. $3x + y = 3$
   $9x - y = -11$

7. _____

8. There were 330 people at a school fundraising dinner. If tickets were $2.50 for children and $4 for adults and ticket sales totaled $1185, how many children attended?

8. _____

Use elimination to solve each system of equations.

9. $2x + 5y = 7$
   $-8x + 5y = 47$

9. _____

10. $-2x + 7y = -17$
    $3x - 7y = 22$

10. _____

Algebra: Concepts and Applications

NAME _____ DATE _____ PERIOD _____

Chapter 13 Quiz A
(Lessons 13–1 through 13–3)

1. Solve the system of equations by graphing.

$x + y = 2$
$2x - y = 7$

1. _____

2. Tell whether the system shown in the graph is *consistent and dependent,* *consistent and independent,* or *inconsistent.*

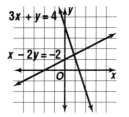

$3x + y = 4$
$x - 2y = -2$

2. _____

3. Determine whether the system at the right has *one* solution, *no* solution, or *infinitely many* solutions. If it has one solution, name it.

$x - 2y = 3$
$4y = 2x + 6$

3. _____

4. Use substitution to solve the system of equations $x = 3y - 2$ and $2x - 3y = 5$.

4. _____

5. What is the solution of the system of equations $5x + 3y = 3$ and $y = 2 - 2x$?

5. _____

NAME _____ DATE _____ PERIOD _____

Chapter 13 Quiz B
(Lessons 13–4 through 13–7)

Use elimination to solve each system of equations.

1. $3x - y = -4$
   $7x - y = -12$

1. _____

2. $-2x + 3y = 18$
   $4x - 5y = -6$

2. _____

For Questions 3–4, use substitution to solve each system of equations.

3. $y = x^2 - 5$
   $y = x + 1$

3. _____

4. $y = x^2 + 2x + 3$
   $y = -2x - 1$

4. _____

5. Solve the system of inequalities by graphing.

$x - 3y < 5$
$2x + y \leq 3$

5.

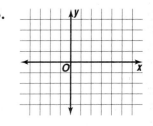

Chapter 13 Cumulative Review

1. Write an equation for the sentence *Eight less than three times a number m equals 10. (Lesson 1–1)*

   1. _____

2. Evaluate $\frac{2a - 5b}{c} + 4d$ if $a = -2$, $b = 4$, $c = -8$, and $d = 5$. *(Lessons 2–3 through 2–6)*

   2. _____

3. Find the mean of the following set of data: 24, 48, 38, 50, 45. *(Lesson 3–3)*

   3. _____

4. Find $6 \div (-0.02)$. *(Lesson 4–3)*

   4. _____

5. Find the percent of decrease from \$140 to \$91. *(Lesson 5–5)*

   5. _____

6. Find the domain of $y = 2x - 3$ if the range is $\{-7, -3, 5, 11\}$. *(Lesson 6–2)*

   6. _____

7. Determine the slope of the line passing through points at $(-2, 4)$ and $(6, -2)$. *(Lesson 7–1)*

   7. _____

8. Simplify $\frac{8x^2y^{-3}}{2x^{-1}y^4}$. *(Lesson 8–3)*

   8. _____

9. Find $(8x^2 - 3x + 1) - (4x^2 - 5x + 3)$. *(Lesson 9–2)*

   9. _____

10. Factor $x^2 - 2x - 15$. *(Lesson 10–3)*

    10. _____

11. Write an equation of the axis of symmetry of the graph of $y = 3x^2 - 12x + 7$. *(Lesson 11–1)*

    11. _____

12. Solve $x^2 + 8x - 20 = 0$ by completing the square. *(Lesson 11–5)*

    12. _____

13. Solve $-3 < 2x + 1 < 9$. *(Lesson 12–5)*

    13. _____

14. Mr. Wilson's bakery donated 240 cookies to a school bake sale. The cookies were packaged in bags of three, which sold for \$0.50, and bags of 12, which sold for \$1.50. When all the cookies were sold, the total collected was \$36. How many bags of three cookies were sold? *(Lesson 13–3)*

    14. _____

15. Use elimination to solve the system of equations $3x + 2y = 10$ and $5x - 2y = 14$. *(Lesson 13–4)*

    15. _____

16. Use substitution to solve the system of equations $y = x^2 - 3x + 11$ and $y = 3x + 2$. *(Lesson 13–6)*

    16. _____

13 Chapter 13 Standardized Test Practice
(Chapters 1–13)

Write the letter for the correct answer in the blank at the right of each problem.

1. Use the order of operations to find the value of $12 - 3 \cdot 2 + 4 \div 2$.
     A. 5   **B.** 7   **C.** 8   **D.** 11   1. _____

2. Simplify $4x(-2) - 5(-3x)$.
     A. $-7x$ **B.** $7x$ **C.** $-23x$ **D.** $23x$ 2. _____

3. Evaluate $\frac{7}{12} - \left(-\frac{1}{3}\right) - \frac{5}{6}$.
     A. $-\frac{7}{6}$ **B.** $\frac{1}{12}$ **C.** $\frac{5}{12}$ **D.** 1   3. _____

4. Evaluate $ab + \frac{c}{d}$ when $a = -\frac{1}{2}$, $b = \frac{2}{3}$, $c = \frac{-1}{8}$, and $d = \frac{3}{4}$.
     A. $-\frac{1}{2}$ **B.** $-\frac{1}{3}$ **C.** $\frac{1}{3}$ **D.** $\frac{3}{4}$ 4. _____

5. For a book review, students must pick one novel from a list of fifteen. They may choose to do a traditional written book report, an oral report, or a book advertisement. Use the Fundamental Counting Principle to determine the number of possible choices for the book review.
     A. 18   **B.** 30   **C.** 45   **D.** 60   5. _____

6. What number is 70% of 130?
     A. 81   **B.** 91   **C.** 101   **D.** 185   6. _____

7. Two dice are rolled. Find the probability that the sum of the two numbers is either a multiple of 3 or an even number.
     A. $\frac{1}{3}$ **B.** $\frac{1}{2}$ **C.** $\frac{2}{3}$ **D.** $\frac{5}{6}$ 7. _____

8. Suppose y varies inversely as x and $y = 16$ when $x = 3$. Find y when $x = 10$.
     A. 4.8   **B.** $5\frac{1}{3}$ **C.** 48   **D.** $53\frac{1}{3}$ 8. _____

9. Write the point-slope form of an equation for the line passing through points at $(3, 8)$ and $(-1, -4)$.
     A. $y - 3 = 3(x - 8)$ **B.** $y + 4 = \frac{1}{3}(x + 1)$
     C. $y - 8 = -3(x - 3)$ **D.** $y - 8 = 3(x - 3)$ 9. _____

10. Write an equation in slope-intercept form of the line perpendicular to the graph of $2x + y = 7$ and passing through the point at $(6, 0)$.
     A. $y = -\frac{1}{2}x + 6$ **B.** $y = \frac{1}{2}x - 3$
     C. $y = 2x - 9$ **D.** $y = -2x + 15$ 10. _____

13

Chapter 13 Standardized Test Practice
(Chapters 1–13) *(continued)*

11. Evaluate $100x^{-2}y^3$ if $x = 5$ and $y = 2$.
    A. 32 B. 300 C. 800 D. 4000 11. _____

12. Find $(4b - 5)(3b - 1)$.
    A. $12b^2 + 5$ B. $12b^2 - 11b - 5$
    C. $12b^2 - 19b + 5$ D. $12b^2 - 9b + 5$ 12. _____

13. Factor $6x^2 - x - 2$.
    A. $(6x - 1)(x + 2)$ B. $(3x - 1)(2x + 2)$
    C. $(3x - 2)(2x + 1)$ D. $(3x + 2)(2x - 1)$ 13. _____

14. Which of the following polynomials is a perfect square?
    A. $4x^2 + 9$ B. $4x^2 - 9$
    C. $4x^2 + 12x - 9$ D. $4x^2 - 12x + 9$ 14. _____

15. Find the coordinates of the vertex of the graph of $y = 2x^2 + 8x + 6$.
    A. $(-2, -2)$ B. $(2, 27)$ C. $(-2, -11)$ D. $(2, 5)$ 15. _____

16. Use the Quadratic Formula to solve $4x^2 + 8x - 21 = 0$.
    A. $\frac{3}{2}, \frac{7}{2}$ B. $\frac{3}{2}, -\frac{7}{2}$ C. $-\frac{3}{2}, -\frac{7}{2}$ D. $-\frac{3}{2}, \frac{7}{2}$ 16. _____

17. Solve $3x - 4 \geq -10$.
    A. $x \geq -2$ B. $x \geq \frac{14}{3}$ C. $x \geq 2$ D. $x \leq \frac{14}{3}$ 17. _____

18. Janelle bought twelve T-shirts, some priced at \$15 and some on sale at \$8. Her total bill, before sales tax, was \$117. How many on-sale T-shirts did she buy?
    A. 8 B. 9 C. 10 D. 11 18. _____

19. Use elimination to solve the system of equations $2x - y = 3$ and $3x + 4y = 21$.
    A. $(4, 5)$ B. $(-3, -9)$ C. $(2, 1)$ D. $(3, 3)$ 19. _____

20. Use substitution to solve the following system of equations.
    $y = x^2 - 4x - 7$
    $y = -6x + 1$
    A. $(4, -23), (-2, 13)$ B. $(-4, 25), (-2, -13)$
    C. $(-4, 25), (2, -11)$ D. $(4, -23), (2, -11)$ 20. _____

Chapter 13 Answer Key

Form 1A

Page 241

1. __B__

2. __D__

3. __C__

4. __B__

5. __D__

6. __B__

7. __C__

8. __A__

9. __B__

Page 242

10. __D__

11. __C__

12. __C__

13. __A__

14. __B__

15. __B__

16. __A__

Bonus __D__

Form 1B

Page 243

1. __C__

2. __A__

3. __D__

4. __B__

5. __C__

6. __D__

7. __C__

8. __B__

9. __D__

Page 244

10. __B__

11. __A__

12. __C__

13. __B__

14. __C__

15. __B__

16. __A__

Bonus __C__

Chapter 13 Answer Key

Form 2A

1. _____ **(2, 5)**

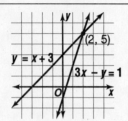

2. _____ **(2, −3)**

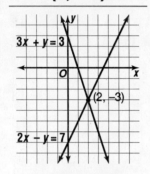

3. _____ **consistent and independent**

4. _____ **consistent and dependent**

5. _____ **(2, −3)**

6. _____ **no**

7. _____ **(−2, −1)**

8. _____ $\left(0, \dfrac{1}{3}\right)$

9. _____ **(60, 32)**

10. _____ **(−8, 27)**

11. _____ **(6, 7)**

12. _____ **(−2, −12)**

13. _____ **(−2, −2), (3, −7)**

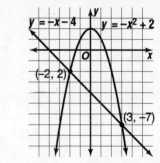

14. _____ **(−2, −2), (3, 13)**

15. _____ **no**

16.

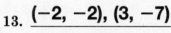

Bonus _____ $2\dfrac{1}{2}$ **lb**

Chapter 13 Answer Key

Form 2B

Page 247

1. ____ **(3, 1)** ____

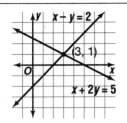

2. ____ **(1, −2)** ____

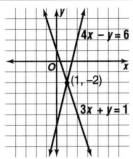

3. ____ **inconsistent** ____

4. ____ **consistent and independent** ____

5. ____ **infinitely many** ____

6. ____ **(−3, −2)** ____

7. ____ **(4, 2)** ____

8. ____ **(2, 3)** ____

9. ____ **(3, −6)** ____

10. ____ **(4, 3)** ____

Page 248

11. ____ **(10, 2)** ____

12. ____ **(−2, −5)** ____

13. ____ **(−1, −3), (2, 0)** ____

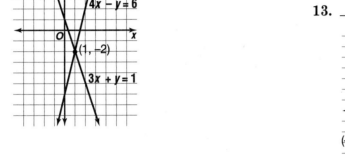

14. ____ **(1, 6)** ____

15. ____ **yes** ____

16.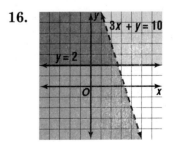

Bonus ____ **27** ____

Chapter 13 Answer Key
Open-Ended Assessment
Sample Answers
Page 249

1. a. $x \geq 3$, $y \geq 8$, $12.5x + 4y \leq 100$

b.

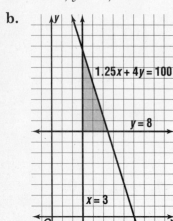

c. a right triangle

d. (3, 8), (3, 15.625), (5.44, 8)

e. The greatest number of pizzas is the largest integer less than or equal to the y-coordinate of the rightmost vertex of the triangle. The greatest number of pizzas is 5 and the greatest number of sandwiches is 15.

f. Count the number of points within the triangle with integral coordinates, i.e., the number of grid intersections on the graph paper if you're using the scale one square = 1 unit.

2. a. $x + y = 46$, $12.5\left(\frac{x}{4}\right) + 4\left(\frac{y}{2}\right) = 128$

b. Substitution, because the coefficients in the first equation are both 1.

c. 32 pizza-eaters, 14 sandwich-eaters

3. a. $c + p = 8$, $c = 3p$

b. Substitution, because the second equation is solved for the variable c.

c. $c = 6$, $p = 2$

Algebra: Concepts and Applications

Chapter 13 Answer Key

Mid-Chapter Test
Page 250

1.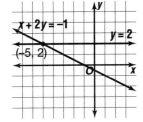

2.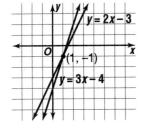

3.   **inconsistent**

4.   **(−2, 4)**

5.   **infinitely many**

6.   **(8, −1)**

7. $\left(-\dfrac{2}{3}, 5\right)$

8.   **90**

9.   **(−4, 3)**

10.   **(5, −1)**

Quiz A
Page 251

1.   **(3, −1)**

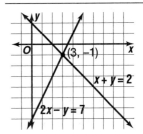

2.   **consistent and independent**

3.   **no**

4.   **(7, 3)**

5.   **(3, −4)**

Quiz B
Page 251

1.   **(−2, −2)**

2.   **(36, 30)**

3.   **(−2, −1), (3, 4)**

4.   **(−2, 3)**

5.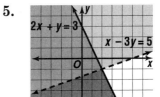

Chapter 13 Answer Key

Cumulative Review
Page 252

1. $3m - 8 = 10$

2. 23

3. 41

4. -300

5. 35%

6. $\{-2, 0, 4, 7\}$

7. $-\dfrac{3}{4}$

8. $\dfrac{4x^3}{y^7}$

9. $4x^2 + 2x - 2$

10. $(x - 5)(x + 3)$

11. $x = 2$

12. $-10, 2$

13. $\{x | -2 < x < 4\}$

14. 48

15. $\left(3, \dfrac{1}{2}\right)$

16. $(3, 11)$

Standardized Test Practice
Page 253

1. C

2. B

3. B

4. A

5. C

6. B

7. C

8. A

9. D

10. B

Page 254

11. A

12. C

13. C

14. D

15. A

16. B

17. A

18. B

19. D

20. C

Write the letter for the correct answer in the blank at the right of each problem.

Name the set or sets of numbers to which each real number belongs. Let N = natural numbers, W = whole numbers, Z = integers, Q = rational numbers, and I = irrational numbers.

1. 0
   A. W, Z   B. W, N   C. W, Z, Q   D. N, W   1. _____

2. $\sqrt{16}$
   A. I   B. N, W, Z   C. N, W, Z, Q   D. I, Q   2. _____

Find an approximation, to the nearest tenth, for each square root.

3. $\sqrt{17}$
   A. 7.3   B. 6.2   C. 4.2   D. 4.1   3. _____

4. $-\sqrt{8}$
   A. no solution   B. -2.8 C. -2.9 D. -3.1 4. _____

5. $\sqrt{27}$
   A. 3.2   B. 5.1   C. 5.2   D. 5.9   5. _____

Find the distance between each pair of points. Round to the nearest tenth, if necessary.

6. $A(0, 3), B(0, -5)$
   A. -2 B. 2   C. 7   D. 8   6. _____

7. $C(1, -1), D(4, 2)$
   A. 2.4   B. 4.2   C. 9   D. 18   7. _____

8. $E(3, 2), F(-4, 2)$
   A. 7   B. 1   C. -1 D. -7 8. _____

Find the value of a if the points are the indicated distance apart.

9. $G(2, a), H(1, 4); d = \sqrt{17}$
   A. 2   B. 1   C. 0   D. -1 9. _____

10. $M(a, 4), N(2, 3); d = \sqrt{10}$
    A. -2 B. -1 C. 0   D. 1   10. _____

Simplify each expression. Leave in radical form.

11. $\sqrt{32}$
    A. $16\sqrt{2}$ B. $4\sqrt{2}$ C. 4   D. $\sqrt{2}$ 11. _____

12. $\sqrt{18} \cdot \sqrt{2}$
    A. 2   B. $\sqrt{3} \cdot \sqrt{2}$ C. $3\sqrt{2}$ D. 6   12. _____

13. $\dfrac{\sqrt{12}}{\sqrt{3}}$
    A. $\dfrac{4\sqrt{3}}{\sqrt{3}}$ B. 4   C. 2   D. $4\sqrt{3}$ 13. _____

14

Chapter 14 Test, Form 1A (continued)

Simplify each expression. Leave in radical form. Use absolute value symbols if necessary.

14. $\dfrac{2}{5 - \sqrt{2}}$

    A. $\dfrac{10 + 2\sqrt{2}}{23}$
    B. $2\sqrt{2}$
    C. $10 + \sqrt{2}$
    D. $\dfrac{5 + 2\sqrt{2}}{2}$

    14. _____

15. $\sqrt{8ab^4}$

    A. $2b^2\sqrt{2}$
    B. $4b\sqrt{2a}$
    C. $2b\sqrt{2a}$
    D. $2b^2\sqrt{2a}$

    15. _____

16. $5\sqrt{3} + 9\sqrt{3}$

    A. 14
    B. 42
    C. $14\sqrt{6}$
    D. $14\sqrt{3}$

    16. _____

17. $14\sqrt{5} - 7\sqrt{5}$

    A. $-7\sqrt{5}$
    B. $7\sqrt{5}$
    C. 7
    D. 35

    17. _____

18. $2\sqrt{2} + 2\sqrt{8}$

    A. $2\sqrt{10}$
    B. $4\sqrt{2}$
    C. $6\sqrt{2}$
    D. 16

    18. _____

19. $\sqrt{24} + \sqrt{54}$

    A. $\sqrt{78}$
    B. 30
    C. 12.5
    D. $5\sqrt{6}$

    19. _____

20. $\sqrt{63} - \sqrt{112} + \sqrt{121}$

    A. $-\sqrt{7} + 11$
    B. $\sqrt{72}$
    C. $11 + \sqrt{7}$
    D. 13.5

    20. _____

Solve each equation. Check your solution.

21. $\sqrt{x} = 4$

    A. 16
    B. 8
    C. 4
    D. 2

    21. _____

22. $\sqrt{a} + 7 = 0$

    A. -7
    B. no solution
    C. $\sqrt{7}$
    D. $-\sqrt{7}$

    22. _____

23. $\sqrt{k - 6} = 6$

    A. 36
    B. 9
    C. 42
    D. $\sqrt{30}$

    23. _____

24. $\sqrt{m + 9} - 5 = 3$

    A. $\sqrt{71}$
    B. -5
    C. 64
    D. 55

    24. _____

25. $p = \sqrt{4p + 5}$

    A. 5
    B. -1
    C. -1 or 5
    D. no solution

    25. _____

Bonus Solve $\sqrt{\dfrac{x}{3}} + 3 = 12$. Check your solution.

    A. 243
    B. 162
    C. 81
    D. 27

    Bonus _____

14

Chapter 14 Test, Form 1B

Write the letter for the correct answer in the blank at the right of each problem.

Name the set or sets of numbers to which each real number belongs. Let N = natural numbers, W = whole numbers, Z = integers, Q = rational numbers, and I = irrational numbers.

1. 1

    A. N, W, Z, Q   **B.** W, N   **C.** W   **D.** N, W, Z   **1.** _____

2. $\sqrt{19}$

    A. Q   **B.** Z   **C.** I   **D.** I, Q   **2.** _____

Find an approximation, to the nearest tenth, for each square root.

3. $\sqrt{21}$

    A. 4.2   **B.** 4.6   **C.** 5.4   **D.** 7.2   **3.** _____

4. $-\sqrt{5}$

    A. −2.2   **B.** −2.1   **C.** 2.2   **D.** no solution   **4.** _____

5. $\sqrt{23}$

    A. 4.9   **B.** 4.8   **C.** 4.5   **D.** 4.0   **5.** _____

Find the distance between each pair of points. Round to the nearest tenth, if necessary.

6. $A(0, 4)$, $B(0, 7)$

    A. −11   **B.** −3   **C.** 3   **D.** 11   **6.** _____

7. $C(2, 1)$, $D(5, 1)$

    A. −3   **B.** 1.7   **C.** 3   **D.** 7   **7.** _____

8. $E(1, 3)$, $F(-1, 2)$

    A. 0   **B.** 2.2   **C.** 2.6   **D.** 3   **8.** _____

Find the value of a if the points are the indicated distance apart.

9. $G(3, a)$, $H(-1, 4)$; $d = 4$

    A. 4   **B.** 2   **C.** 0   **D.** −1   **9.** _____

10. $M(a, 2)$, $N(3, 3)$; $d = \sqrt{10}$

    A. −1   **B.** 0   **C.** 1   **D.** 2   **10.** _____

Simplify each expression. Leave in radical form.

11. $\sqrt{108}$

    A. $36\sqrt{3}$ **B.** $3\sqrt{3}$ **C.** $6\sqrt{3}$ **D.** 11   **11.** _____

12. $\sqrt{8} \cdot \sqrt{2}$

    A. $3\sqrt{2}$ **B.** 2   **C.** $\sqrt{3} \cdot \sqrt{2}$ **D.** 4   **12.** _____

13. $\dfrac{\sqrt{50}}{\sqrt{2}}$

    A. $\dfrac{25}{\sqrt{2}}$ **B.** 5   **C.** $\dfrac{5}{\sqrt{2}}$ **D.** 25   **13.** _____

                  Algebra: Concepts and Applications

Chapter 14 Test, Form 1B *(continued)*

Simplify each expression. Leave in radical form. Use absolute value symbols if necessary.

14. $\dfrac{3}{2 - \sqrt{2}}$

   A. $\dfrac{3 + 3\sqrt{2}}{2}$ **B.** $\dfrac{6 + 3\sqrt{2}}{2}$ **C.** $3 + \sqrt{2}$ **D.** $\dfrac{6 - 3\sqrt{2}}{2}$

   14. _____

15. $\sqrt{50b^4}$

   A. $5b\sqrt{2}$ **B.** $5\sqrt{2b}$ **C.** $25\sqrt{2b}$ **D.** $5b^2\sqrt{2}$

   15. _____

16. $3\sqrt{2} + 4\sqrt{2}$

   A. $7\sqrt{2}$ **B.** $12\sqrt{2}$ **C.** 14 **D.** $14\sqrt{2}$

   16. _____

17. $8\sqrt{7} - 5\sqrt{7}$

   A. $3\sqrt{7}$ **B.** $-3\sqrt{7}$ **C.** -3 **D.** 21

   17. _____

18. $4\sqrt{3} + \sqrt{27}$

   A. $12\sqrt{3}$ **B.** $13\sqrt{3}$ **C.** $7\sqrt{3}$ **D.** 21

   18. _____

19. $\sqrt{18} - \sqrt{32}$

   A. $-\sqrt{14}$ **B.** no solution   **C.** $-\sqrt{2}$ **D.** $7\sqrt{2}$

   19. _____

20. $\sqrt{80} + \sqrt{45} - \sqrt{125}$

   A. $12\sqrt{5}$ **B.** $-2\sqrt{5}$ **C.** $2\sqrt{5}$ **D.** 0

   20. _____

Solve each equation. Check your solution.

21. $\sqrt{y} = 7$

   A. 7 **B.** 49 **C.** $\sqrt{7}$ **D.** $\sqrt{7}$ or $-\sqrt{7}$

   21. _____

22. $\sqrt{b} + 6 = 0$

   A. no solution   **B.** 36 **C.** $\sqrt{6}$ **D.** $-\sqrt{6}$

   22. _____

23. $\sqrt{d - 6} = 5$

   A. $\sqrt{31}$ **B.** 19 **C.** $\sqrt{19}$ **D.** 31

   23. _____

24. $\sqrt{n + 8} + 6 = 11$

   A. 33 **B.** 25 **C.** 17 **D.** -3

   24. _____

25. $p = \sqrt{2p + 3}$

   A. -1 or 3 **B.** -1 **C.** 3 **D.** no solution

   25. _____

Bonus Solve $\sqrt{\dfrac{x}{2}} = 6$. Check your solution.

   A. 72 **B.** 36 **C.** 18 **D.** 12

   Bonus _____

14

Chapter 14 Test, Form 2A

Name the set or sets of numbers to which each real number belongs. Let N = natural numbers, W = whole numbers, Z = integers, Q = rational numbers, and I = irrational numbers.

1. $\frac{1}{2}$

1. _____

2. -4

2. _____

Find an approximation, to the nearest tenth, for each square root.

3. $\sqrt{11}$

3. _____

4. $-\sqrt{39}$

4. _____

5. $\sqrt{50}$

5. _____

Determine whether each number is rational or irrational. If it is irrational, find two consecutive integers between which its graph lies on the number line.

6. $-\sqrt{64}$

6. _____

7. $\sqrt{71}$

7. _____

Find the distance between each pair of points. Round to the nearest tenth, if necessary.

8. $A(0, 4), B(1, 4)$

8. _____

9. $C(-1, 1), D(4, 1)$

9. _____

10. $E(0, 2), F(3, 5)$

10. _____

11. $G(3, 3), H(-1, -2)$

11. _____

Find the value of a if the points are the indicated distance apart.

12. $J(-2, a), K(-4, 1); d = \sqrt{20}$

12. _____

13. $L(3, -2), M(a, -4); d = \sqrt{5}$

13. _____

14. $N(3, a), P(5, 4); d = \sqrt{13}$

14. _____

Simplify each expression. Leave in radical form.

15. $\sqrt{2} \cdot \sqrt{18}$

15. _____

16. $\sqrt{200}$

16. _____

Simplify each expression. Leave in radical form. Use absolute value symbols if necessary.

17. $\dfrac{\sqrt{44}}{\sqrt{4}}$

17. _____

18. $\sqrt{25ab^4}$

18. _____

19. $\sqrt{32x^2}$

19. _____

20. $\sqrt{121y^4z^6}$

20. _____

Simplify each expression.

21. $5\sqrt{5} + 2\sqrt{5}$

21. _____

22. $18\sqrt{7} - \sqrt{7}$

22. _____

23. $-6\sqrt{2} + 5\sqrt{2}$

23. _____

24. $6\sqrt{7} + 3\sqrt{7} - 12\sqrt{7}$

24. _____

25. $\sqrt{32} + \sqrt{18}$

25. _____

26. $3\sqrt{27} + \sqrt{3}$

26. _____

27. $8\sqrt{4} + 9\sqrt{4} - 15\sqrt{4}$

27. _____

Solve each equation. Check your solution.

28. $\sqrt{x} = 81$

28. _____

29. $\sqrt{z} = -11$

29. _____

30. $\sqrt{5a} = 5$

30. _____

31. $\sqrt{k + 2} = 5$

31. _____

32. $\sqrt{51 - m} = 7$

32. _____

33. $p = \sqrt{p + 6}$

33. _____

Bonus Solve $\sqrt{\dfrac{128}{x}} - 8 = 0$. Check your solution.

Bonus _____

14

Chapter 14 Test, Form 2B

Name the set or sets of numbers to which each real number belongs. Let N = natural numbers, W = whole numbers, Z = integers, Q = rational numbers, and I = irrational numbers.

1. 0.1

2. $\sqrt{7}$

1. _____

2. _____

Find an approximation, to the nearest tenth, for each square root.

3. $\sqrt{7}$

4. $-\sqrt{41}$

5. $\sqrt{53}$

3. _____

4. _____

5. _____

Determine whether each number is rational or irrational. If it is irrational, find two consecutive integers between which its graph lies on the number line.

6. $-\sqrt{81}$

7. $\sqrt{67}$

6. _____

7. _____

Find the distance between each pair of points. Round to the nearest tenth, if necessary.

8. $A(1, 3), B(1, 5)$

9. $C(5, 2), D(5, -2)$

10. $E(1, 1), F(3, 2)$

11. $G(4, 0), H(6, 3)$

8. _____

9. _____

10. _____

11. _____

Find the value of a if the points are the indicated distance apart.

12. $J(2, a), K(-3, -2); d = \sqrt{34}$

13. $L(-3, 1), M(a, 2); d = \sqrt{2}$

14. $N(2, a), P(5, -4); d = \sqrt{13}$

12. _____

13. _____

14. _____

Simplify each expression. Leave in radical form.

15. $\sqrt{9} \cdot \sqrt{4}$

16. $\sqrt{500}$

15. _____

16. _____

Simplify each expression. Leave in radical form. Use absolute value symbols if necessary.

17. $\dfrac{\sqrt{56}}{\sqrt{8}}$

17. _____

18. $\sqrt{9ab^4}$

18. _____

19. $\sqrt{50x^2}$

19. _____

20. $\sqrt{100y^2z^4}$

20. _____

Simplify each expression.

21. $2\sqrt{5} + 2\sqrt{5}$

21. _____

22. $6\sqrt{7} - \sqrt{7}$

22. _____

23. $-3\sqrt{2} + 2\sqrt{2}$

23. _____

24. $2\sqrt{7} + 3\sqrt{7} + \sqrt{7}$

24. _____

25. $\sqrt{8} + \sqrt{18}$

25. _____

26. $2\sqrt{12} + \sqrt{3}$

26. _____

27. $3\sqrt{4} + 2\sqrt{4}$

27. _____

Solve each equation. Check your solution.

28. $\sqrt{x} = 9$

28. _____

29. $\sqrt{z} = -1$

29. _____

30. $\sqrt{2a} = 2$

30. _____

31. $\sqrt{k + 2} = 2$

31. _____

32. $\sqrt{13 - m} = 3$

32. _____

33. $p = \sqrt{2p - 1}$

33. _____

Bonus Solve $\sqrt{\dfrac{16}{x}} = 2$. Check your solution.

Bonus _____

14

Chapter 14 Open-Ended Assessment

Instructions: Demonstrate your knowledge by giving a clear, concise solution for each problem. Be sure to include all relevant drawings and to justify your answers. You may show your solution in more than one way or investigate beyond the requirements of the problem.

1. In the chart below, write four examples from each set of numbers.

Natural	Whole	Rational	Irrational

2. Find an approximation to the nearest tenth for $-\sqrt{10}$. Then graph that value on the number line.

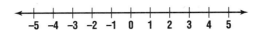

3. Name a point that is exactly 4 units horizontally or vertically from $(3, -5)$.

4. Write a fraction with a radical expression in the denominator that can be simplified by multiplying both numerator and denominator by a conjugate. Then write your fraction in simplified form.

5. Find an exact value for the perimeter of the triangle shown.

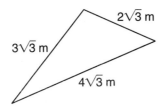

6. Explain why you must check all solutions when you solve a radical equation.

NAME _____ DATE _____ PERIOD _____

Chapter 14 Mid-Chapter Test
(Lessons 14–1 through 14–3)

Determine whether each number is rational or irrational. If it is irrational, find two consecutive integers between which its graph lies on the number line.

1. $\sqrt{12}$

1. _____

2. $-\sqrt{4}$

2. _____

3. $\sqrt{144}$

3. _____

4. $\sqrt{17}$

4. _____

5. $\sqrt{81}$

5. _____

Find the distance between each pair of points. Round to the nearest tenth, if necessary.

6. $A(-3, -1)$, $B(3, 0)$

6. _____

7. $C(-3, -2)$, $D(2, 1)$

7. _____

8. $E(1, -2)$, $F(2, 1)$

8. _____

Find the value of a if the points are the indicated distance apart.

9. $G(a, -1)$, $H(-10, 1)$; $d = \sqrt{5}$

9. _____

10. $J(-4, -1)$, $K(a, 2)$; $d = \sqrt{73}$

10. _____

11. $L(-4, a)$, $M(4, -1)$; $d = 8$

11. _____

Simplify each expression. Leave in radical form.

12. $\sqrt{200}$

12. _____

13. $-\sqrt{12} \cdot \sqrt{3}$

13. _____

14. $\sqrt{5} \cdot \sqrt{5}$

14. _____

Simplify each expression. Use absolute value symbols if necessary.

15. $\sqrt{4a^4}$

15. _____

16. $\sqrt{3b^2}$

16. _____

NAME _____ DATE _____ PERIOD _____

Chapter 14 Quiz A
(Lessons 14–1 and 14–2)

Find an approximation, to the nearest tenth, for each square root.

1. $\sqrt{30}$　　　　　　　　　　　　　　　　1. _____

2. $-\sqrt{2}$　　　　　　　　　　　　　　　　2. _____

3. $\sqrt{13}$　　　　　　　　　　　　　　　　3. _____

4. $\sqrt{500}$　　　　　　　　　　　　　　　4. _____

Find the distance between each pair of points. Round to the nearest tenth, if necessary.

5. $A(1, -1), B(4, -1)$　　　　　　　　　　　5. _____

6. $C(1, -1), D(-1, 1)$　　　　　　　　　　　6. _____

7. $E(0, 0), F(2, 2)$　　　　　　　　　　　　7. _____

NAME _____ DATE _____ PERIOD _____

Chapter 14 Quiz B
(Lessons 14–3 through 14–5)

Simplify each expression. Leave in radical form.

1. $\sqrt{17} \cdot \sqrt{17}$　　　　　　　　　　1. _____

2. $\sqrt{32} \cdot \sqrt{2}$　　　　　　　　　　2. _____

3. $\dfrac{\sqrt{243}}{\sqrt{3}}$　　　　　　　　　　3. _____

4. $2\sqrt{2} + 7\sqrt{2}$　　　　　　　　　　4. _____

5. $6\sqrt{3} - 4\sqrt{3}$　　　　　　　　　　5. _____

6. $\sqrt{32} + \sqrt{2}$　　　　　　　　　　6. _____

Solve each equation. Check your solution.

7. $\sqrt{a - 11} = 3$　　　　　　　　　　　7. _____

8. $\sqrt{\dfrac{x}{2}} = 1$　　　　　　　　　　8. _____

1. Name the property shown by the statement below. *(Lesson 1–3)*

$$7 + x + 13 = 13 + 7 + x$$

1. _____

2. Name the quadrant in which point $(-2, 5)$ is located. *(Lesson 2–2)*

2. _____

3. Find the solution of $x - \frac{1}{3} = \frac{1}{3}$ if the replacement set is

$x = \left\{0, \frac{1}{3}, \frac{2}{3}, 1\right\}$. *(Lesson 3–4)*

3. _____

4. Find $5\frac{1}{2} \div \frac{1}{2}$. *(Lesson 4–3)*

4. _____

5. Solve $\frac{3}{8} = \frac{y}{56}$. *(Lesson 5–1)*

5. _____

6. If there are 16 ounces in one pound, how many ounces are in $3\frac{1}{4}$ pounds? *(Lesson 6–5)*

6. _____

7. Write an equation in point-slope form of the line with slope -2 and y-intercept 3. *(Lesson 7–2)*

7. _____

8. Simplify $\frac{16x^6y^2}{8x^2y^4}$. *(Lesson 8–3)*

8. _____

9. Find $(8c + 18d) + (4c - 8d)$. *(Lesson 9–2)*

9. _____

10. Find the greatest common factor of $8x^2y^3$, $12x^3y^6$, and $36x^4y^9$. *(Lesson 10–1)*

10. _____

11. Solve $7g^2 - 7 = 0$. Check your solution. *(Lesson 11–4)*

11. _____

12. Solve $\frac{x}{2} \leq 12$. Check your solution. *(Lesson 12–3)*

12. _____

13. What is the solution of the system $y = \frac{1}{2}x + 3$ and $2x = y$? *(Lesson 13–3)*

13. _____

14. Solve $\sqrt{\frac{500}{y}} = 10$. *(Lesson 14–5)*

14. _____

14

Chapter 14 Standardized Test Practice
(Chapters 1–14)

Write the letter for the correct answer in the blank at the right of each problem.

1. Which score occurs most frequently in the stem-and-leaf plot at the right?

   A. 2   **B.** 22
   C. 32   **D.** 34

Stem	Leaf
2	8
3	1 2 2 2 4 4
4	2 6 7 7 $2 \mid 8 = 28$

   1. _____

2. Simplify $-y + 5y$.

   A. $-6y$ **B.** $4y$ **C.** $-4y$ **D.** $6y$

   2. _____

3. Which of the following is a true statement about the data set below?

   $$35, 38, 42, 42, 45, 64, 68, 70$$

   A. The mode is 45.   **B.** The median is 42.
   C. The range is 25.   **D.** The mean is 50.5.

   3. _____

4. The results shown by a tree diagram are called

   A. integers.   **B.** reciprocals.
   C. outcomes.   **D.** solutions.

   4. _____

5. Solve $\frac{x}{x + 1} = \frac{4}{5}$.

   A. 5   **B.** 4   **C.** 1   **D.** 0.8

   5. _____

6. Which of the following is a linear equation?

   A. $y = \frac{1}{2}x$ **B.** $\frac{1}{x} + \frac{1}{y} = 3$ **C.** $y = 2x^2$ **D.** $xy = 3$

   6. _____

7. A line passing through the point at (2, 1) with slope 3 also passes through the point at

   A. (5, 1).   **B.** (0, −5).   **C.** (1, 0).   **D.** (−1, 3).

   7. _____

8. Which of the following is equivalent to $(-6)(x)(x)(x)(y)(y)$?

   A. $-6xy^5$ **B.** $6xy$ **C.** $-6(xy)^2$ **D.** $-6x^3y^2$

   8. _____

9. The expression $(x - 2)(x + 3)$ is equivalent to

   A. $x^2 + x - 6$.   **B.** $x^2 - x - 6$.
   C. $x^2 + x + 6$.   **D.** $x^2 - x + 6$.

   9. _____

10. The expression $12k^2 - 10k - 8$ is equivalent to

    A. $(6k - 1)(2k + 8)$.   **B.** $(4k + 2)(4k - 3)$.
    C. $(4k - 2)(3k - 4)$.   **D.** $2(2k + 1)(3k - 4)$.

    10. _____

14

Chapter 14 Standardized Test Practice
(Chapters 1–14) *(continued)*

11. Identify the equation of the graph shown.
   A. $y = x^2 - 3x + 4$
   B. $y = x^2 - x - 2$
   C. $y = x^2 + x + 2$
   D. $y = x^2$

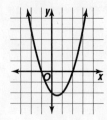

11. _____

12. What value of c makes the trinomial $a^2 + 24a + c$ a perfect square?
   A. 576   B. 144   C. 24   D. 12

12. _____

For Questions 13–14, solve each inequality. Check your solution.

13. $a + 7 > 13$
   A. $\{a \mid a > 6\}$ B. $\{a \mid a > 7\}$ C. $\{a \mid a > 20\}$ D. $\{a \mid a > -6\}$

13. _____

14. $-x - 2 < -21$
   A. $\{x \mid x < -19\}$ B. $\{x \mid x > 23\}$ C. $\{x \mid x > 19\}$ D. $\{x \mid x < -17\}$

14. _____

15. Which of the following is a solution of $y = 2x + 1$ and $y = -x + 2$?
   A. The system has no solution.   B. $\left(\frac{1}{3}, 1\frac{2}{3}\right)$
   C. $\left(\frac{1}{3}, \frac{2}{3}\right)$ D. $(0, 0)$

15. _____

16. $(0, 0)$ is a solution of which of the following systems?
   A. $y > x$ and $y < -x^2$ B. $y \geq x^2 - 1$ and $y < 2$
   C. $y = x^2$ and $y = 2$ D. $y = x$ and $y = x + 1$

16. _____

17. Name the set of numbers to which $\sqrt{8}$ belongs.
   A. irrational   B. integers   C. whole   D. natural

17. _____

18. The distance between $(-1, 2)$ and $(0, 1)$ is
   A. $\sqrt{3}$.   B. 1.   C. $\sqrt{2}$.   D. 2.

18. _____

19. Simplify $\sqrt{28}$.
   A. 5.5   B. 5   C. 7   D. $2\sqrt{7}$

19. _____

20. Simplify $2\sqrt{7} + 5\sqrt{7}$.
   A. $7\sqrt{14}$ B. 49   C. 7   D. $7\sqrt{7}$

20. _____

Chapter 14 Answer Key

Form 1A

1. C
2. C
3. D
4. B
5. C
6. D
7. B
8. A
9. C
10. B
11. B
12. D
13. C

14. A
15. D
16. D
17. B
18. C
19. D
20. A
21. A
22. B
23. C
24. D
25. A
Bonus A

Form 1B

1. A
2. C
3. B
4. A
5. B
6. C
7. C
8. B
9. A
10. B
11. C
12. D
13. B

14. B
15. D
16. A
17. A
18. C
19. C
20. C
21. B
22. A
23. D
24. C
25. C
Bonus A

Chapter 14 Answer Key
Form 2A

1. Q

2. Z, Q

3. 3.3

4. -6.2

5. 7.1

6. rational

7. irrational; between 8 and 9

8. 1

9. 5

10. 4.2

11. 6.4

12. 5 or -3

13. 4 or 2

14. 1 or 7

15. 6

16. $10\sqrt{2}$

17. $\sqrt{11}$

18. $5b^2\sqrt{a}$

19. $4|x|\sqrt{2}$

20. $11y^2|z^3|$

21. $7\sqrt{5}$

22. $17\sqrt{7}$

23. $-\sqrt{2}$

24. $-3\sqrt{7}$

25. $7\sqrt{2}$

26. $10\sqrt{3}$

27. 4

28. 6561

29. no solution

30. 5

31. 23

32. 2

33. 3

Bonus 2

Algebra: Concepts and Applications

Chapter 14 Answer Key

Form 2B

1. _____ Q _____   17. _____ $\sqrt{7}$ _____

2. _____ I _____   18. _____ $3b^2\sqrt{a}$ _____

                                 19. _____ $5|x|\sqrt{2}$ _____

3. _____ 2.6 _____   20. _____ $10|y|z^2$ _____

4. _____ −6.4 _____

5. _____ 7.3 _____   21. _____ $4\sqrt{5}$ _____

                                 22. _____ $5\sqrt{7}$ _____

                                 23. _____ $-\sqrt{2}$ _____

6. _____ rational _____   24. _____ $6\sqrt{7}$ _____

7. _____ irrational; between 8 and 9 _____   25. _____ $5\sqrt{2}$ _____

                                 26. _____ $5\sqrt{3}$ _____

                                 27. _____ 10 _____

8. _____ 2 _____

9. _____ 4 _____

10. _____ 2.2 _____   28. _____ 81 _____

11. _____ 3.6 _____   29. _____ no solution _____

                                 30. _____ 2 _____

                                 31. _____ 2 _____

12. _____ 1 or −5 _____   32. _____ 4 _____

13. _____ −2 or −4 _____   33. _____ 1 _____

14. _____ −2 or −6 _____

15. _____ 6 _____   Bonus _____ 4 _____

16. _____ $10\sqrt{5}$ _____

Open-Ended Assessment
Sample Answers
Page 269

1.

Natural	Whole	Rational	Irrational
3	0	3	$\sqrt{2}$
5	2	$-\frac{1}{2}$	$\sqrt{3}$
6	3	$\frac{5}{3}$	1.442...
7	4	$-\sqrt{9}$	2.04004...

2. -3.2

3. $(7, -5), (-1, -5), (3, -1),$ or $(3, -9)$

4. $\dfrac{2}{2 - \sqrt{3}}, 4 + 2\sqrt{3}$

5. $9\sqrt{3}$ m

6. Squaring each side of an equation may produce results that do not satisfy the original equation.

Chapter 14 Answer Key

Mid-Chapter Test
Page 270

1. irrational;
between 3 and 4

2. rational

3. rational

4. irrational;
between 4 and 5

5. rational

6. 6.1

7. 5.8

8. 3.2

9. −9 or −11

10. 4 or −12

11. −1

12. $10\sqrt{2}$

13. 6

14. 5

15. $2a^2$

16. $|b|\sqrt{3}$

Quiz A
Page 271

1. 5.5

2. −1.4

3. 3.6

4. 22.4

5. 3

6. 2.8

7. 2.8

Quiz B
Page 271

1. 17

2. 8

3. 9

4. $9\sqrt{2}$

5. $2\sqrt{3}$

6. $5\sqrt{2}$

7. 20

8. 2

Chapter 14 Answer Key

Cumulative Review
Page 272

1. Commutative Property of Addition

2. quadrant II

3. $\dfrac{2}{3}$

4. 11

5. 21

6. 52

7. $y - 3 = -2x$

8. $\dfrac{2x^4}{y^2}$

9. $12c + 10d$

10. $4x^2y^3$

11. $-1, 1$

12. $\{x \mid x \leq 24\}$

13. $(2, 4)$

14. 5

Standardized Test Practice
Page 273

1. C

2. B

3. D

4. C

5. B

6. A

7. B

8. D

9. A

10. D

Page 274

11. B

12. B

13. A

14. C

15. B

16. B

17. A

18. C

19. D

20. D

Algebra: Concepts and Applications

15

Chapter 15 Test, Form 1A

Write the letter for the correct answer in the blank at the right of each problem.

Find the excluded value(s) for each rational expression.

1. $\dfrac{7a}{3a - 1}$

    A. $\dfrac{1}{3}$ **B.** $3a$ **C.** a **D.** $7a$

    1. _____

2. $\dfrac{x^2 + 3x + 2}{x^2 - x - 6}$

    A. 6 **B.** $-2, 3$ **C.** $2, 3$ **D.** $-2, -3$

    2. _____

Simplify each rational expression.

3. $\dfrac{9}{27}$

    A. $\dfrac{1}{9}$ **B.** $\dfrac{1}{4}$ **C.** $\dfrac{1}{3}$ **D.** $\dfrac{1}{2}$

    3. _____

4. $\dfrac{x^2 - 4x}{3(x - 4)}$

    A. $\dfrac{x}{3}$ **B.** $\dfrac{x^2}{3}$ **C.** $x - 4$ **D.** $\dfrac{x - 4}{3}$

    4. _____

Find each product.

5. $\dfrac{4x}{3y} \cdot \dfrac{y^2}{2}$

    A. $\dfrac{2}{3}$ **B.** $\dfrac{2x}{3}$ **C.** $\dfrac{2xy}{3}$ **D.** $\dfrac{2x}{3}$

    5. _____

6. $\dfrac{a^2 - 16}{a + 2} \cdot \dfrac{3a + 6}{a^2 - 3a - 4}$

    A. $\dfrac{3(a - 4)}{a + 1}$ **B.** $\dfrac{3(a + 4)(a + 3)}{a + 1}$ **C.** $\dfrac{3(a + 4)}{a + 1}$ **D.** $\dfrac{3(a - 4)}{(a + 1)(a + 2)}$

    6. _____

Find each quotient.

7. $\dfrac{3ab}{c} \div \dfrac{3}{4c}$

    A. $\dfrac{9ab}{4c^2}$ **B.** $12ab$ **C.** $\dfrac{ab}{c}$ **D.** $4ab$

    7. _____

8. $\dfrac{g^2 + 3g + 2}{4} \div \dfrac{g + 2}{8}$

    A. $\dfrac{g + 1}{2}$ **B.** $2(g + 1)$ **C.** $\dfrac{g + 2}{2}$ **D.** $2(g + 2)$

    8. _____

9. $(x^2 + 5x) \div (x + 5)$

    A. x **B.** $x + 5$ **C.** x^2 **D.** $\dfrac{x}{5}$

    9. _____

10. $(k^2 - k - 20) \div (k - 5)$

    A. $k + 4$ **B.** $k - 5$ **C.** $k - 4$ **D.** $\dfrac{k + 4}{k - 5}$

    10. _____

11. Find $(4y^2 - 9y + 2) \div (4y - 1)$.

    A. $\dfrac{y - 2}{4y}$ B. $\dfrac{y}{4}$ C. $y - 2$ D. $y + 2$ 11. _____

For Questions 12–14, find each sum or difference. Write in simplest form.

12. $\dfrac{8}{14b} - \dfrac{3}{14b}$

    A. $\dfrac{11}{14b}$ B. $\dfrac{5}{b}$ C. 5 D. $\dfrac{5}{14b}$ 12. _____

13. $\dfrac{7}{3e} + \dfrac{-5}{e}$

    A. $\dfrac{2}{3}$ B. $\dfrac{12}{3e}$ C. $\dfrac{4}{e}$ D. $\dfrac{-8}{3e}$ 13. _____

14. $\dfrac{12}{x - 3} - \dfrac{9}{x - 3}$

    A. $\dfrac{1}{x - 3}$ B. $\dfrac{1}{x}$ C. $\dfrac{3}{x}$ D. $\dfrac{3}{x - 3}$ 14. _____

15. Find the LCM for $14x^2$ and $12xy$.

    A. $84x^2y$ B. $2x$ C. $14x^2y$ D. $48x^2y$ 15. _____

16. Write $\dfrac{2}{ab}$ and $\dfrac{3}{ac}$ with the same LCD.

    A. $\dfrac{2c + 3b}{abc}$ B. $\dfrac{5}{abc}$ C. $\dfrac{2c}{abc}, \dfrac{3b}{abc}$ D. $\dfrac{5}{a^2bc}$ 16. _____

17. Find $\dfrac{y}{3} - \dfrac{y}{7}$ in simplest form.

    A. $-\dfrac{y}{4}$ B. $\dfrac{4y}{21}$ C. 0 D. $\dfrac{2y}{14}$ 17. _____

Solve each equation. Check your solution.

18. $\dfrac{h}{4} = \dfrac{6 - h}{8}$

    A. 6 B. 3 C. 2 D. $\dfrac{1}{2}$ 18. _____

19. $\dfrac{1 - x}{x} + \dfrac{2 - x}{x} = 7$

    A. -2 B. $\dfrac{1}{3}$ C. $\dfrac{3}{5}$ D. 2 19. _____

20. $\dfrac{1}{3y} + \dfrac{1}{y} = \dfrac{1}{3}$

    A. $\dfrac{1}{12}$ B. $\dfrac{1}{4}$ C. $\dfrac{4}{3}$ D. 4 20. _____

Bonus Solve $\dfrac{8}{a^2 - 5a + 6} = \dfrac{1}{a - 2} + \dfrac{2}{a - 3}$. Check your solution.

    A. $\dfrac{13}{2}$ B. 5 C. $\dfrac{5}{3}$ D. 0 **Bonus** _____

15 Chapter 15 Test, Form 1B

Write the letter for the correct answer in the blank at the right of each problem.

Find the excluded value(s) for each rational expression.

1. $\dfrac{a}{a + 7}$

    A. -7 **B.** 0   **C.** 1   **D.** 7   1. _____

2. $\dfrac{x + 4}{(x + 4)(x + 3)}$

    A. 0   **B.** $\dfrac{1}{x + 3}$ **C.** $-3, -4$ **D.** 3, 4   2. _____

Simplify each rational expression.

3. $\dfrac{8}{20}$

    A. $\dfrac{1}{8}$ **B.** $\dfrac{1}{3}$ **C.** $\dfrac{2}{5}$ **D.** $\dfrac{4}{5}$ 3. _____

4. $\dfrac{(x + 2)(x - 5)}{(x - 5)(x + 3)}$

    A. $\dfrac{2}{3}$ **B.** $x + \dfrac{2}{3}$ **C.** $x + 2$ **D.** $\dfrac{x + 2}{x + 3}$ 4. _____

Find each product.

5. $\dfrac{gh}{gm} \cdot \dfrac{m}{n}$

    A. h **B.** $\dfrac{h}{n}$ **C.** 1   **D.** $\dfrac{hm}{nh}$ 5. _____

6. $\dfrac{2a + 2}{a^2 - 4} \cdot \dfrac{a + 2}{a^2 + a}$

    A. $\dfrac{2}{a(a - 2)}$ **B.** $\dfrac{(a + 2)^2}{a^2 + a - 4}$ **C.** $\dfrac{a + 2}{a - 2}$ **D.** $\dfrac{2}{a - 2}$ 6. _____

Find each quotient.

7. $\dfrac{x^2}{y} \div \dfrac{x}{y^2}$

    A. $\dfrac{x}{y}$ **B.** $\dfrac{x^3}{y^3}$ **C.** xy **D.** $\dfrac{x^2}{y^2}$ 7. _____

8. $\dfrac{4c^2}{b + 3} \div \dfrac{4c}{b + 3}$

    A. $\dfrac{4c^2}{(b + 3)^2}$ **B.** $\dfrac{c}{b + 3}$ **C.** c **D.** 1   8. _____

9. $(12a - 3) \div (4a - 1)$

    A. $\dfrac{1}{3a}$ **B.** 3   **C.** 4   **D.** $\dfrac{1}{3}$ 9. _____

10. $(8b^2 + 20b) \div (2b + 5)$

    A. $\dfrac{b}{5}$ **B.** $\dfrac{b}{b + 5}$ **C.** $b + 4$ **D.** $4b$ 10. _____

11. Find $(d^2 + 5d + 6) \div (d + 3)$.
    A. $d + 2$ **B.** $d - 3$ **C.** $d + 3$ **D.** $d - 2$

11. _____

For Questions 12–14, find each sum or difference. Write in simplest form.

12. $\frac{6}{g} + \frac{7}{g}$

    A. $\frac{13}{g}$ **B.** 13   **C.** $13g$ **D.** $\frac{13}{2g}$

12. _____

13. $\frac{5k}{2} - \frac{4k}{2}$

    A. 0   **B.** k **C.** $\frac{k}{2}$ **D.** $\frac{k}{0}$

13. _____

14. $\frac{m}{3} + \frac{2m}{3}$

    A. $\frac{3m}{9}$ **B.** m **C.** $\frac{3m}{6}$ **D.** $\frac{m}{2}$

14. _____

15. Find the LCM for $4a$ and $6ab$.
    A. $12a^2b$ **B.** $24a^2b$ **C.** $10ab$ **D.** $12ab$

15. _____

16. Write $\frac{2}{x^2}$ and $\frac{3}{x}$ with the same LCD.

    A. $\frac{5x}{x^2}$ **B.** $\frac{5}{x^2}$ **C.** $\frac{2}{x^2}, \frac{3x}{x^2}$ **D.** $\frac{6}{x^3}$

16. _____

17. Find $\frac{y}{10} - \frac{y}{20}$ in simplest form.

    A. $-\frac{y}{10}$ **B.** $\frac{y}{20}$ **C.** $-\frac{1}{10}$ **D.** $-\frac{y}{20}$

17. _____

Solve each equation. Check your solution.

18. $\frac{4x}{6} + \frac{x}{3} = 2$

    A. $\frac{5}{6}$ **B.** 1   **C.** 2   **D.** 3

18. _____

19. $\frac{x}{4} = \frac{x + 10}{12}$

    A. 5   **B.** $\frac{40}{16}$ **C.** $\frac{5}{2}$ **D.** 2

19. _____

20. $\frac{2}{a} + \frac{24}{3a} = -\frac{5}{2}$

    A. -10 **B.** -4 **C.** $-\frac{2}{5}$ **D.** $\frac{1}{4}$

20. _____

Bonus Solve $\frac{x + 1}{x} + \frac{x - 1}{x} = 4x$. Check your solution.

     A. 1   **B.** $\frac{1}{2}$ **C.** $\frac{1}{3}$ **D.** -3

Bonus _____

15 Chapter 15 Test, Form 2A

Find the excluded value(s) for each rational expression.

1. $\dfrac{6m}{2m + 5}$

1. _____

2. $\dfrac{3s}{(s - 1)(s + 3)}$

2. _____

Simplify each rational expression.

3. $\dfrac{8x}{10y}$

3. _____

4. $\dfrac{a(a + 7)}{b(a + 7)}$

4. _____

Find each product.

5. $\dfrac{3(x + y)}{4} \cdot \dfrac{4}{5(x + y)}$

5. _____

6. $\dfrac{5a + 25}{3a} \cdot \dfrac{6a}{2a + 10}$

6. _____

Find each quotient.

7. $\dfrac{x^2 + 7x + 12}{x^2} \div \dfrac{(x + 3)}{x}$

7. _____

8. $\dfrac{a^2 - 16}{5a} \div (a - 4)$

8. _____

9. $(x^3 + 2x^2 + 2x + 1) \div (x + 1)$

9. _____

10. $(9k^2 - 6k) \div (3k - 2)$

10. _____

11. $(a^2 - 2a - 63) \div (a + 7)$

11. _____

12. $(3x^2 - 10x - 8) \div (3x + 2)$

12. _____

Find each sum or difference. Write in simplest form.

13. $\dfrac{11}{k} + \dfrac{9}{k}$

13. _____

14. $\dfrac{12t}{17} - \dfrac{5t}{17}$

14. _____

15. $\dfrac{8y}{y + 2} + \dfrac{-6y}{y + 2}$

15. _____

16. $\dfrac{5x - 9}{2y - 3} - \dfrac{3x - 6}{2y - 3}$

16. _____

Algebra: Concepts and Applications

17. Find the LCM for $x^2 - 4$ and $x^2 + 4x + 4$.

17. _____

18. Write $\frac{8a}{b}$ and $\frac{a}{b^2}$ with the same LCD.

18. _____

Find each sum or difference. Write in simplest form.

19. $\frac{3}{4xy} + \frac{4}{y^2}$

19. _____

20. $\frac{7}{3x} + \frac{5}{2x}$

20. _____

21. $\frac{4}{yz} - \frac{2}{xy^2}$

21. _____

Solve each equation. Check your solution.

22. $\frac{1}{3x} + \frac{1}{x+1} = \frac{1}{2}$

22. _____

23. $\frac{x}{8} = \frac{x+4}{12}$

23. _____

24. $\frac{y}{7} = \frac{y-2}{21}$

24. _____

25. $\frac{-4}{x+1} + \frac{1}{x} = \frac{-7}{x}$

25. _____

Bonus Solve $\frac{-4}{x^2 + 3x + 2} = \frac{3}{x+1} + \frac{4}{x+2}$.

Bonus _____

15

Chapter 15 Test, Form 2B

Find the excluded value(s) for each rational expression.

1. $\dfrac{6}{m(m + 1)}$

1. _____

2. $\dfrac{4s}{s^2 + 3s}$

2. _____

Simplify each rational expression.

3. $\dfrac{15}{30}$

3. _____

4. $\dfrac{a + 3}{4(a + 3)}$

4. _____

Find each product.

5. $\dfrac{4(x - y)}{x} \cdot \dfrac{x}{x - y}$

5. _____

6. $\dfrac{8a}{a + 7} \cdot \dfrac{2a + 14}{16a}$

6. _____

Find each quotient.

7. $\dfrac{b^2}{b - 6} \div \dfrac{b}{b - 6}$

7. _____

8. $5cd \div \dfrac{10c}{d}$

8. _____

9. $(e^2 - e - 12) \div (e - 4)$

9. _____

10. $(6x + 9) \div (2x + 3)$

10. _____

11. $(a^2 + 11a + 30) \div (a + 5)$

11. _____

12. $(2x^2 + 7x + 3) \div (2x + 1)$

12. _____

Find each sum or difference. Write in simplest form.

13. $\dfrac{9}{k} + \dfrac{8}{k}$

13. _____

14. $\dfrac{8t}{21} - \dfrac{5t}{21}$

14. _____

15. $\dfrac{4y}{y + 2} + \dfrac{-y}{y + 2}$

15. _____

16. $\dfrac{p}{8} + \dfrac{3p}{8}$

16. _____

17. Find the LCM for $x^2 + 3x + 2$ and $x^2 + 5x + 6$.

17. _____

18. Write $\dfrac{3}{w}$ and $\dfrac{4}{w^2}$ with the same LCD.

18. _____

Find each sum or difference. Write in simplest form.

19. $\dfrac{3}{x} + \dfrac{x+3}{y}$

19. _____

20. $\dfrac{5}{3x} + \dfrac{2}{x}$

20. _____

21. $\dfrac{3}{a-1} - \dfrac{4}{2a-2}$

21. _____

Solve each equation. Check your solution.

22. $\dfrac{1}{2x} + \dfrac{1}{x} = \dfrac{3}{8}$

22. _____

23. $\dfrac{x}{5} = \dfrac{x+4}{9}$

23. _____

24. $\dfrac{3y}{2} = \dfrac{7+y}{4}$

24. _____

25. $\dfrac{6}{x+2} = \dfrac{2}{x-4}$

25. _____

Bonus Solve $\dfrac{-14}{x^2-1} = \dfrac{2}{x+1} + \dfrac{3}{x-1}$.

Bonus _____

15 Chapter 15 Open-Ended Assessment

Instructions: Demonstrate your knowledge by giving a clear, concise solution for each problem. Be sure to include all relevant drawings and to justify your answers. You may show your solution in more than one way or investigate beyond the requirements of the problem.

1. Simplify $\dfrac{3x - 15}{x^2 - 2x - 15}$.

2. What is the quotient when $\dfrac{14ac^2 + 21bc^2}{4a^2 - 9b^2}$ is divided by $\dfrac{c^2}{2a - 3b}$?

3. Find the width of the rectangle with the length and area shown.

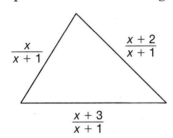

$x - 3$ cm

area $= 4x^2 - 5x - 21$ cm^2

4. Find the perimeter of the triangle shown.

$\dfrac{x}{x + 1}$

$\dfrac{x + 2}{x + 1}$

$\dfrac{x + 3}{x + 1}$

5. Write two rational expressions with unlike denominators in which one of the denominators is the least common denominator of the rational expressions.

6. A kayaker paddling at a steady rate travels 10 miles with the river current. She can travel only 4 miles against the current in the same amount of time. If the rate of the current is 8 miles per hour, what is the kayaker's rate without the current? (*Hint:* Use the formula $d = rt$.)

15

Chapter 15 Mid-Chapter Test
(Lessons 15–1 through 15–3)

Find the excluded value(s) for each rational expression.

1. $\dfrac{x}{x + 6}$

1. _____

2. $\dfrac{x + 1}{(x + 1)(x - 2)}$

2. _____

Simplify each rational expression.

3. $\dfrac{8}{14}$

3. _____

4. $\dfrac{(x + 1)(x - 3)}{(x - 3)(x + 2)}$

4. _____

5. $\dfrac{x^2 - 7x - 8}{x^2 - 1}$

5. _____

Find each product.

6. $\dfrac{4a}{3b} \cdot \dfrac{3b^2}{8}$

6. _____

7. $\dfrac{5(m - n)}{3} \cdot \dfrac{3}{10(m - n)}$

7. _____

Find each quotient.

8. $\dfrac{e^2}{3f} \div \dfrac{e^3}{6f}$

8. _____

9. $\dfrac{x^2 - 9}{y^2 + 4y} \div \dfrac{x + 3}{y + 4}$

9. _____

10. $\dfrac{b^2 - 3b}{a^2 + 5a} \div \dfrac{b}{a}$

10. _____

11. $(18k - 24) \div (3k - 4)$

11. _____

12. $(x^2 + 7x) \div (x + 7)$

12. _____

13. $(b^3 - 7b^2) \div (b - 7)$

13. _____

14. $(3x^2 - 7x + 2) \div (x - 2)$

14. _____

15. $(x^3 + 2x^2 + 4x + 3) \div (x + 1)$

15. _____

16. $(y^3 + 5y^2 - 2y - 24) \div (y + 4)$

16. _____

   Algebra: Concepts and Applications

NAME _____ DATE _____ PERIOD _____

Chapter 15 Quiz A
(Lessons 15–1 and 15–2)

1. Find the excluded value(s) for $\dfrac{k+4}{k-5}$.

1. _____

Simplify each rational expression.

2. $\dfrac{9}{27}$

2. _____

3. $\dfrac{x^2 - 8x}{3(x - 8)}$

3. _____

For Questions 4–5, find each product.

4. $\dfrac{14x^2}{12y^2} \cdot \dfrac{18y^3}{21x}$

4. _____

5. $\dfrac{3a^2}{4b} \cdot \dfrac{6c^3}{5a}$

5. _____

6. Find $\dfrac{9a^3b^2}{4} \div \dfrac{6ab^3}{2}$.

6. _____

NAME _____ DATE _____ PERIOD _____

Chapter 15 Quiz B
(Lessons 15–3 through 15–6)

Find each quotient.

1. $(y^2 - 7y + 10) \div (y - 5)$

1. _____

2. $(a^2 - 5a - 36) \div (a - 9)$

2. _____

Find each sum or difference. Write in simplest form.

3. $\dfrac{7}{15p} - \dfrac{3}{15p}$

3. _____

4. $\dfrac{2}{t + 8} + \dfrac{6}{t + 8}$

4. _____

5. $\dfrac{b}{3} - \dfrac{b}{9}$

5. _____

6. $\dfrac{x}{x + 1} + \dfrac{2x}{x - 1}$

6. _____

Solve each equation. Check your solution.

7. $\dfrac{4}{x} + \dfrac{5}{x} = 3$

7. _____

8. $\dfrac{2}{y - 1} = \dfrac{18}{8y - 4}$

8. _____

1. Write an equation for the sentence below. *(Lesson 1–1)*
   The product of a number k and 17 is equal to 68.

   1. _____

2. Find $-15 + (-3)$. *(Lesson 2–3)*

   2. _____

3. Write $\frac{3}{8}$, 4.2, 0.95, 1.7, and -3 in order from least to greatest.
   (Lesson 3–1)

   3. _____

4. Find $-\frac{3}{8}\left(-\frac{1}{3}\right)$. *(Lesson 4–1)*

   4. _____

5. Use the percent proportion to find 8% of 250. *(Lesson 5–3)*

   5. _____

6. If y varies inversely as x and $y = 4$ when $x = 9$, find y when
   $x = 2$. *(Lesson 6–6)*

   6. _____

7. Write an equation in point-slope form of the line with slope $-\frac{1}{3}$
   and y-intercept 7. *(Lesson 7–2)*

   7. _____

8. Simplify $-\sqrt{\frac{25}{49}}$. *(Lesson 8–5)*

   8. _____

9. Find $(x + 2y)(2x + y)$. *(Lesson 9–4)*

   9. _____

10. Factor $7k^3 - 7k$. *(Lesson 10–5)*

    10. _____

11. Describe how the graph of $y = \frac{1}{2}x^2$ changes from its parent
    graph of $y = x^2$. Then name the vertex. *(Lesson 11–2)*

    11. _____

12. Solve $-\frac{1}{2} \le a + \frac{1}{3}$. *(Lesson 12–2)*

    12. _____

13. What is the solution of the system $y = x + 5$ and $3x = -2y$?
    (Lesson 13–3)

    13. _____

For Questions 14–15, solve each equation. (Lesson 14–5)

14. $\sqrt{\frac{x}{3}} + 2 = 7$

    14. _____

15. $\frac{\sqrt{y - 3}}{y} = \frac{1}{4}$

    15. _____

16. Simplify $\frac{m^2 - 25}{m^2 - 3m - 10}$. *(Lesson 15–1)*

    16. _____

Algebra: Concepts and Applications

15 Chapter 15 Standardized Test Practice
(Chapters 1–15)

Write the letter for the correct answer in the blank at the right of each problem.

1. Which is the equation for the sentence below?

   The quotient of five and a number n is one half.

   A. $5n = \frac{1}{2}$ **B.** $\frac{5}{n} = \frac{1}{2}$ **C.** $5 = \frac{1}{2} \cdot n$ **D.** $\frac{n}{5} = 1\frac{1}{2}$

   1. _____

2. Simplify $-5x + (-2x)$.

   A. $-7x$ **B.** $-3x$ **C.** $7x$ **D.** 3

   2. _____

3. Which of the following is *not* a true statement about the set of data below?

   $$5, 8, 12, 12, 12, 14, 18, 20$$

   A. The mode is 12.
   B. The median is 12.
   C. The range is 25.
   D. The mean is larger than either the mode or the median.

   3. _____

4. The product of two negative integers is
   A. undefined.   **B.** zero.
   C. always positive.   **D.** always negative.

   4. _____

5. One letter from the word CANADA is chosen at random. What is the probability that a letter A is chosen?

   A. 5   **B.** 3   **C.** $\frac{1}{2}$ **D.** $\frac{1}{6}$

   5. _____

6. Which of the following is a linear equation?

   A. $y = \frac{1}{x}$ **B.** $y - x = 17$ **C.** $y = x^2$ **D.** $xy = 12$

   6. _____

7. Determine the slope of the line passing through points at (4, 1) and (0, −2).

   A. $-\frac{5}{2}$ **B.** $-\frac{4}{3}$ **C.** $\frac{3}{4}$ **D.** undefined

   7. _____

8. Which of the following is equivalent to $\frac{a^9}{a^3}$?

   A. $\frac{a^7}{a}$ **B.** a^3 **C.** 6   **D.** $\frac{1}{a^6}$

   8. _____

9. Which expression is equivalent to $z^2 - 25$?
   A. $(z - 5)(z - 5)$ **B.** $(z - 5)^2$
   C. $(z + 25)(z - 25)$ **D.** $(z + 5)(z - 5)$

   9. _____

10. The expression $5x$ is the GCF of which pair of monomials?
    A. 5 and x **B.** x and x^5
    C. $5xy$ and $15xz$ **D.** $10xy$ and $12wx$

    10. _____

11. Which exponential function does *not* have a *y*-intercept of 1?

    A. $y = 2^x$ **B.** $y = 0.5^x$ **C.** $y = -5^x$ **D.** $y = 10^x$ **11.** _____

12. What value of *c* makes the trinomial $r^2 + 12r + c$ a perfect square?

    A. 4   **B.** 6   **C.** 24   **D.** 36   **12.** _____

For Questions 13–14, solve each inequality.

13. $\frac{a}{4} > 3$

    A. $\{a \,|\, a > 7\}$ **B.** $\{a \,|\, a > 12\}$ **C.** $\left\{a \,|\, a > \frac{3}{4}\right\}$ **D.** $\{a \,|\, a > -1\}$ **13.** _____

14. $\frac{3}{4}x - 5 < -11$

    A. $\{x \,|\, x < -8\}$ **B.** $\{x \,|\, x > 8\}$ **C.** $\{x \,|\, x > -8\}$ **D.** $\{x \,|\, x < 8\}$ **14.** _____

15. Which of the following is a solution of $y = 3x + 2$ and $2x + y = 2$?

    A. The system has no solution.   **B.** $(0, 0)$

    C. $(0, 2)$ **D.** $(3, 2)$ **15.** _____

16. $(0, 0)$ is a solution of which of the following systems?

    A. $y = x^2$ and $y = -x^2 - 1$ **B.** $y = x^2$ and $y = x$

    C. $y = x^2$ and $y = 2x - 5$ **D.** $y = x$ and $y = x + 1$ **16.** _____

For Questions 17–18, simplify each expression.

17. $\dfrac{\sqrt{80}}{\sqrt{10}}$

    A. $2\sqrt{2}$ **B.** $\dfrac{4\sqrt{20}}{\sqrt{10}}$ **C.** $\sqrt{8}$ **D.** $\dfrac{5\sqrt{4}}{\sqrt{10}}$ **17.** _____

18. $\dfrac{\sqrt{17}}{\sqrt{34}}$

    A. $\dfrac{\sqrt{2}}{2}$ **B.** $\dfrac{1}{2}$ **C.** $\dfrac{1}{4}$ **D.** $\dfrac{1}{1.414}$ **18.** _____

For Questions 19–20, find each sum or difference. Write in simplest form.

19. $\dfrac{1}{2xy} + \dfrac{3}{yz}$

    A. $\dfrac{3}{2xyz}$ **B.** $2xyz$ **C.** $\dfrac{z + 2x}{xyz}$ **D.** $\dfrac{z + 6x}{2xyz}$ **19.** _____

20. $\dfrac{h}{3} - \dfrac{h}{5}$

    A. $-\dfrac{2h}{15}$ **B.** $\dfrac{h}{2}$ **C.** $\dfrac{h}{8}$ **D.** $\dfrac{2h}{15}$ **20.** _____

Chapter 15 Answer Key

Form 1A

Page 281

1. __A__

2. __B__

3. __C__

4. __A__

5. __C__

6. __C__

7. __D__

8. __B__

9. __A__

10. __A__

Page 282

11. __C__

12. __D__

13. __D__

14. __D__

15. __A__

16. __C__

17. __B__

18. __C__

19. __B__

20. __D__

Bonus __B__

Form 1B

Page 283

1. __A__

2. __C__

3. __C__

4. __D__

5. __B__

6. __A__

7. __C__

8. __C__

9. __B__

10. __D__

Page 284

11. __A__

12. __A__

13. __C__

14. __B__

15. __D__

16. __C__

17. __B__

18. __C__

19. __A__

20. __B__

Bonus __B__

Chapter 15 Answer Key

Form 2A

Page 285

1. $-\dfrac{5}{2}$

2. $1, -3$

3. $\dfrac{4x}{5y}$

4. $\dfrac{a}{b}$

5. $\dfrac{3}{5}$

6. 5

7. $\dfrac{x + 4}{x}$

8. $\dfrac{a + 4}{5a}$

9. $x^2 + x + 1$

10. $3k$

11. $a - 9$

12. $x - 4$

13. $\dfrac{20}{k}$

14. $\dfrac{7t}{17}$

15. $\dfrac{2y}{y + 2}$

16. $\dfrac{2x - 3}{2y - 3}$

Page 286

17. $(x + 2)^2(x - 2)$

18. $\dfrac{8ab}{b^2}, \dfrac{a}{b^2}$

19. $\dfrac{3y + 16x}{4xy^2}$

20. $\dfrac{29}{6x}$

21. $\dfrac{4xy - 2z}{xy^2z}$

22. $2, -\dfrac{1}{3}$

23. 8

24. -1

25. -2

Bonus -2

Chapter 15 Answer Key
Form 2B

1. $0, -1$

2. $0, -3$

3. $\dfrac{1}{2}$

4. $\dfrac{1}{4}$

5. 4

6. 1

7. b

8. $\dfrac{d^2}{2}$

9. $e + 3$

10. 3

11. $a + 6$

12. $x + 3$

13. $\dfrac{17}{k}$

14. $\dfrac{t}{7}$

15. $\dfrac{3y}{y + 2}$

16. $\dfrac{p}{2}$

17. $(x + 1)(x + 2)(x + 3)$

18. $\dfrac{3w}{w^2}, \dfrac{4}{w^2}$

19. $\dfrac{3y + x^2 + 3x}{xy}$

20. $\dfrac{11}{3x}$

21. $\dfrac{1}{a - 1}$

22. 4

23. 5

24. 1.4

25. 7

Bonus -3

Chapter 15 Answer Key

Open-Ended Assessment
Sample Answers
Page 289

1. $\dfrac{3}{x+3}$

2. 7

3. $4x + 7$ centimeters

4. $\dfrac{3x+5}{x+1}$

5. $\dfrac{5}{xy}, \dfrac{2}{x}$

6. $18\dfrac{2}{3}$ or 18.67 miles per hour

Chapter 15 Answer Key

1. -6

2. $-1, 2$

3. $\dfrac{4}{7}$

4. $\dfrac{x + 1}{x + 2}$

5. $\dfrac{x - 8}{x - 1}$

6. $\dfrac{ab}{2}$

7. $\dfrac{1}{2}$

8. $\dfrac{2}{e}$

9. $\dfrac{x - 3}{y}$

10. $\dfrac{b - 3}{a + 5}$

11. 6

12. x

13. b^2

14. $3x - 1$

15. $x^2 + x + 3$

16. $y^2 + y - 6$

1. 5

2. $\dfrac{1}{3}$

3. $\dfrac{x}{3}$

4. xy

5. $\dfrac{9ac^3}{10b}$

6. $\dfrac{3a^2}{4b}$

1. $y - 2$

2. $a + 4$

3. $\dfrac{4}{15p}$

4. $\dfrac{8}{t + 8}$

5. $\dfrac{2b}{9}$

6. $\dfrac{x(3x + 1)}{x^2 - 1}$

7. 3

8. 5

Chapter 15 Answer Key

Cumulative Review
Page 292

1. $17k = 68$

2. -18

3. $-3, \frac{3}{8}, 0.95, 1.7, 4.2$

4. $\frac{1}{8}$

5. 20

6. 18

7. $y - 7 = -\frac{1}{3}x$

8. $-\frac{5}{7}$

9. $2x^2 + 5xy + 2y^2$

10. $7k(k - 1)(k + 1)$

11. widens; $(0, 0)$

12. $\{a | a \geq -\frac{5}{6}\}$

13. $(-2, 3)$

14. 75

15. 4 or 12

16. $\dfrac{m + 5}{m + 2}$

Standardized Test Practice
Page 293

1. B

2. A

3. C

4. C

5. C

6. B

7. C

8. A

9. D

10. C

Page 294

11. C

12. D

13. B

14. A

15. C

16. B

17. A

18. A

19. D

20. D

Algebra: Concepts and Applications

Semester Test
(Chapters 1–8)

Write the letter for the correct answer in the blank at the right of each problem.

For Questions 1–4, refer to the figure at the right. The figure shows the ages of runners in a senior's race.

Stem	Leaf
6	7 8 8 9
7	1 3 4 4 5 7
8	0 0 1 1 1 $6\mid7 = 67$

1. How many runners were younger than 70 years?

   A. 4   **B.** 5   **C.** 6   **D.** 7   1. _____

2. What was the difference in age between the oldest and youngest runner in this group?

   A. 81   **B.** 67   **C.** 14   **D.** 12   2. _____

3. Which term describes the difference in age between the oldest and youngest runner?

   A. mean   **B.** range   **C.** mode   **D.** median   3. _____

4. Which of the following has a value of 81?

   A. mean   **B.** range   **C.** mode   **D.** median   4. _____

For Questions 5–6, name the quadrant in which each point is located.

5. (10, 2)

   A. I   **B.** II   **C.** III   **D.** IV   5. _____

6. (−1, −8)

   A. I   **B.** II   **C.** III   **D.** IV   6. _____

7. A student has 4 shirts and 2 pairs of jeans to wear. How many different shirt and jean outfits are possible?

   A. 6   **B.** 8   **C.** 12   **D.** 16   7. _____

8. Which of the following statements about multiplicative inverses is true?

   A. A reciprocal is the same as a multiplicative inverse.

   B. Two numbers with a sum of 1 are multiplicative inverses.

   C. The numbers $\frac{1}{2}$ and −2 are multiplicative inverses.

   D. The numbers −7 and 7 are multiplicative inverses.   8. _____

9. Solve $\frac{x+1}{8} = \frac{x-2}{4}$.

   A. −4   **B.** $\frac{1}{2}$ **C.** $\frac{3}{2}$ **D.** 5   9. _____

10. A scale model of a sailboat is 6 inches long. If the sailboat is 30 feet long, find the scale of the model.

   A. 1 in. = $\frac{1}{2}$ ft   **B.** 1 ft = 6 in.   **C.** 2 in. = 60 ft   **D.** 1 in. = 5 ft   10. _____

Semester Test
(Chapters 1–8) *(continued)*

11. What number is 30% of 140?

    A. 420   **B.** 110   **C.** 46.67   **D.** 42   **11.** _____

12. Which of the following is the domain of $\{(-3, 2), (-2, 3), (-1, 5), (0, 7)\}$?

    A. $\{3, 2, 1, 0\}$ **B.** $\{2, 3, 5, 7\}$

    C. $\{-3, -2, 2, 3\}$ **D.** $\{-3, -2, -1, 0\}$ **12.** _____

13. The table lists the coordinates of points whose graphs are on a straight line. Find the values a, b, and c.

    A. $a = -2, b = -2, c = 0$

    B. $a = 2, b = 2, c = 0$

    C. $a = -1, b = 2, c = 3$

    D. $a = -2, b = 1, c = 1$

x	y
-3	-6
a	-4
-1	b
0	c
1	2

    13. _____

14. The relation $\{(-3, 2), (-2, 3), (m, n), (0, 2), (-1, 1)\}$ is a function. Which of the following could be substituted for (m, n)?

    A. $(-3, 5)$ **B.** $(-2, 1)$ **C.** $(1, 2)$ **D.** $(-1, 0)$ **14.** _____

15. Determine the slope of the line through points at $(-2, 5)$ and $(6, 3)$.

    A. -4 **B.** $-\dfrac{7}{9}$ **C.** $-\dfrac{1}{4}$ **D.** 1 **15.** _____

16. Which of the following statements about the graph of $y = \dfrac{1}{4}x - 4$ is correct?

    A. The graph has a negative slope.

    B. The graph crosses the y-axis at $(0, -4)$.

    C. The graph shows an inverse variation.

    D. The graph passes through only the first and fourth quadrants.   **16.** _____

17. Which pair of equations represents perpendicular lines?

    A. $y = x$ and $y = 2x$ **B.** $y = -3x$ and $y = 3x$

    C. $y = 5x + 1$ and $y = 5x + 3$ **D.** $y = \dfrac{1}{4}x + 2$ and $y = -4x + 2$ **17.** _____

18. Write the expression $5 \cdot 5 \cdot 5 \cdot 7 \cdot 7$ using exponents.

    A. $5^2 \cdot 7^2$ **B.** $5 \cdot (57)^2$ **C.** $5^3 \cdot 7^2$ **D.** $(35)^2$ **18.** _____

19. Which of the following numbers is 5.4×10^{-3} written in standard form?

    A. 0.00054   **B.** 0.0054   **C.** 0.054   **D.** 54,000   **19.** _____

20. Which of the following is closest to 6?

    A. $\sqrt{6}$ **B.** $\sqrt{34}$ **C.** $\sqrt{40}$ **D.** $\sqrt{66}$ **20.** _____

Semester Test
(Chapters 1–8) *(continued)*

For Questions 21–22, write an equation for each sentence.

21. The sum of x and 7 equals 25.

21. _____

22. The quotient of 17 and y is 4.

22. _____

23. Find the value of $\frac{24 - (9 \times 2)}{3}$.

23. _____

24. Name the property shown by $5 \cdot (4 \cdot x) = (5 \cdot 4) \cdot x$.

24. _____

25. Order the numbers $-51, 4, 0, -1, -4, 53$ from greatest to least.

25. _____

Write the ordered pair that names each point.

26. P

26. _____

27. Q

27. _____

Find each sum, difference, or product.

28. $9 + (-2)$

28. _____

29. $-7 - (-8)$

29. _____

30. $1.2 - (-6.2)$

30. _____

31. $\frac{9}{5} - \frac{4}{5}$

31. _____

32. $8(3.4)$

32. _____

Replace each ● with $<$, $>$, or $=$ to make a true sentence.

33. 5.7 ● 5.70

33. _____

34. 0.68 ● -6.08

34. _____

Solve each equation. Check your solution.

35. $|c - 4| = 5$

35. _____

36. $8m = 72$

36. _____

37. $-2p + 4 = 6$

37. _____

38. $15 = 45(x \div 6)$

38. _____

39. Find the percent of increase from $32 to $36.

39. _____

40. Find the probability that a letter chosen at random from the word SEMESTER is not an E.

40. _____

41. What does a probability of 0 mean?

41. _____

42. Find the domain of $y = x + 5$ if the range is $\{-4, -1, 0, 3\}$.

42. _____

43. Use the fact that there are 12 inches in one foot to find the number of inches in $14\frac{1}{2}$ feet.

43. _____

44. Does the graph show *direct variation* or *inverse variation*? Explain.

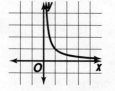

44. _____

45. The line shown in the figure passes through points at $(4, -1)$ and $(0, 5)$. Write an equation in point-slope form of the line.

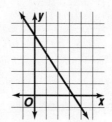

45. _____

46. Determine the slope and y-intercept of the graph of the equation $y = -2x + 7$. Then graph the equation.

46. _____

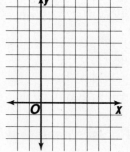

47. Change $y = -\frac{1}{4}x - 8$ so that the graph of the new equation has the same slope but is shifted up 2 units.

47. _____

Simplify each expression.

48. $(x^2y)(xy^3)$

48. _____

49. $\dfrac{b^5}{b^{-3}}$

49. _____

50. $-\sqrt{\dfrac{144}{100}}$

50. _____

Semester Test
(Chapters 9–15)

Write the letter for the correct answer in the blank at the right of each problem.

1. Which polynomial has the greatest degree?

    A. 7   **B.** $-4x^4$ **C.** $6x^2$ **D.** x **1.** _____

2. Find $(8y^2 - 7y) + (5y - y^2)$.

    A. $7y^2 - 2y$ **B.** $6y^2 - 2y$ **C.** $13y^2 - 8y$ **D.** $8y^2 - 13y$ **2.** _____

3. What is the GCF of $7m$, $28m^2$, and $14mn$?

    A. $7m$ **B.** $2m^2$ **C.** $4mn$ **D.** m **3.** _____

For Questions 4–5, factor each polynomial.

4. $9ab + 28c + 9b$

    A. $9(ab + 3c + b)$ **B.** $9b(a + 1)$

    C. $9b(a + 4c + 1)$ **D.** prime   **4.** _____

5. $64 - k^2$

    A. $(8 - k)(8 + k)$ **B.** $(8 - k)^2$

    C. $(8 + k)^2$ **D.** prime   **5.** _____

6. Describe how the graph of $y = (x - 3)^2$ changes from the parent graph of $y = x^2$.

    A. It shifts up 3 units.   **B.** It shifts left 3 units.

    C. It shifts down 3 units.   **D.** It shifts right 3 units.   **6.** _____

7. Find the roots of $x^2 + 5x - 14 = 0$.

    A. 2, −7   **B.** −2, 7   **C.** 2, 7   **D.** −2, −7   **7.** _____

8. Which is an equation for this graph?

    A. $y = 2^x$ **B.** $y = 2^x - 3$

    C. $y = -2^x$ **D.** $y = x - 2$

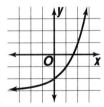

    8. _____

9. The statement $x + 3 < 6$ or $x > 8$ is an example of a(n)

    A. boundary.   **B.** intersection.

    C. union.   **D.** compound inequality.   **9.** _____

10. The set $\{x \,|\, x > 4\}$ is a solution of which of the following statements?

    A. $x = 4$ **B.** $(x + 4)^2 > 0$ **C.** $x + 2 > 6$ **D.** $-x > -4$ **10.** _____

11. Solve $-9k < -45$.

    A. $\{k \,|\, k < -5\}$ **B.** $\{k \,|\, k > -5\}$ **C.** $\{k \,|\, k < 5\}$ **D.** $\{k \,|\, k > 5\}$ **11.** _____

12. Which of the following statements about systems of equations is true?
   A. A system of equations is a set of two or more inequalities.
   B. A system is consistent and independent if the equations have the same slope.
   C. A consistent and dependent system of equations has infinitely many solutions.
   D. An inconsistent system of equations has one solution.

12. _____

For Questions 13–14, identify the solution to each system of equations.

13. $y = 2x - 5$ and $y = x - 3$
   A. $(2, -1)$ **B.** $(2, 1)$ **C.** $(0, -5)$ **D.** $(1, -2)$

13. _____

14. $y = x^2 + 1$ and $y = 2x$
   A. $(0, 1)$ **B.** $(0, 0)$ **C.** $(1, 1)$ **D.** $(1, 2)$

14. _____

15. Which number is an integer but *not* a whole number?
   A. -1 **B.** $\sqrt{2}$ **C.** 2 **D.** 2.5

15. _____

16. Which number is closest in value to 11?
   A. 5.5^2 **B.** $\sqrt{144}$ **C.** $\sqrt{115}$ **D.** $\sqrt{100}$

16. _____

17. The graph at the right shows a pair of points at $(3, 4)$ and $(6, 8)$. Find the distance between the points.
   A. 3   **B.** 4
   C. 5   **D.** 6

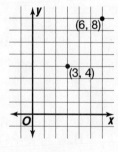

17. _____

18. What is the reciprocal of $x - 1$?
   A. $x + 1$ **B.** $1 - x$ **C.** $-\dfrac{1}{x-1}$ **D.** $\dfrac{1}{x-1}$

18. _____

Find each quotient.

19. $\dfrac{x^2 - 4}{3x} \div \dfrac{x - 2}{6x}$
   A. $\dfrac{(x+2)(x-2)}{18x^2}$ **B.** $x - 2$ **C.** $2(x + 2)$ **D.** $\dfrac{x-2}{x}$

19. _____

20. $(2m^2 - 3m - 27) \div (m + 3)$
   A. $m - 9$ **B.** $2m - 9$ **C.** $m + 9$ **D.** $2m - 3$

20. _____

21. Arrange the terms of $7 - 4x^2 + 2x - 8x^3$ so that the powers of x are in ascending order.

21. _____

For Questions 22–25, find each product.

22. $a^3(3a - 8a^2)$

22. _____

23. $(b + 12)(b - 2)$

23. _____

24. $(m + 3)(m - 8)$

24. _____

25. $(7k - 8)(7k + 8)$

25. _____

26. Find $(18x^3 + 14x^5) \div 2x$.

26. _____

For Questions 27–29, factor each trinomial.

27. $x^2 + 7x + 12$

27. _____

28. $2y^2 - y - 3$

28. _____

29. $b^2 + 12b + 36$

29. _____

30. Find the equation of the axis of symmetry and the coordinates of the vertex of the parabola $y = x^2 + x - 6$.

30. _____

31. Solve $17g^2 - 17 = 0$.

31. _____

32. Find the value of c that makes $a^2 + 22a + c$ a perfect square.

32. _____

33. Use the Quadratic Formula to solve $4x^2 - 16x - 1 = 0$.

33. _____

34. Write an inequality for this graph.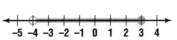
-5 -4 -3 -2 -1 0 1 2 3 4

34. _____

Solve each inequality.

35. $\frac{1}{2}x + 6 > 3$

35. _____

36. $-5 \leq y + 2 < 9$

36. _____

37. $|b - 10| \leq 5$

37. _____

Semester Test
(Chapters 9–15) *(continued)*

38. The equation of the dashed line in this graph is $y = 2x + 1$. Identify the inequality that is shown in the graph.

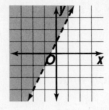

38. _____

For Questions 39–42, solve each system of equations.

39. $y = 3x$ and $y = -x + 2$

39. _____

40. $y = -x + 1$ and $y = \frac{1}{2}x - \frac{1}{2}$

40. _____

41. $2x + 3 = y$ and $2x - 5 = y$

41. _____

42. $2(x + y) = -2$ and $3y - 4x = 4$

42. _____

43. Solve the system $y > 1$ and $y > -x$ by graphing. If the system does not have a solution, write *no solution*.

43.

For Questions 44–46, simplify each expression. Leave in radical form. Use absolute value symbols if necessary.

44. $\sqrt{75}$

44. _____

45. $\sqrt{500a^2b}$

45. _____

46. $2\sqrt{18} + 2\sqrt{27}$

46. _____

47. Solve $\sqrt{-2d} = 3$.

47. _____

48. Simplify $\frac{5p^2qr^4}{10pr^3}$.

48. _____

Find each sum or difference.

49. $\frac{7}{3x} + \frac{1}{6x}$

49. _____

50. $\frac{7}{f} - \frac{1}{f + 2}$

50. _____

Final Test
(Chapters 1–15)

Write the letter for the correct answer in the blank at the right of each problem.

1. Evaluate $5xy + 2z$ if $x = -3$, $y = 2$, and $z = -5$.
   - **A.** -40
   - **B.** -20
   - **C.** 0
   - **D.** 20

   1. _____

2. Which of the following is *not* a way of organizing statistical data?
   - **A.** population
   - **B.** frequency table
   - **C.** line graph
   - **D.** histogram

   2. _____

3. Find $(-4ab)(-3c)$.
   - **A.** $12abc$
   - **B.** $-12ab$
   - **C.** $12bc$
   - **D.** $-12abc$

   3. _____

4. The value that occurs most frequently in a set of data is called the
   - **A.** mean.
   - **B.** median.
   - **C.** range.
   - **D.** mode.

   4. _____

5. Solve $|k - 2| = 4$.
   - **A.** 0 or -4
   - **B.** $\varnothing$
   - **C.** 2 or -2
   - **D.** 6 or -2

   5. _____

6. Find $8b(1.7f)$.
   - **A.** $9.7bf$
   - **B.** $8.7bf$
   - **C.** $2.5bf$
   - **D.** $13.6bf$

   6. _____

7. Solve $\frac{8}{20} = \frac{m}{250}$.
   - **A.** 80
   - **B.** 96
   - **C.** 100
   - **D.** 238

   7. _____

8. If $g(x) = -7x + 2$, find $g(-6)$.
   - **A.** -44
   - **B.** -40
   - **C.** $\frac{8}{7}$
   - **D.** 44

   8. _____

9. The graph at the right shows the pair of points at $(-4, -2)$ and $(-1, -1)$. Determine the slope of the line through the two points.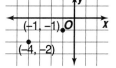
   - **A.** $\frac{1}{3}$
   - **B.** $-\frac{3}{5}$
   - **C.** -1
   - **D.** $-\frac{5}{3}$

   9. _____

10. Find the equation of the line in this graph.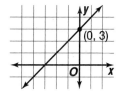
    - **A.** $y = 3$
    - **B.** $y = x - 3$
    - **C.** $y = x + 3$
    - **D.** $y = -x + 3$

    10. _____

11. Simplify $\frac{48b^6}{12b^2}$.
    - **A.** $3b^4$
    - **B.** $4b^3$
    - **C.** $3b^3$
    - **D.** $4b^4$

    11. _____

12. Find $(-8x^2y^3 - 3xy^2) + (5x^2y^3 - xy^2)$.
   A. $3x^2y^3 - 2xy^2$
   B. $-7x^2y^3$
   C. $-3x^2y^3 - 4xy^2$
   D. $-11x^2y^3 - 4xy^2$

   12. _____

13. Factor $8ab^2 + 16ab$.
   A. $24ab^2$
   B. $24a^2b^3$
   C. $8a^2(b + 2)$
   D. $8ab(b + 2)$

   13. _____

14. Factor $2p^2 - 9p + 10$.
   A. $(2p - 5)(p - 2)$
   B. $(p - 5)(p - 2)$
   C. $(p - 4)(p + 10)$
   D. $(p - 1)(p + 20)$

   14. _____

15. What is the equation of the parabola that moves the parent graph of $y = x^2$ down 10 units?
   A. $y = x^2 + 10$
   B. $y = x^2 - 10$
   C. $y = (x - 10)^2$
   D. $y = (x + 10)^2$

   15. _____

For Questions 16–17, solve each inequality.

16. $-x + 1 < -\dfrac{1}{2}$
   A. $x > -\dfrac{1}{2}$
   B. $x < \dfrac{3}{2}$
   C. $x > \dfrac{3}{2}$
   D. $x < \dfrac{1}{2}$

   16. _____

17. $|b + 2| < -1$
   A. $\varnothing$
   B. $b < -3$
   C. $b < 1$
   D. $b < -1$

   17. _____

18. Which system of equations is shown in the graph?
   A. $y = x + 2$ and $y = -\dfrac{1}{2}x$
   B. $y = x + 2$ and $y = -\dfrac{1}{2}x - 1$
   C. $y = x - 2$ and $y = -\dfrac{1}{2}x - 1$
   D. $y = x - \dfrac{1}{2}$ and $y = x + 2$

   18. _____

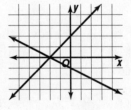

19. Which of the following numbers is *not* a member of the set of rational numbers?
   A. -1
   B. 0
   C. $\dfrac{1}{7}$
   D. $\sqrt{6}$

   19. _____

20. To divide $\dfrac{7}{x + 2}$ by $\dfrac{x - 2}{14}$, you can multiply $\dfrac{7}{x + 2}$ by which of the following?
   A. $\dfrac{x + 2}{7}$
   B. $14(x - 2)$
   C. $0.14x - 0.28$
   D. $\dfrac{14}{x - 2}$

   20. _____

21. Simplify $9k - 4 + 2k$.

21. _____

22. Order the numbers -23, 15, -13, -2, 14, and 5 from least to greatest.

22. _____

For Questions 23–24, write the ordered pair that names each point.

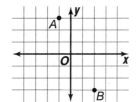

23. A

23. _____

24. B

24. _____

25. Find $63 \div (-9)$.

25. _____

26. Find $\frac{-11}{5} + \frac{6}{5}$.

26. _____

27. Evaluate $\frac{f}{4}$ if $f = \frac{1}{5}$.

27. _____

Solve each equation.

28. $6x + 5 = 23$

28. _____

29. $3(y - 7) = y + 3$

29. _____

For Questions 30–31, find each number.

30. 12% of 3600

30. _____

31. 150% of 28

31. _____

32. Find the domain of $y = x + 3$ if the range is $\{-1, 1, 3, 5\}$.

32. _____

33. A lake is 120 fathoms deep. Use the fact that there are 6 feet in a fathom to tell the depth of the lake in feet.

33. _____

34. Suppose y varies inversely as x and $y = 5$ when $x = 20$. Find x when $y = 2$.

34. _____

35. Write an equation of the line in slope-intercept form with slope $\frac{1}{3}$ that crosses the y-axis at $(0, -2)$.

35. _____

36. Write 7 cubed using an exponent.

36. _____

37. Simplify $\sqrt{\frac{81}{225}}$.

37. _____

Final Test
(Chapters 1–15) *(continued)*

38. Find the length of the missing side of the right triangle.

35 ft

28 ft

38. _____

For Questions 39–40, find each product.

39. $-5a^2(a^2 - 6a + 7)$

39. _____

40. $(6y + 5)(2y + 3)$

40. _____

41. Factor the polynomial $s^2 + 25$. If the polynomial cannot be factored, write *prime*.

41. _____

42. Find the roots of $2x^2 - 5x + 1 = 0$. If exact roots cannot be found, state the consecutive integers between which the roots are located.

42. _____

43. Find the value of c that makes $g^2 - 18g + c$ a perfect square.

43. _____

44. Write an inequality for this graph.

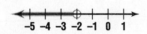

-5 -4 -3 -2 -1 0 1

44. _____

45. Solve the system of equations $y = 2x - 10$ and $x - y = 7$.

45. _____

46. Solve the system of inequalities $x > 2$ and $y \le x + 3$ by graphing. If the system does not have a solution, write *no solution*.

46.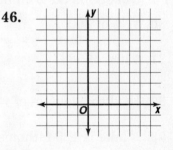

47. Find the distance between the points at $(0, 2)$ and $(3, 6)$.

47. _____

48. Simplify $\sqrt{75a^2b^3c}$. Use absolute value symbols if necessary.

48. _____

49. Simplify $\dfrac{y^2 - 6y + 9}{y^2 - 3y}$.

49. _____

50. Solve $\dfrac{x}{2} + \dfrac{5x}{10} = -2$.

50. _____

Semester Test (Chapters 1–8)
Answer Key

1. ___A___

2. ___C___

3. ___B___

4. ___C___

5. ___A___

6. ___C___

7. ___B___

8. ___A___

9. ___D___

10. ___D___

11. ___D___

12. ___D___

13. ___A___

14. ___C___

15. ___C___

16. ___B___

17. ___D___

18. ___C___

19. ___B___

20. ___B___

Semester Test (Chapters 1–8)
Answer Key

Page 303

21. $x + 7 = 25$

22. $\dfrac{17}{y} = 4$ or $17 \div y = 4$

23. 2

24. Associative Property ($\times$)

25. $53, 4, 0, -1, -4, -51$

26. $P(3, 2)$

27. $Q(-1, -2)$

28. 7

29. 1

30. 7.4

31. 1

32. 27.2

33. $=$

34. $>$

35. -1 or 9

36. 9

37. -1

38. 2

Page 304

39. 12.5%

40. $\dfrac{5}{8}$

41. The event is impossible.

42. $\{-9, -6, -5, -2\}$

43. 174 in.

44. Inverse variation; as x increases, y decreases and as x decreases, y increases.

45. $y + 1 = -\dfrac{3}{2}(x - 4)$ or $y - 5 = -\dfrac{3}{2}x$

46. slope $= -2$, y-intercept $= 7$

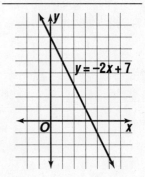

$y = -2x + 7$

47. $y = -\dfrac{1}{4}x - 6$

48. $x^3 y^4$

49. b^8

50. $-\dfrac{6}{5}$ or -1.2

1. __B__

2. __A__

3. __A__

4. __D__

5. __A__

6. __D__

7. __A__

8. __B__

9. __D__

10. __C__

11. __D__

12. __C__

13. __A__

14. __D__

15. __A__

16. __C__

17. __C__

18. __D__

19. __C__

20. __B__

Semester Test (Chapters 9–15)
Answer Key

Page 307

21. $7 + 2x - 4x^2 - 8x^3$

22. $3a^4 - 8a^5$

23. $b^2 + 10b - 24$

24. $m^2 - 5m - 24$

25. $49k^2 - 64$

26. $9x^2 + 7x^4$

27. $(x + 3)(x + 4)$

28. $(2y - 3)(y + 1)$

29. $(b + 6)^2$

30. $x = -\frac{1}{2}; \left(-\frac{1}{2}, -6\frac{1}{4}\right)$

31. $1, -1$

32. 121

33. $\frac{4 + \sqrt{17}}{2}, \frac{4 - \sqrt{17}}{2}$

34. $\{x | -4 < x \le 3\}$

35. $\{x | x > -6\}$

36. $\{y | -7 \le y < 7\}$

37. $\{b | 5 \le b \le 15\}$

Page 308

38. $y > 2x + 1$

39. $\left(\frac{1}{2}, \frac{3}{2}\right)$

40. $(1, 0)$

41. no solution

42. $(-1, 0)$

43.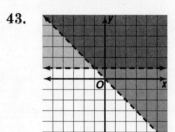

44. $5\sqrt{3}$

45. $10|a|\sqrt{5b}$

46. $6\left(\sqrt{2} + \sqrt{3}\right)$ or $6\sqrt{2} + 6\sqrt{3}$

47. $-\frac{9}{2}$

48. $\frac{pqr}{2}$

49. $\frac{5}{2x}$

50. $\frac{6f + 14}{f(f + 2)}$ or $\frac{6f + 14}{f^2 + 2f}$

Final Test (Chapters 1–15)
Answer Key

Page 309

1. __A__

2. __A__

3. __A__

4. __D__

5. __D__

6. __D__

7. __C__

8. __D__

9. __A__

10. __C__

11. __D__

Page 310

12. __C__

13. __D__

14. __A__

15. __B__

16. __C__

17. __A__

18. __B__

19. __D__

20. __D__

Final Test (Chapters 1–15)
Answer Key

Page 311

21. $11k - 4$

22. $-23, -13, -2, 5, 14, 15$

23. $A(-1, 3)$

24. $B(2, -3)$

25. -7

26. -1

27. $\dfrac{1}{20}$

28. 3

29. 12

30. 432

31. 42

32. $\{-4, -2, 0, 2\}$

33. 720 ft

34. 50

35. $y = \dfrac{1}{3}x - 2$

36. 7^3

37. $\dfrac{3}{5}$ or 0.6

Page 312

38. 21 ft

39. $-5a^4 + 30a^3 - 35a^2$

40. $12y^2 + 28y + 15$

41. prime

42. between 0 and 1, between 2 and 3

43. 81

44. $x < -2$

45. $(3, -4)$

46.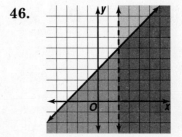

47. 5 units

48. $5|ab|\sqrt{3bc}$

49. $\dfrac{y - 3}{y}$

50. -2